The Daily Lives of Muslims

The Daily Lives of Muslims

Islam and Public Confrontation in Contemporary Europe

NILÜFER GÖLE

Translated by Jacqueline Lerescu

ZED

Zed Books

LONDON

The Daily Lives of Muslims: Islam and Public Confrontation in Contemporary Europe was first published in French in 2015 as *Musulmans au quotidien: une enquête européenne sur les controverses autour de l'islam* by Editions La Découverte, 9 Bis Rue Abel Hovelacque, 75013 Paris, France.

This edition published in 2017 by Zed Books Ltd,
The Foundry, 17 Oval Way, London SE11 5RR, UK.

www.zedbooks.net

Typeset in Adobe Caslon Pro by seagulls.net
Index by John Barker
Cover design by www.alice-marwick.co.uk
Cover photo © Ian Teh/Panos

A catalogue record for this book is available from the British Library.

ISBN 978-1-78360-954-3 hb
ISBN 978-1-78360-953-6 pb
ISBN 978-1-78360-955-0 pdf
ISBN 978-1-78360-956-7 epub
ISBN 978-1-78360-957-4 mobi

FSC www.fsc.org MIX Paper from responsible sources FSC® C013604

CONTENTS

PREFACE TO THE FRENCH-LANGUAGE EDITION

AFTER THE JANUARY 2015 ATTACKS, 'MAKING SOCIETY' DESPITE TERROR

This unplanned foreword was, alas, written on 28 January 2015, three weeks after terrorist attacks struck the heart of Paris. This foreword was necessary because this book's intention, the fruit of four years of research, which I finished writing two weeks before the events, is to provide readers with keys to understanding the lived realities of Europeans of Muslim culture. These realities cannot be ignored by those who wonder about the killers' motivations while somewhat confusedly recognizing that these sectarian terrorists have no relationship to the daily life of the immense majority of European Muslims and the new public culture to whose creation they contribute.

A NEW BREAK IN THE EUROMUSLIM COLLECTIVE MEMORY

All attacks create a break in time. In an instant, the course of daily life is upended and the social contract is shattered, leading to polarization in society. After the shock and the profound emotion it elicits, we first pay homage to those who lost their lives. Next, we try to repair the damage, to fix the social fractures. Sometimes, we are able to isolate the moment of terror, close the parenthesis and mourn for those who cannot begin again. Sometimes, this instant of terrorism interferes with long-term temporality, leading to a series of unforeseeable events from which we cannot emerge unscathed.

The crimes of January 2015 are probably among the latter. The assassination of eight cartoonists and editors of *Charlie Hebdo* and two of their friends present in the offices, three police officers and four Jewish citizens, taken hostage in a kosher supermarket in Vincennes, signaled a turning point. These targeted massacres carried out by French-born terrorists under the pretext of 'avenging' the Prophet Mohammed exacerbated the feeling of uneasiness towards Islam across Europe. Two founding values of contemporary Western democracy, the defence of freedom of expression and the fight against anti-Semitism, seemed to have been gunned down by terrorist weapons. These killings could possibly derail European history and that of its Muslims.

There is a before and an after this date, as there was after the Al-Qaeda attacks on September 11. But unlike the United States, Europe – and particularly France – has a long shared history with Islam and Muslims, a relationship forged in the long term as well as the present. It is precisely this interwoven nature of the dynamics between Muslims and European societies that this book seeks to demonstrate. It situates terrorist acts against *Charlie Hebdo* in a European perspective and brings to light its harbingers. In fact, the January 2015 attacks in Paris took place as part of a chain of events and controversies resulting from the representation of the sacred symbols of Islam. The 1989 fatwa against Salman Rushdie, the author of *The Satanic Verses*, the 2004 assassination of Theo Van Gogh, the director of the film *Submission*, and the publication of caricatures of the Prophet Mohammed in a Danish newspaper in 2005 are shocks engraved on the collective Euromuslim memory. A transversal dynamic between London, Amsterdam, Copenhagen and Paris has been created.

Beyond the differences between national contexts and the separation between Sunni and Shia, a European cartography of controversies surrounding Islam has been progressively drawn. As in the case of *Charlie Hebdo*, it is around the representation of Islam in the written and visual arts and through the use of satire that the violence of these controversies is revealed: the pictorial representation of Islam in the arts and the recourse to critical humor provoke the violence of these reactions. And as was tragically revealed in the case of *Charlie Hebdo*, it is some of those who share the cultural heritage of May '68 who collide with Islam and its visible forms in public life in Europe.

The writer Michel Houellebecq is one of the most emblematic figures of the turbulent meeting of these two cultures. In his novels, he captures the feeling of the times, the worries of a disenchanted and depressed generation that is perplexed by the rise of Islam. In his novel *Submission*, he anticipates a French society penetrated by Islam, a country that elects a Muslim president named Muhammad. The hero, who is working on a dissertation at the Sorbonne on Joris-Karl Huysmans, is a 'misanthropic and solitary aesthete' looking for spiritual comfort in Catholic liturgy. He ends up converting to Islam, repeating the ritual prayer in the Grand Mosque in Paris. In 2022, Islam becomes the religion of France, just as it does for the protagonist. This successfully blurs distinctions between fiction and politics, the author and the hero, his phobia about Islam and his disenchanted attraction to religion. Far from remaining confined to literary circles, this book caused a sensation: it led to a strongly mediatized polemic that forced politicians and intellectuals to react. *Charlie Hebdo* was no exception: the novelist was on the cover of the issue that appeared on the day of the attacks. The cartoonist Luz, one of the survivors of the killing, depicted the author, dressed as a wizard, announcing his own submission to Islam: 'In 2015, I will lose my teeth, in 2022, I will observe Ramadan.' The book went on sale on 7 January 2015, a fateful date, just like his novel *Platform*, which came out just before the attacks of September 11.

The French counterculture of the 1970s was shaped by the critique of conservative 'values', inherited from the influence of the Catholic Church, and by the mobilization for sexual liberation. During this period, a new wave of secularization penetrated the cultural domain and the private sphere, with equality of the sexes and libertine behavior on its horizon. For many, the May '68 movement became the symbol of the emancipation of women and sexual minorities. *Charlie Hebdo*, which in 1970 succeeded *L'Hebdo Hara-Kiri* (created in 1969), is one of the avant-garde centers of this counterculture. Its cartoonists and columnists, who became famous for their impertinent pens that attacked all forms of religious hegemony and public morality, are the legendary figures of this generation. In France, the tradition of humor and outrageousness goes back to the sixteenth century, as proven by the works of François Rabelais, a hedonist if ever there was one. But the humor of *Charlie Hebdo*'s first leaders is inscribed in the emancipatory movements of the left in favor of oppressed minorities.

Forty years later, times have changed. If the 'sixty-eighters' movements remain in a certain imaginary as an eternal youth, enamored of ideals of justice, a number of the new ideas promoted by their actors have since become banal. And the Church's influence has disappeared in a society where sexual liberty no longer collides with a moral authority. Religious norms and the visibility of Islam's symbols have appeared since the 1990s in a secularized and sexually emancipated society. Since then, the direct inheritors of the most ardent defenders of freedom of expression, the young cartoonists at the new *Charlie Hebdo*, could consider it logical to extend the battles of their predecessors against the Church's influence to that of Islam today, notably in its terrorist offshoots in the Muslim world. But in so doing, they have often endorsed dominant media representations of Islam which are exaggeratedly skewed and caricatured without taking into account its diversity and, above all, the thoughts and feelings of their fellow Muslim citizens, nor their precarious status as a minority.

These binary representations do not leave any room for gray areas, a multiplicity of points of view, the work of interpretation, learning, or transformation through debate. Media mechanisms accentuate the assumed specificities of protagonists, and exaggerate and exacerbate cultural differences. The stereotypical references which result from this process feed controversies. The confrontation that crystallizes between defenders of freedom of expression and those who call for the protection of the sacred thus worsens, pushing aside multiple audiences of ordinary people.

In this context, freedom of expression and secularism seem to have become incantatory values, a façade behind which the so-called spokespeople of the majoritarian society take refuge to preserve their intellectual comfort. Instead of facilitating social links to others or inviting them to share their opinions, the thus 'falsified' values – to use a term from the historian of secularism Jean Baubérot – of some increase inequality today, maintaining a deafness towards Europeans of Muslim culture or confession. This lack of recognition, when it is not a form of public humiliation based on religious and cultural singularity, feeds their resentment. Constantly asked by the media to express their allegiance to the value of freedom of expression, European Muslims are much more rarely asked to freely explain their points of view on the subjects of controversies.

The problem here is not an antagonism based on the values of French society, between those who have a sense of humor and those who do not. The problem is that the voices on the fringes of society, those of ordinary Muslims, their presence, their points of view, their sense of humor – all remain unheard. This phenomenon is obviously made worse by acts of violence committed in the name of Islam. The young killers who targeted *Charlie Hebdo*, the police and Hyper Cacher suppressed the voices of French citizens of Muslim culture of all generations, believers or not. They shattered the possibility of another interpretation of the images, the expression of a multiplicity of visions, in order to impose with force and violence what is sacred and non-negotiable to them. In a purely ideological conception of sharia, sectarians and anti-Semites want to impose their authority on Muslims by forcing them to break away from their fellow European citizens and join them.

Nonetheless, in contrast to the Rushdie affair a quarter of a century earlier, a number of Muslims condemned the attacks of January 2015 and distanced themselves from them without hesitation. They adopted the slogan 'Not in my name,' introduced by British citizens of Muslim culture after the atrocities committed by Daesh in 2014. Common citizens of Muslim culture thus put themselves forward personally to publicly assert their condemnation of these killings. The innumerable commentaries prompted by the terrorist attacks have once more moved different perceptions of Islam and Muslims to the fore. For some, Islamic terrorism is explainable by characteristics within Islam, while for others it is the geopolitical and socio-economic conditions of Europeans of Muslim culture that is the cause. For religious authority in contemporary Islam, the role of blasphemy and fatwas has again become a source of questioning. The recruitment of young people, the identity of terrorists, their social trajectory, the reasons for their radicalization, the role of the internet, the feeling of injustice, and the wars in Iraq and Syria have also been mentioned. Attention has been drawn to the reasons for the failure to integrate Muslim populations. Housing projects, which through semantic slippage have become 'ghettos,' schools and prisons have been identified as places which have consolidated these problems, from learning disabilities to delinquency. Obviously, all these questions must be asked. But the fact remains that terrorist attacks have reinforced representations of Islam and Muslims as social as well as religious 'problems.'

In this context, ordinary Muslims, pushed to the side as insignificant or simply considered as unrepresentative of the 'big problems in society,' are becoming a bit less visible. Those who benefit from upward social mobility and belong to the new middle classes – young professionals, lawyers, doctors, entrepreneurs – and those who work in the service sector, cultural media and the arts, hoping to combine their singularity, their faith and their culture with their citizenship, are pushed aside. All those who do not see a contradiction between wearing a headscarf, praying, eating halal, circumcising male children, burying their relatives in Muslim cemeteries and joining French society are not heard. However, it is their very presence in public life, their visibility, which has 'caused a problem' in the majoritarian society since the 1980s. And it is precisely the quest for citizenship by these ordinary Muslims and their calls for visibility that have been hindered and weakened by the terrorist attacks.

THE 11 JANUARY RALLY, OR HOW TO MAKE SOCIETY

On 11 January 2015, days after these attacks, the massive demonstration in Paris from Place de la République to Place de la Nation, along with others across France, showed society's determination not to fall into the terrorists' trap of polarization. Without slogans against Islam or Muslims, without even a mention of the assassins, these gatherings proved that it is possible to avoid a politics of fear and hostility against Islam and Muslims. These were not gatherings against an adversary, but the expression of a society affirming itself. This movement showed another form of expressing citizenship without aiming to transcend the differences among the people or within the nation.

People came in great numbers, in families with children, holding handwritten signs, with giant pencils made of paper they constructed at home. All of society was thus revealed to itself, mixed and multilingual, under the flags of Europe and the whole world. A new design for making society was thus tested in public space by the gathering of Parisians and all others. Through this performativity in the public sphere a reappropriation of the quotidian, the street and the future was expressed.

Gathering was also a way of expressing singularity, expressing one's point of view, showing one's face to others and to neighbors, in order to share, exchange and construct links. Like the image of two people, arms linked, one holding a sign that read 'I'm a Muslim and I like Jews,' the other proudly showing another that read 'I'm a Jew and I like Muslims.' This symbolic gesture shows the necessary link between Jews and Muslims sharing the same soil, the same daily life where kosher and halal lifestyles mix. Gathering thus becomes a type of transformative experience for people in the presence of one another, forming a collective.

With restraint and humor, the participants wanted to show that they would not give in to the fear of terrorism. At once a slogan and a logo, the *slogo* 'Je suis Charlie' provided a personal tone and united participants in tears and empathy. 'Charlie' became a sympathetic figure around the world. He was adopted in solidarity with the victims, but also in sympathy for France. 'Charlie' also led to a reflection on the reasons why some do not identify with the humorous editorial line of *Charlie Hebdo*. The fact remains that, as after May '68, France once again stands as an inspirational center for a new democratic imaginary, with the determination of its citizens to make society in difficult times.

The gatherings also led to a new meaning for the European community, created in the streets by citizens. A way of making community by bringing together differences was made available, a 'cosmopolitics' as the philosophers Étienne Balibar and Isabelle Stengers propose. In order to do so, Euroskepticism must be left aside. Because it is first and foremost in Europe that democratic stakes are raised and we can begin to construct the daily life of a public culture opposing violence with civility.

This book, the result of a European inquiry on 'Muslims in daily life,' resonates with the before and after of the *Charlie Hebdo* events and the anti-Semitic attack in Vincennes. In effect, it studies the European genealogy of controversies surrounding Islam. Without being restricted to the media level of debates and the question of the supposed incompatibility of Islam with 'European values,' its narrative line delves into the universe of ordinary people. It thus allows for the discovery of the creation of a new public culture in which ordinary Muslims are the creative actors. It is neither about optimism nor pessimism. Social science researchers have the duty to illuminate present dynamics as well as horizons of the possible. A responsibility to participate in 'making society' requires, beyond a 'sociological imaginary,' the meticulous and patient actions of the artisanal work of weaving together cultures and people. Without obscuring differences of opinion and starting with causes that spark controversy, this book demonstrates the emergence of a new public culture with the concerns of truth, justice and beauty. I thus hope to propose an antidote to the ills in our societies and contribute to changing the intellectual paradigm through a cultural renewal.

Nilüfer Göle

28 January 2015

PREFACE TO THE ENGLISH-LANGUAGE EDITION

ISLAM AS A POST-MIGRATORY PHENOMENON

We are witnessing a crucial moment in which the 'Islamic question' has become a decisive element, an overriding symbol of difference against which national identities are dressed and political agendas are set in the Western world. A cluster of different problems – namely global jihadist terrorism, recent crises involving refugees from the Middle East, and Muslim migrant minorities in European countries – have been amalgamated as part of an Islamic problem that Western countries are currently facing. Increasing securitization – nominally to prevent terrorism – the rise of neo-populist movements against a Muslim presence in Europe, and the closing down of frontiers against the flow of refugees are becoming common political traits observable in many European countries. A fusion between different categories of people, refugees, terrorists and migrants, in spite of the differences in their historical trajectories, social aspirations and political strategies, has led to the reification of an Islam deprived of a human face and real-life situations.

This book attempts to disclose the multiplicity of voices used by Muslims, and in doing so to open up our understanding of the everyday politics affecting Muslim minorities living in different cities of Europe. 'Islam is plural' is a widely accepted motto, but also an intrinsic part of European reality, a fact mostly ignored. Muslim migrants are people with diverse ethnic origins, believers and non-believers, men and women, belonging to different branches of Islam, who have been pushed into migrating for various reasons, whether it be war, oppression or economic misery. They come from different waves and temporalities of migration, including those from the second and third generation, those living in countries with a colonial past, and those who find themselves in destination countries without any historical familiarity or linguistic skills. However, Muslim migrants have become part of everyday life in European cities, as they increasingly settle over time with their families and change the outlook of their neighborhoods. Their sense of belonging shifts from their countries of origin to their countries of residence. The environment of migration fades away, to be replaced by the concerns of everyday life and the claims of one's neighborhood, school and workplace.

Islam gains visibility in Europe at this particular stage as a post-migration phenomenon. It seems paradoxical that those who have already integrated into host countries feel most confident asserting their Islamic identity, thereby making manifest their religious difference. In this respect, Islamic faith serves mostly as a support for identity formation among members of the second and third generation, becoming the common denominator among Muslims of different national backgrounds and ethnic origins. Post-migrant Islam signals the distancing of migrants from any given ethno-religious identities. The terms that designate Muslims by their 'migrant origins' ('*issue de l'immigration*'), or in reference to the national cultural backgrounds of their parents, are widely criticized as not only inadequate but also discriminatory towards Muslim citizens of Europe. Thus, Islam is redefined in isolation from the national cultures of migrants, instead embracing a universal sense of belonging.

In contrast to their parents, the present generation of migrant Muslims are not intimidated in making manifest their religion in public and look for ways of reconciling their faith practices with their secular life environment. For most of them, Islam is neither an obstacle to living in Western societies, nor an ideology of rupture. Contrary to the view of global jihadists, they aspire to participation, and by claiming Islamic faith they are not thereby turning against the societies in which they live. Access to education, the acquisition of professional skills, and engagement in associative life and in politics all provide youthful members of migrant communities with an upward social mobility and contribute to the formation of Muslim middle classes. For the mainstream discourse, which frames Islam as a 'problem,' equating migrants with failed integration, and Muslim youth with crime and violence, the existence of Muslim middle classes is scarcely noticeable. Issues related to religious extremism, segregation in suburban areas, academic failure in state schools and indoctrination in prisons appear as problem areas. In an atmosphere of hostility toward Islam, new discourses surrounding citizenship claims by Muslim middle classes emerging throughout western Europe are undermined.

VISIBLE MUSLIMS IN DAILY LIFE

During the last three decades, the visibility of Islam in public life – that is, the appearance of religious signs and the practices of Muslim minorities – have occupied the forefront of societal debates in European countries. Being visibly Muslim conveys a sense of incongruity with social norms and creates an impediment to their recognition as ordinary citizens. They are 'ordinary Muslims,' in daily life people who pursue educational strategies, acquire linguistic skills, master codes of conduct and interact in public life. Yet living in accordance with religious prescriptions, namely women's covering of their faces and bodies, daily praying, eating halal and adherence to the sacredness of Islam, render them 'visible' and problematic for the majoritarian societies of Europe. The term 'ordinary Muslim' therefore signals a tension between being a visible Muslim and being accepted within the everyday life practices of European societies.

Why does the visibility of Islam in public life engender such resentment and rejection among the majority populations of host countries? Perhaps it is because some of the widely accepted presuppositions about religion, secularism and public life are being challenged by the ways Muslims are carving out a space in Europe.

A Muslim presence in the public sphere challenges the idea that religion should be a private matter. However, religious faith has an incorporated personal dimension as well as a public one. It is not only about abstract faith, but also a corporeal ritual, a daily practice, that intensifies the experience of faith. An embodied act of faith is a source of self-discipline and guidance in modern life, a ritual and a discursive practice, learned individually and in private, but also collectively. In the context of migration, the transmission of religious knowledge and practice within the family loses its vitality, replaced by the proliferation of religious and cultural institutes that provide a place for Islamic learning, rehearsal of faith and religious socialization for the youth of the community. In a secular environment, religious faith becomes a learned corpus of knowledge and a matter of permanent surveillance of one's piety. The personal incorporation of Muslim faith as well as its public manifestations are refashioned within the social fabric of European secular countries. Although Islam is often debated from the outside, though not within, as a religion with a political agenda, the personal and public manifestations of Islam are becoming decisive in the transformation of public life in Europe.

The majority of Muslims who follow the Islamic prescriptions of covering, praying, dietary habits and holding to sacred symbols are ordinary actors of Islam. They are differentiated in their various ways of living out their faith, being pious, holding values of sexual modesty and sharing of cultural habits. Manifestations of Islamic faith do not inevitably imply that someone is affiliated with extremist groups. The performative elements of religious practice are, however, often perceived as an aggressive, radical assertion of Islam and a rejection of prevalent Western values. We observe a non-correspondence between the subjective meanings that Muslims attribute to their faith and the public perceptions of Islam as a threat. The gap indicates a problem of understanding between a migrant religion and the culture of the majority, a meaning that is 'lost in translation' and subject to misconceptions.

The process of accommodation necessitates a cross-cultural understanding and opening up of shared public space. Access to the public sphere is not open to all citizens, and frequently even less so to Muslims. Rather, it is subject to limitations, exclusions and restrictions. The Muslim presence and related citizenship discourses in Europe are played out in the public domain, putting to the test Western democracy's capacity to include or exclude, to recognize or reject. Obviously, the public sphere is not a neutral, empty space, free of power relations, but is regulated by different technologies of governance and is subject to negotiation with citizens. The question of who has the power of knowledge, and thereby the means to make use of discursive and legislative power, to name and differentiate between faith and threat, between a familiar sign and an ostentatious one, between 'us' and 'them,' is becoming a crucial one. Yet power is not only vertical, imposed from the top down. Public debate on Islam necessitates Muslim representation, in the form of people who speak credibly about religious tradition, faith leaders, Muslim civil society and umbrella organizations. Controversies about Islam generate a remodeling of the public sphere, not always in conformity with the intention of political actors.

I have identified four main clusters of controversy around Islam that have appeared in Europe since the end of the 1980s – namely the headscarf issue, the construction of mosques, halal food and visual representations of Islam. Each public controversy stems from an Islamic prescription. Each chapter examines the theological and subjective meanings that Muslims attach to Islamic prescriptions, in the form of covering, praying, dietary habits and the safeguard of the sacred. The presence of Muslim actors becomes controversial and 'visible' to the extent that they pursue their faith whilst entering into zones of contact with other non-Muslim citizens. There is therefore a spatial element, the intrusion of the Muslim 'stranger' into life-worlds supposedly reserved for the 'native' inhabitants. The headscarf worn by first-generation migrant women working in factories and cleaning up schools was not considered to be a culturally disturbing symbol, and therefore not visible to the public eye. It is the covering of young students in state schools that became a public affair, as is well illustrated in French debates. Similarly, the prayer rooms in peripheral urban industrial zones have not been a source of major public debate. However, the construction of mosques in the center of cities, whether in Germany or in Italy, has become a major political issue for urban inhabitants. It is the social mobility of Muslims, their move from work settings and peripheral areas to centers of education and urban life, that engenders resentment and rejection. It is both a spatial transgression and an infraction of common consensual norms. On the one hand, they have succeeded in achieving upward social mobility, leaving the peripheral zones reserved for migrants and claiming access to the 'epicenter' of societies, namely cities, schools and politics, where societal values are produced and disseminated. On the other hand, such social mobility is not an indicator of cultural assimilation. On the contrary, by holding to religious symbols and practices Muslims express a sense of identity and belonging, which in the eyes of many non-Muslim citizens represents an infraction against prevalent secular cultural norms.

Nevertheless, the separation of Islamic religion from migrant culture leads to unprecedented accommodations within the cultural fabric of European countries. Muslim practices are neither exclusively religious nor cultural; rather they are creative accommodations between contemporary sensibilities, cultural trends and Islamic faith practices. Islam as a means for guidance in the daily lives of Muslims helps them to make distinctions between what is licit and illicit, and to redraw boundaries between halal and haram in secular life-worlds. In that respect, I speak of the formation of 'halal lifestyles.' The creation of an inclusive mosque for Muslim sexual minorities, halal *jambon*, and the burkini are among the most extreme but illustrative examples. They exemplify the way Muslim subjectivities shaped by everyday life practices are challenging established norms, whether defined by orthodox religious or secular Western actors.

EMPOWERING ISLAM

Muslims manifest their faith in public, thereby becoming visible minorities with distinctive styles and modes of conduct. Islam, along with providing guidance on ethics and good conduct, provides actors of faith with the authority to use a political language. It is a marker of distinction for a higher ethical self, but also a language for assertiveness, a source of empowerment for Muslims to act in society.

Contemporary actors of Islam turn the religion of the migrant subaltern into a tool for asserting personal identity and collective power. In voluntarily adopting symbols of stigma and religious idiom, Muslim actors transfigure and update Islam. The meaning of Muslim veiling requires readjustment – often identified with the seclusion of women, its meaning is transformed by young women who pursue success in education, professional life and public standing in European countries. Islam has a transformative effect on shared public spaces, ranging from mosque-building to halal markets to the domains of art and fashion. In each domain, it becomes part of a larger societal issue, necessitating cross-cultural debate. The issue of mosques in Europe is not debated exclusively in terms of their role as places of prayer for Muslims, but also as a common concern for the inhabitants of the city. Their architectural form becomes decisive in setting the conditions for a shared public space. Similarly, halal dietary habits which concern Muslim consumers have become part of a larger debate on animal rights and vegetarianism. This necessitates updating the religious arguments concerning ritual slaughtering practices in light of concerns about animal suffering, the phenomenon of mass consumption driving the meat industry, and the needs of Muslims living in European countries.

Contemporary actors of Islam, among whom converts play an important role, can speak to different publics, articulate religious and cultural codes, communicate cross-culturally and successfully move between multiple identities. They gain the symbolic power of public recognition among Muslims but also within broader society.

The election of Sadiq Khan on 5 May 2016 as the first Muslim mayor of London is an illustration of a successful accommodation between being British and being a Muslim. His political career has followed the dynamics of an emerging migrant middle class and related discourses of citizenship, as well as different ways of combining Muslim identity with a broader sense of belonging to British society. His journey has been similar to those of the 'ordinary Muslims' who gave their voices to this book – he is of migrant origin and emphasizes his own disadvantaged background as the son of an immigrant Pakistani bus driver. He studied law and joined the Labour Party when very young. Access to higher education and his engagement in politics account for his upward social mobility. In his speeches, he stresses social justice and promises to be a 'mayor for all Londoners' of all faiths and ethnicities.

He is not claiming to represent a 'Muslim community' (the very existence of such an entity is in question), nor speaking exclusively as a Muslim. He promises to tackle Islamophobia along with anti-Semitism and homophobia. He says he will support organizations that aim to bring people from different backgrounds together, such as the Big Iftar and Mitzvah Day initiatives. However, Islamic extremism on the one hand and Islamophobia on the other make it difficult, as he puts it, 'to be Brit, Muslim and Londoner.' As a Muslim, it is difficult not to take a public stance in the face of events such as the 7/7 jihadist terrorist attacks in London, or Donald Trump's promise to ban Muslims entering America during the US presidential campaign.

BEYOND EUROPE

Beyond Europe, the Western world is becoming an anachronism. The election of Donald Trump announces the changing of the canvas for cultural values – namely multiculturalism, an open society, recognition of differences, rights for minorities, and the feminization of culture. He has capitalized on the rising discourse of Islamophobia across the Western world, stoked up anti-establishment resentments, expressed hostility towards cultural liberal cosmopolitan elites, promised anti-globalization politics, does not shy away from an anti-feminist stance and has asserted his leadership with virile boldness.

Trump and Khan seem to be diametrically opposed. Khan sees himself as a global citizen, defending the idea that we all have multiple identities and that most of us have some sort of migrant heritage in us. His vision for London is that of a global city, where citizens with different ethnic, racial and religious backgrounds struggle to make their way in everyday life. He puts ordinary citizens at the core of his project, aiming to better the lives of the disadvantaged in their neighborhoods, schools and workplaces. He believes in building from the ground up a cross-cultural society and finding ways of linking Europe and Muslims.

When one speaks of European Islam, one has in mind the cooperation between governments and Muslim representative organizations in order to promote mainstream Islam or prevent religious extremism. It is European Islam I have studied in this book, in proximity with ordinary citizens, as it emerges in a given locality, in a city, in a shared public place that necessitates accommodations in everyday life practices. Controversies divide but also function as an interface between Muslims and non-Muslim citizens in the making of European Islam.

Europe is not, generally speaking, an idea that people are passionate to defend. In the 2016 UK referendum on the European Union, it was 'Brexit' rather than 'Brin' that became the buzzword and captured the public mood. This all changes when the debate concerns European Islam. Islam represents a hot zone, provokes controversies and scandals, mobilizes people and their emotions, and causes actors to gain visibility whether they endorse or contest Islam. In unprecedented ways, Islam has become the accelerator of Europe.

The controversies emerge in particular cities of Europe, in different places, but the themes are recurrent, circulating from one national context to another, gaining a transnational momentum.

Some of the controversies remain local or national, others become European and global. There is a process of mutual learning that emerges from the controversies. These controversies affect our mental mapping of Europe, particularly countries of immigration such as France, Germany and Great Britain. Furthermore, the minaret referendum in Switzerland and the cartoon controversy in Denmark have changed the European landscape and introduced other cases into the collective memory.

The future of the European democratic public sphere, whether it is headed in an inclusive or an exclusive direction, will depend on the social lessons that are drawn from the controversies. Will the headscarf and burka ban in France be taken as a model to be imitated or one not to be repeated? Will the election of Sadiq Khan as mayor of London set a role model for young migrant Muslims, encouraging them to engage in the political domain, or will it remain a moment of exception in European politics? Two different strategies coexist in European politics – the first based on the belief in an open multicultural society providing channels of participation for Muslim migrants, the second based on a nation closing down its frontiers, forbidding Muslims from accessing public life.

European countries are converging in having difficulty dealing with Islam and a Muslim presence. The politics of multiculturalism and the recognition of minority religious rights have shaped liberal European democracies in the past. However, we have witnessed during the last three decades the fact that both frames of thought are subject to criticism. The end of multiculturalism, and its incompatibility with the question of Islam, has become a widely accepted conviction. It is simplistically equated with cultural relativism, and criticized for leaving the patriarchal, traditional elements of oppression within the communities intact. Furthermore, critics of multiculturalism argue that the lack of interaction between different communities has not only led to cultural clashes, but also provided a potential enclave for radicalization and terrorism.

The discourse of religious freedom for minority groups has not provided a frame of recognition for Islam. The controversial debates are around secular norms, giving priority to the rights of women, animals and children over religious freedom. Hence Islamic veiling is not framed as the individual right of a religious minority group but as a sign of the submission of women that contradicts feminist principles of gender equality. Similarly halal slaughtering is not qualified as a religious right, as has been the case for the kosher tradition and *shechita*, but as an archaic practice disrespectful of animal rights. Controversies around Islam tend to be framed within a discourse of incompatibility between cultures, and a hierarchy of civilizations. The pillars of European culture are reinforced around secularism and rights discourse, in confrontation with Muslim claims, the reinforcing of the politics of identity and the rejection of cultural pluralism. Distinctions between 'us' and 'them' have propagated an atmosphere of hostility across Europe, and beyond. Islamophobic discourses are spreading in public debates, and the call for a combative politics against the 'Islamization of Europe' has both gained popularity and set political agendas.

The neo-populist movements are not replicas of the old xenophobic movements of the far right. They adopt the mainstream norms of sexuality and secularity and turn them into a politics of enmity, defending ethno-nationalism against the effects of migration and globalization. Whilst leftist liberal movements, identified as they are with the establishment, elitism and globalism, lose ground, Eurosceptic, anti-global, nativist movements gain in strength. Nationalist nativism stresses a sense of belonging with racist connotations, defending the right of the autochthones against newcomers and those perceived as 'strangers.' The latter represent all those with multiple attachments – migrants, refugees, but also all those who need freedom of access to public life, inter-connectivity with the global world, intellectuals, artists, journalists, and elites, including business. (In that respect it is ironic to observe liberal parties of the Anglo-Saxon tradition defending protectionist anti-globalization politics.) How to turn the clash of cultures into an opportunity for elaborating common norms and restoring a civic public culture? This book attempts to identify the conditions for an inclusive public sphere, free from violence, that releases the potential for collectively creating new forms of living together.

Nilüfer Göle

1 December 2016

INTRODUCTION

European Muslims: From Collage to Interweaving

Since the end of the twentieth century, the Muslim presence in Europe has been evident in urban landscapes. These Muslims, from diverse ethnic and religious backgrounds, are nonetheless an integral part of local life. We pass them in the street, at school, and in places of leisure. But this presence does not leave majoritarian society dispassionate. Faced with the arrival of newcomers with different ways of life in spaces that are familiar to them, disarray takes over. The publicly visible daily lives of Islam disturb the collective imaginary of European countries shaped by the secular values of freedom and a non-religious way of life. From one end of Europe to the other, series of controversies test modalities of the Muslim presence with the underlying question: is Islam compatible with Western values or not?

THE GROWING TENSION OF TWO REALITIES

London, a cosmopolitan city known for its ethnic pluralism and multiculturalism, has not escaped the social malaise spreading across Europe. In 2013, two British artists, Gilbert and George, sought to capture in a series of photo collages the tensions, fears and the perceptible feeling of defiance in the East End neighborhood.[1] Witnesses of the arrival of new ethnicities with other religions, occupations and behaviors that changed the atmosphere in this neighborhood, they decided to give their interpretation of the present. The East London streets they had known, with their signs and billboards, bobos riding bikes and mothers pushing strollers, these peaceful, familiar and reassuring scenes were disappearing little by little, giving way, it seemed to them, to the portents of a catastrophe.

Through this series of photomontages, the artists sought to announce 'truths' about the modern world. They aimed to represent the complex coexistence of religions, politics, beliefs and lifestyles – from radical extremism to capitalist secularism – with the only common line of the daily realities of urban life in the second decade of the twenty-first century. 'Our era is going through a modern war, a war of values,'[2] they affirm. Their different images present us with streets lined with tandoori restaurants, veiled women, radical imams and young people dressed in hooded sweatshirts. In the middle of this heteroclite assembly are superposed self-portraits of the two artists, Gilbert and George, in their regular attire of suit and tie in tweed as well as a myriad of small candies that worryingly resemble bombs ...

We have before our eyes an ultracontemporary urban landscape where cultural practices, beliefs, and political convictions are juxtaposed in a hodgepodge source of unease. The distinctive traits of Muslim migrants and 'native' British placed side by side create a disconcerting effect. Gilbert and George, homosexuals, atheists, defenders of sexual liberty, work alongside Muslims, intriguing figures from here and elsewhere. Silhouettes of women in black burkas give a medieval quality to the bustling streets of London; but with their sneakers and laptop cases they are also the familiar figures of our era. By putting together the ephemeral encounters in the street and dissonant realities – ultramodernity and religious extremism – the artist duo creates a shock effect in the face of a daily situation that seems to them potentially explosive.

The small fake bombs are a reminder of the anxieties over terrorism, war, arbitrary violence and destruction. Shiny and metallic, of identical shape and size, these objects are in reality doses of nitrous oxide, a new drug popular among young people. The inhalation of this gas causes a state of euphoria, laughter and hallucinations. Particularly in East London, near the famous Brick Lane mosque, you can find street dealers of these cartridges of 'laughing gas.'[3] These objects at once recall bombs and drugs, thus intentionally bringing up the question of the relationship between decadence and violence. Faces are hidden behind veils and masks. Entitled 'Scapegoat,' this series reveals the climate of paranoia in a society marked by a culture of reciprocal criticism and hostility.

This figural representation of contemporary reality recalls the media's treatment of the Islam 'problem.' The pop art style and newspaper photomontages overstate, as does the media, the differential traits of Muslims and privilege an affective immediacy, more particularly repulsion and fear. The growing tension between two realities and two worlds is presented as a collision, as a war where different kinds of values face off and as a shock of civilizations, a thesis that has gained ground since September 11, 2001 The destruction of New York's twin towers by Al-Qaeda's aerial attacks is a form of 'urbicide,'[4] the murder of civilians as well as the destruction of the life of society and the reassuring routine of the everyday. The event reunited in violence people separated by time, place and culture, superposing a disturbing and surreal collage of images of New York and Kabul, George Bush and Bin Laden.[5] Jihadi terrorist acts target public places and places of passage – streets, train stations, subways, and buses; meeting places – cafés, nightclubs, and youth camps; places of worship – synagogues and mosques; places of exchange – schools, banks, markets and malls; places of patrimony – museums and libraries; in sum, all the places where links are created between members of a collectivity. It is the heart of public life that is targeted in attacks that weaken democratic coexistence.

Europe finds itself at present confronted by the emergence of a new world and emblematic figures of Islam in the center of its public life. Europe, which escaped the influence of the Church, fought a sexual revolution and is living a new wave of secularization that adheres to the rights of sexual minorities, is today facing the 'Islam problem.' It is in this new 'ultramodern' stage that the confrontation between actors of sexual democracy, with feminists and homosexuals at the forefront, is emerging with actors of European Islam. Religious migrant citizens and non-religious 'native' citizens share the same public space without having the impression of belonging to the same space/time.

Common public life creates an interface and proximity without, however, producing real ties or recognition between citizens with divergent convictions.

TO UNDERSTAND THE ENIGMA CREATED BY THE EMERGENCE OF ISLAM IN THE EUROPEAN PUBLIC SPHERE: TURNING TO AN INQUIRY

How do we represent this contradictory if not antagonistic reality, according to whose perspective we take? Some 'native' inhabitants fear finding themselves stripped of power over their lives as minorities in their own countries, even targeted by an 'anti-white racism.'[6] As for them, Muslims often complain of suffering generalized Islamophobia, of being questioned on every aspect of Islam, of being constantly suspect for their convictions and their belonging, of not sharing the values of their host countries. How can we understand modalities of belonging of a new world in the heart of Europe that inspires a sufficiently strong sense of defiance that it feeds conspiracy theories? In his essay Énigmes et complots (*Enigmas and Conspiracies*), the sociologist Luc Boltanski leads a real detective inquiry into scientific inquiries. From crime novels to spy novels, he defines enigma via a singularity 'that we can qualify as *abnormal*, which conflicts with the way things appear in conditions assumed to be *normal*, so that the mind cannot inscribe this worrisome strangeness into the field of reality.'[7] By 'the world,' he means 'everything that happens' in a sporadic manner and that is impossible to fully master, an 'eruption of the *world* into *reality*.'[8]

Thus, to represent the new European reality disturbed by the sporadic and unmastered appearance of Islam, to understand how its presence in European public spaces produces the effect of a worrisome strangeness, inquiry, the principal tool of sociology, is in order. This was the objective of the research project EuroPublicIslam whose results this book aims to reproduce for a wide audience.[9] This project's acronym explicitly designates the exploration of zones of encounters between Islam and Europe. In order to understand the enigma that the appearance of Islam creates in the fabric of European public space, we had to simultaneously deconstruct Islam *and* Europe as macro-historical and sociological categories; in this perspective, we conducted an inquiry among ordinary citizens with many faces, ethnicities and convictions while accounting for their daily interactions.

I conducted this inquiry over four years, from 2009 to 2013. with a group of researchers and doctoral students from the School for Advanced Studies in the Social Sciences. We selected a series of public controversies that arose over the course of this period as entry points into the field. This cartography of controversy served as my guide for constructing a research itinerary and choosing locations for the inquiry spread across twenty-one cities in different European countries.[10]

Controversies emerged when Muslims demanded the possibility of following Islamic prescriptions in their daily life in Europe. This was not a question of simple media phenomena, because these controversies were linked to precise events occurring in specific places and involving Muslim and non-Muslim citizens. Each controversial event created a public field, made different actors appear, mobilized a certain rhetoric, and deployed a particular repertoire of actions. On the European level, constructing a mosque, wearing the veil, eating halal and understanding the sacred are the recurrent subjects of media controversies. However, these affairs still unfold in daily reality in a given moment in well-defined places and with identifiable people. The terrain of inquiry thus consisted of questioning the people who were involved or those who felt they were affected, by going to the places where these controversies appeared. We questioned them individually in the framework of semi-directive interviews, as well as collectively in discussion groups. The individual interviews demonstrated the singularity of personal experiences and the individual ways in which each person interprets and lives his or her faith. The group discussions allowed us to go beyond binary oppositions and perceive the possibility, or not, of the emergence of new perspectives. The complete transcript of the data collected in the field took up more than three thousand pages and a sixty-minute documentary film that was made from the video recordings of group discussions.[11]

In this inquiry, we appealed first to ordinary citizens of Muslim culture rarely invited to participate in media debates. Among them were practicing and non-practicing Muslims from different ethnic origins – Pakistanis, Turks, Algerians … – as well as young natives of Europe or children of interreligious marriages. Some women wore the headscarf, others did not, but they nonetheless claimed their Muslim identity as consumers who prefer to eat halal and organic, as the faithful who want a new mosque in their city, and as converts who defend the Islamic patrimony in Europe. Our inquiry also gave a voice to 'ordinary Muslims' in Europe today, on whom public controversies are focused but who are absent from media and political debates. The aim of this research was to include their voices and reverse the unequal geometry of the media field without forgetting to make heard the viewpoints of non-Muslims, which are often pushed aside in a paradoxical way from the staging of the 'Muslim problem.'

In the frame of this sociological research, the category 'Muslims' was exploded, but it was also enriched by evidence of nuance and differences among different people according to their ethnic origins, their trajectory as immigrants, and their relationships to belief and to European norms. Our questions focused on different notions of Islam, the boundary between the permissible and the forbidden, and what was the product of their own choices or that of Islamic prescriptions.

Those who participated in our inquiry were those who hoped to interact, reflect and debate together. Ready to give their time to respond to a semi-directive interview for over an hour and a half, or to participate in a group discussion and for four hours debate the realities of European Islam, they proved their interest and their engagement in the affairs of the city. At the end of our research, they all expressed their satisfaction at having had the occasion to simply talk about themselves and at having not been, for once, called on to address problems related to integration and discrimination or their position on Islamic radicalism. In our research, they found an occasion for listening and exchange with their fellow citizens. They often expressed their desire to continue this experience of encounter and dialogue among themselves.

The inquiry, carried out on the level of European cities, was conducted in French and English, but also in German, Italian, Spanish, Dutch, Turkish and Bosnian. Despite linguistic differences and national specificities, we observed across Europe clear dynamics of convergence in public affairs surrounding Islam. In fact, the study of controversies allows for the adoption of a transversal methodology, while the particularities of national contexts appear in individual accounts and in the use of political language. We thus discovered in the participants' comments the ambient rhetoric of the country in which they lived, such as the principle of secularism for the French, the duty of memory for Germans, the rights of sexual minorities for the Danes, multiculturalism for the Brits, freedom of provocation for the Dutch, or Catholicism for the Italians ...

THE NEW WEAVING OF EUROPE BY ITS CITIZENS, MUSLIM OR NOT

This inquiry thus charts the appearance of religious and cultural difference in European realities among 'ordinary' citizens in their daily lives. By making visible their differences in public life, Muslims are questioning common sense, norms and majoritarian values in Europe. The question is whether an image of Europe is emerging beyond the collage of mutually foreign realities. This is why we looked for possibilities, among dissimilar actors, to 'make public' conditions for sharing the same space/time.

All social science researchers find themselves confronted by the tension between the necessity of leading empirical research and that of creating a conceptual framework which gives the keys to understanding social facts, keys for a better world. We aim to construct a theoretical corpus and a method; we aim to create a style that bears the researcher's imprint in her way of seeing and giving sense to the world. How was I going to account for the multiplicity of faces and voices, of this new world in the heart of Europe that was emerging around the affairs of Islam? This is how the occupation of carpet weaver presented itself. The Anatolian women who spent long hours facing the frame of a rug are part of my childhood memories. During our visits to rug weavers' workshops, I saw them from behind, seated in front of threads of all colors hung vertically; they knotted these colored threads one by one, making knots in parallel rows, and the speed of their movements and the skill of their hands left us in admiration. This image is at once familiar and distant for me. I was never envious of this occupation: the artisanal work of women weaving was the opposite of the scientific work to which I aspired.[12] So it is with some embarrassment but also with relief that I realized that this forgotten image would give me the key: Europe was being woven like a rug around these controversies and these knots, with the faces and voices of actors of different ethnic origins, religious beliefs, and political convictions. It is with these threads of all colors that the recurring motifs appear as a European composition. These motifs bear the same styles across cultures and make evident the transformations in details in zones of encounter and borrowing between different cultures.[13]

The occupation of weaver can be found in Europe's Hellenistic heritage. This specifically feminine occupation has its roots in its meaning in Greek mythology. Since antiquity, weaving has been a sign of women's passion for creating beautiful works, of resisting pleasure and occupying a central role in the economy of the *oikos*, the home. But beyond that, these 'women's works' are the source of metaphors and carriers of meaning in the affairs of the home as well as in those of the city: it is they who reel in the threads of rivalries and marital deceptions, the thread of war or of the unified city.[14]

A people's style or culture is not defined by its transformations as a whole, but by the microscopic changes that occur in the details, in ways of doing, thinking, living, dressing, connecting, and being together. The entry of Islam into Europe is occurring in the cultural domain where women are the central figures of its transformation. Women appear as a central knot in controversies surrounding Islam and in societies' debates. The way in which they occupy their places in social life is transforming the boundaries between private and public spheres, determining the unraveling of present conflicts.

As long as the realities of concurrent cultures are juxtaposed in a 'collage,' they remain foreign to one another, making it impossible to make a society. As we can see in the works of the British artists, this collage of identities in binary oppositions, of Muslims versus Europeans, is potentially 'explosive.' Without interaction, there is no possibility of becoming familiar, evolving together, mutually transforming – in sum, of making a society. Our research was structured around the creation of an alternative space for encounter and dialogue, a space that brought people together. Unlike a 'collage,' Europe recreated itself before our eyes as a rug woven from many threads of citizens, Muslim and non-Muslim, as a collective and almost anonymous product, but with the distinctive motifs that indicate new ways of acting, and helping public creativity emerge, the only bulwark for the democratic exceptionalism of Europe.

Above all, it is this realization that I have tried to report in this book, which cannot pretend to retrace in detail all the richness of the lessons of this long, collective inquiry.[15] After an examination of the often very violent context of media, political or literary controversies born of the new Muslim presence in Europe (Chapter 1), I return to the more discrete emergence of new 'Muslim voices' (Chapter 2) that have accompanied them, justifying the framework of an 'Experimental Public Sphere' (EPS) that we put into place in various European cities: a framework that I believe is more efficient than the many opportunistic opinion polls that reveal 'what Islam is really doing to Europe.' In any case, it greatly helped me in proposing in the following chapters, the heart of the book, other ways of looking at the realities of public manifestations of European Islam masked by media controversies: street prayers, the construction of mosques, polemics on 'blasphemy,' the women's headscarf, references to sharia, halal lifestyles, and the relationship to the 'Jewish question' (Chapters 3 to 9). Finally, I explain in the conclusion why creative freedom is a European exception, capable, in my opinion, of constructing a horizon of possibility with 'its Muslims.'

ACKNOWLEDGMENTS

This book is the product of questioning about contemporary Islam that I have been leading with some obstinacy since the late 1980's. My goal was to better understand the emergence in Muslim societies of new faces of Islam – young women, intellectuals, public figures – who are fighting to be recognized in universities, in public debates or in parliament. Rather than via the axis of political Islam, I focused on the study of the entry of Islam into the public sphere via these new actors. In order to understand the internal dynamics of Islam today and the challenges that its practice poses for the secular values of contemporary societies,

I opted to research the importance of the Islamic veil, the subjectivity of Muslim women and their daily interpretation of faith, thus displacing the boundaries between private and public life. Since 2001, I have been pursuing my research at the École des hautes études en sciences sociales (School for Advanced Studies in the Social Sciences, or EHESS) in Paris. I would like to thank my colleagues for integrating me into this school, particularly Michel Wieviorka, who believed in my work. My seminars at EHESS were organized around the theme of contemporary Islam and its modes of visibility in public life in European countries. The definition of the intimate and of the public, the organization of interior and exterior spaces, the values of the sacred and of sexuality in Islam comprised an important part of my reflection. In the course of teaching, I defined the field of studying Islam by putting into perspective multiple modernities in order to identify the uniqueness of these practices and experiences. My seminars gave me the occasion to deepen these themes with my PhD students and colleagues. I am immensely grateful to EHESS, a unique institution of its kind in France, which allows researchers to explore new frontiers of knowledge without being confined to one cultural area or scientific discipline. It is the only community to which I belong with such pleasure and ease.

My seminars allowed me to construct new working hypotheses and envisage the fieldwork necessary for confronting these hypotheses with the realities of Islam in Europe. It is within the framework of the call for applications for the 'Ideas Programme' of the European Union's Seventh Framework Programme that I developed the EuroPublicIslam project. Awarded an ERC Advanced Grant, which aims to encourage innovative projects under the direction of a primary researcher, this project allowed me to lead this work in the field on controversies surrounding Islam in Europe.

EuroPublicIslam realized the alchemy between the conceptual framework developed in my seminars and the empirical inquiry on the ground. Thanks to the four-year funding of the project, I was able to develop an experimental methodology of the public sphere and lead an inquiry in twenty-one European cities. I created a group of researchers with my doctoral and post-doctoral students who were familiar with my conceptual framework. For these young researchers, this research revealed itself as a place for transmission and apprenticeship in the career of sociologist. Each of them participated in the project for one to two years at different stages of its development, and carried out different tasks, including, for example, establishing a cartography of controversies, preparing documents for fieldwork, conducting interviews, creating discussion groups, directing a documentary film, and organizing two international colloquia; they also contributed to two collective works that came out of this research. All the interviews were conducted by members of the team, while I myself led the group discussions, the 'Experimental Public Sphere' (EPS).

This group of young researchers included Cagla Aykac, Julie Billaud, Zehra Cunillera, Francesca De Micheli, Valentina Frate, Anahita Grisoni, Warda Hadjab, Rachid Id Yassine, Bochra Kammarti and Simone Maddanu. Each of them worked at the same time on the subjects of their various dissertations: public figures of Islam in Europe, Afghan women, young theologians in Europe, patrimony and museums in Morocco, women artists in Egypt, naturopathics and the cult of well-being, love and intimacy among young European Muslims, Islam and European regionalism, Islamic finance, and Muslim youth in Italy, respectively. Six of them defended their dissertations and received their PhDs during the course of the project (2009–13) –Francesca De Micheli already had a PhD in sociology before joining the team. Administrative support for the project was initially provided by Erden Göktepe, then by Dounia Bergaoui and Thibault Dilly. All of them are today pursuing careers as researchers, instructors and directors in European institutions or elsewhere in the world. Without them, research with such a scope, conducted in twenty-one European cities, would not have been possible. I thank them all.

The EuroPublicIslam project was housed at Reid Hall, the Parisian campus of Columbia University in New York. For more than a century, Reid Hall has welcomed students, professors, and artists in the spirit of sharing, exchange and transmission of knowledge. I want to thank Danièle Haasc Dubosc, the director of Reid Hall in 2009, and Nebahat Avcioglu, then the research coordinator, for their hospitality, which allowed me to realize my dream: working in a space previously occupied by architects. This space played a decisive role in the functioning of this research. In fact, I had conceived of our workplace as a workshop, in that a workshop is a place turned inwards, towards production – the architectural workshop working on a competition or a weaving workshop, to reprise the metaphor of this inquiry. Unlike 'offices' and 'research centers,' the workshop allowed me to work in an artisanal spirit, to protect my need for communication, and to save me from the position of expert and from the individualism that generally dominates in offices. The space of the workshop was a place for the gestation of knowledge, introducing a different, slower, continuous and necessary temporality to research in the social sciences. In conformity with the project's questions, at once turned towards the public sphere and towards intimate subjectivity, this intermediate space allowed for mediation between two approaches.

Without François Gèze, president of Éditions La Découverte until 2014, this book would never have seen the light of day in this form. Thanks to his talent as an editor, he helped and even forced me to leave my perspective in the workshop and turn towards the exterior world, sharing my reflections and writing with a view to communication with a large audience. I had the immense privilege of benefitting from his reading, which was as attentive as it was demanding. He had already put his faith in me by publishing *The Forbidden Modern*.[16] Today, I am very happy to be publishing *Les Musulmans au quotidien* at La Découverte, and I hope that this book will open a space for alternative reflection, going against the grain, about European Islam.

I want to thank my friend Catherine Orsot Cochard, who in her detailed readings pushed me to clarify my writing and abandon my language tics and scientific jargon. Among my doctoral students, only Zehra Cunillera was present in the research team during all stages of the project, from the beginning until the final phase. With Warda Hadjab, also a doctoral student, she accompanied me and assisted in the editing and publishing phase. They also supervised the publication of two collective works that came out of the EuroPublicIslam project. It was a great pleasure to share work with them on a daily basis. I want to express my friendship and gratitude to them.

The EuroPublic Islam project has helped new problems emerge. The fertility of a project can be measured by its capacity to spread in its wake new themes and new projects. At the heart of political stakes, we saw new esthetic and artistic dimensions appear in the public field. Since then, I have been exploring this path of interdisciplinarity between art and politics, notably around the construction of mosques in Berlin and Istanbul, in collaboration with architects and art historians. EuroPublicIslam has also demonstrated the necessity of rethinking the Jewish question in relation to current controversies surrounding Islam and public space. In view of this, I created a study group, A Shared Perspective of Jews and Muslims for Europe, composed of researchers from the Van Leer Institute in Jerusalem, the Istanbul Policy Center at Sabanci University, the Mercator Foundation in Berlin and CESPRA at EHESS.

Among those who had confidence in my obstinacy in my most intimate circles, there is of course my husband, Asaf Savas Akat, a humanist intellectual and passionate economist. Quite simply, I owe him an enormous thank-you. Without the feeling of solidarity between us, our communal life would have been a life of exile.

This book is dedicated to all those who participated in its research in twenty-one European cities. I warmly pay tribute to them. From Toulouse to Cordoba, from Sarajevo to Geneva, from Paris to Istanbul, they gave their time to engage in these debates. I thank them for it. I would have liked to name each one of them and quote their words in their entirety for all. I hope that they will find themselves in the motifs of this European rug – their anonymous work – that is emerging before our eyes. I am very grateful to them, beyond the framework of this research, for showing us the possibility of another future for us all.

1

Europe: No Entry for Islam?

The *flâneur*, an emblematic figure of modernity since Baudelaire, is distinguished by the freedom of walking, observing as a spectator, and experiencing daily life in the urban landscape. In contemporary societies in a migratory flux, the immigrant replaces this figure, displaces himself, traverses boundaries and integrates himself into new landscapes and new cities. But unlike the *flâneur*, he cannot move without crashing into obstacles, and his freedom of circulation is permanently called into question.

Orhan Pamuk, the Turkish author and Nobel laureate, describes in an allegorical way the obstacles that the walker/immigrant encounters. He quickly understands the meaning of discrimination: 'The inscription is there to remind some that they are allowed to enter, and others that they are not … the message that they wish to share is probably the following: not all may enter here! Just as they authorize some to cross the threshold, they chase away others who wish to enter without being entitled to do so …'[1] Behind the banner, we hear the voices of those who fear being invaded by these new arrivals: '"Too many people from outside are coming in", they say. "We cannot accept everyone …" and they reach the logical conclusion: one day, people on the inside will come together to discuss how to limit access.' People on the inside want to protect their privileges, their material goods, their tastes, and their habits. Orhan Pamuk's text illustrates the dynamics of interdependence, the definition of an 'us' in relation with the Other, the structuring effect the stranger has on European identity. By adopting this double view, the author aims to reveal the emotional register of those who reinforce these boundaries out of fears of identity and those who find themselves in front of closed doors, feeling humiliated and excluded. This quest for identity, this game of opposing forces between those who reinforce barriers and those who transgress them, aptly describes the choreography occurring in European public life. Contemporary public debates and controversies surrounding immigration and Islam shape rules of integration, boundaries of exclusion and conditions for participation in the definition of an 'us' among European citizens.

In their countries, controversies surrounding Islam in European countries have occupied the forefront of society for more than a quarter-century. In 1989 both the 'headscarf affair' in France and the fatwa against Salman Rushdie, the author of *The Satanic Verses*, in England, were a prelude. These two very different events – one focused on the religious practices of young French female citizens, the other the act of a state outside the European Union which sought to impose Islamic law beyond its boundaries – made the presence of Islam in Europe readily visible – a threatening presence.

THE FATWA AND THE VEIL: THE IRRUPTION OF ISLAM IN EUROPE

Wearing the veil is for certain young Muslim women a quotidian and peaceful act that concerns only a small minority. The fatwa pronounced against a British author of Indian origin, from a Muslim family, because the book he wrote was seen as blasphemous towards Islam, the Koran and the Prophet, was a death sentence. These two events, while entirely dissimilar and occupying different spaces, put a spotlight on Islam and stirred controversy in the European public sphere. The archaic forces of sharia law and the covering of women entered the collective European imaginary with a bang, as in both cases Islam breached secular European space. The fatwa signaled the collapse of boundaries and the loss of a comforting sense of separation from the Muslim world.

Europeans discovered with surprise and anger that Islam's power was not circumscribed to distant Muslim lands, but a phenomenon situated in the heart of European countries, which saw this as a threat to intellectuals, writers, artists and women. The headscarf affair – the appearance of a feminine form of Islam – heightened this sense of troubling proximity. The emergence of Islam was seen as a step backwards which threatened women's rights and freedom of expression and cast doubt on these hard-won rights obtained through battles against the Church's influence through the secularization of political power. Terms from the religious lexicon, such as blasphemy, submission and corporeal punishment, emerged in the secular European public field.

The fatwa against Rushdie in England and the presence of a minority of young women wearing the veil in France created a conflictual situation that has lasted for decades. In the aftermath of these affairs, the feeling of intrusion produced a change in the repertoire of European public debates. Arguments against the presence of Islam mobilized around two pillars: sexual equality and freedom of thought. From here followed an opposition between sacred laws and freedom, on the one hand, and the values of piety and sexuality on the other. Opinions crystallized around secular values, redefining identity by distinguishing between 'us' and 'them,' aimed at blocking Islam. In some European countries, 'No Entry' signs were raised to prevent Muslims from showing their difference, diminishing their visibility in the public sphere.

The anxiety caused by the alterity of Muslim presence incited European publics – sometimes at the initiative of public powers – to define their cultures' distinct traits that constitute their national identity in order to establish conditions for the integration of migrants. Principles taken for granted, such as 'secularism,' were submitted to rigorous testing in France; didn't Muslim populations' religious claims constitute a potential danger for secularism? New themes emerged, such as *Leitkultur* in Germany, in order to assert the dominance of the 'culture of reference' in the face of the establishment of significant foreign communities from majority Muslim backgrounds. Through the debates in these two countries, the notion of secularism was revisited in France and *Leitkultur* was forged in Germany in order to force an active recognition of the dominant culture's values. These notions evoke 'French exceptionalism' and 'German cultural essentialism' and exalt the specificity of national identity, leading to a hierarchization of the relationships between cultures. Over the course of these debates, these notions, potentially models of integration, took on new meaning, becoming exclusionary instead.

SECULARISM AND *LEITKULTUR*: BASES OF IDENTITY

In France, the strength and richness of secularism as a political principle are derived from its capacity to organize coexistence, as Jean Baubérot,[2] a historian of secularism, has written. Secularism is based on the articulation of four principles: the separation of Church and state, the neutrality of public authority with regard to different beliefs, freedom of conscience, and equal rights. In France, according to Baubérot, debates on Islam and the banning of religious symbols in the public sphere led to the hypertrophying of the principle of neutrality: it was interpreted as the neutralization of public space and not as the neutrality of the arbiter who requires all parties to respect the rules. He considers this extensive conception of neutrality as 'repressive secularism,' or secularism which suppresses 'the religious expression that the 1905 law previously authorized.' Baubérot is the only member of the Stasi Commission[3] to abstain from voting on the proposed law on the application of the principle of secularism and the banning of the ostensible wearing of religious symbols in public schools.

A shift occurred in the interpretation and application of the principle of secularism regarding Muslims and the signs that demonstrate their religious affiliation. Secularism conceived in relation to Christianity was confronted with a religion exterior to the Christian vision of the world.[4] In this forced encounter with Islam, secularism was reinterpreted so that the question of the visibility of religious symbols, public space and feminism occupy a central place in the discursive field of secularism. At present, secularism – a concept at once remote, philosophical and juridical – has entered contemporary language and occupies a preponderant role in public debates; discussing secularism today implicitly signals Islam. A new oppositional pair has thus been created with two notions which are difficult to compare but which are nonetheless brought together and equated. If the pairing of secularism–Islamic veil was neither thinkable nor pertinent twenty years ago, today these terms are inseparable.[5] Despite the indignation of those who opposed the reduction of the principle of secularism to a 'scrap of cloth,' the Islamic veil has become dominant in debates on secularism in France.

Unlike the multiculturalist model, the French model has been criticized for its 'blindness' to differences. Nevertheless, this capacity to disregard difference is an advantage. In the civic tradition of secularism, a reversal has occurred: Muslims are regarded in particular in order to scrutinize their difference and judge them based on whether they fail to respect the principle of secularism, adopt or interiorize it. The secular tradition has lost its aptitude for indifference and become a standard system of identity; it has become a condition for integration imposed on Muslim immigrants. Political powers have put out circulars to survey the application of secularism in hospitals and public service cafeterias by opposing specific religious requests.

France has witnessed the emergence of an interrogation of identity. Now the question 'What is a Frenchman?'[6] occupies a central place. On television and in newspapers and books, historians, intellectuals and politicians debate this topic. The constitutive elements of national identity – cultural values – are presented as an indispensable condition for the integration of Muslim immigrants. The creation of a 'Ministry of Immigration, Integration, National Identity and Codevelopment' in 2007 is the most explicit illustration of the equation between national identity and the political desire to address the question of integration via culture and identity.[7]

France is not an exception. In Germany, a similar questioning of national identity has occurred. The 2010 publication of Thilo Sarrazin's *Germany Does Away with Itself*, an instant bestseller, and the debates it stirred, was at the root of a restructuring of the public field around the idea of the nation and its relationship to Islam. Considering Islam as an impediment to integration and progress, Sarrazin, an establishment figure, a member of the Social Democrat party (SPD) and director of the Bundesbank, gives an alarmist interpretation of the economic and cultural decline of Germany.[8] He uses cultural arguments based on statistics to denounce the failure to integrate the Muslim, Turkish and Arab communities. For him, Germany risks losing its economic competitiveness, cultural heritage, its very 'substance,' through the demographic expansion of segments of the population he judges 'less educated and less intelligent.'[9] He deplores the fact that most Turks in Germany don't recognize Angela Merkel as Chancellor and do not accept Germany as their native land – *Heimat*.[10] Thilo Sarrazin admits his dismay in the face of a Germany whose culture is changing: 'I don't want my grandchildren and great-grandchildren to live in a mostly Muslim country where Turkish and Arabic are widely spoken, women wear headscarves and the day is measured out by the muezzin's call to prayer.'[11]

It has been previously noted that 'Sarrazin' is ironically one of the names given to the Muslim peoples along the Mediterranean coasts in Europe of the Middle Ages. Thilo Sarrazin's response to allegations of racism is that he is a European 'bastard,' and that his name comes from his paternal ancestors, originally from the South of France, where the term '*sarrasin*' commonly designated 'Arab pirates.' Asked whether he hates Turks, Thilo Sarrazin responds that his physical features, notably his mustache and salt-and-pepper hair, make him resemble a Turk of a certain age and allow him to pass unnoticed in Kreutzberg, Berlin's Turkish quarter.[12]

Sarrazin has garnered popular success because he had the 'courage' to disobey the law of silence and knock down taboos on questions of immigration at the risk of being accused of racism. He was forced to step down from his post at the Bundesbank, and the SPD began procedures to expel him. Despite the fierce criticism opposing his views, Sarrazin has received international popular support. Not to be outdone, the German media has called him everything from 'the people's hero' in *Der Spiegel*, a critical weekly news magazine; to a 'taboo breaker' in *Focus*, a right-wing weekly news magazine; but also a 'living room racist' in *TAZ*, a left-wing daily paper.

'Can you become German?'[13] This question implies that access to German citizenship is complex in this nation with its particular history, where, unlike in France, citizenship was defined not by 'right of birthplace' but by 'right of blood' – *jus sanguinis*. In 2000, Germany revised its citizenship laws. Restrictions imposed on the recognition of dual citizenship remained in place, but the principle of descent was relaxed. The right wing of parliament stirred a debate on the 'culture of reference' – *Leitkultur-Debatte*

– in order to defend a hierarchy between cultures and dispute the dual allegiance of citizens, notably Turkish immigrants. The question of cultural integration, which was a juridical and political issue, was pushed into the field of culture.

Paradoxically, the notion of *Leitkultur* was forged in 1998 by Bassam Tibi, a professor of political science of Syrian descent in Göttingen and an eminent public figure who defended an enlightened form of Islam and Europe's reconciliation with Islam. By choosing the term *Leitkultur*, Bassam Tibi attempted to map the values and norms that he sees as constituting European modernity and which are potential markers in the integration of migrants and Muslims. For him, the acceptance and appreciation of these values by Muslims constitutes a major criterion for choosing allegiance with Europe. In the course of these debates, the idea of *Leitkultur* took on new meaning according to whether the focus was on the national or the European context. Today, there are multiple constitutive features of *Leitkultur*: the defense of German culture and the rejection of multiculturalism, the condemnation of cultural relativism and the requirement of absolute loyalty to the dominant culture. The notion of *Leitkultur* has played a major role in Germany in provoking debates on the question of national identity and especially by reorienting immigration policy as a cultural matter. The adoption of German social norms has become a prerequisite for participation in the national community.

The well-established distinction between the German culturalist model and French universalism has thus been blurred in the course of debates on Islam. In France, these debates have led to the reaffirmation of the principle of secularism, inherent to the notion of French exceptionalism. Currently, the universalist ideal of French civilization has taken on the trappings of cultural particularism, converging with the German model it used to critique. The idea that not all civilizations are equal, which implies that Islam subjugates women and prohibits freedom of expression, is affirmed in opposition to cultural relativism and multicultural policies. In both cases, values are seen as a condition for the integration of Muslims in the national community.

THE INVALIDATION OF MULTICULTURALISM

The return to national identity, the affirmation of the specificity of European cultural values, the necessity to defend the superiority of Western civilization, all this has had as a consequence the abandoning of any approach based on multiculturalism and cultural relativism.

The first criticisms of multiculturalism were formulated in the Netherlands, despite its pride as a model of multicultural society. The writer and journalist Paul Scheffer, an intellectual star of the liberal left, opened the debate in January 2000 with an article entitled 'The multicultural drama.'[14] This article shook the left wing's partisans as the author underscored the fragility of a 'society open to immigration' as a failure of the integration of ethnic minorities. Scheffer criticized multiculturalism because of the threat he felt it held for social harmony. We cannot avoid conflicts, the author declared, and we can no longer tolerate cultural conservatism in the name of respecting the traditions of others. Multiculturalism is criticized not only because it leads to the separation of communities, but especially because it legitimizes cultural conservatism in that it accepts retrograde traditions, like honor killings, in the name of cultural heritage. Thus the author invalidates multiculturalism, which he believes leads to the indifference and negligence made evident by policies towards immigrant and Muslim populations.

The fatwa against Salman Rushdie in 1989, the Al-Qaeda attacks in New York in 2001, and the assassination of Theo van Gogh in the streets of Amsterdam in 2004 have reinforced European publics' sense of fragility and insecurity and have, in their eyes, validated the thesis of the failure of multiculturalism. The irruption of violence has undermined the image of a calm, unshakeable and tolerant society.

The announcement of the end of multiculturalism has two contradictory implications. The critics of this notion consider questions of immigration and Islam a matter of collective conscience and a public affair. In accordance with the central hypothesis of this book, the question of Islam has become a de facto public affair in that it is seen as something which concerns us all, not only Muslim communities. In this view, the criticism of multiculturalism changes the problem of immigration completely, inviting all citizens to join the debate and favoring its framing as a matter for debate in the public sphere. The multicultural policies, which are the emanation of the state, are informed by the principle of verticality between the state and communities. If critics of multiculturalism modify this hierarchic power structure, it is because they have brought down the question of immigration and Islam to the public arena, calling on collective conscience and inviting citizens to assume responsibility and get involved in public affairs. An open society assumes that all traditions are subjected to critical review. In this first implication, immigration and Islam are not questions best left to the state, but instead complex factors within the city that must be debated and examined.

However, the critical examination of multiculturalism paradoxically leads to the desire to exclude Islam as well. In this orientation, multiculturalism is presented as a burden, which hides Europeans' feelings of culpability, an obstacle that must be pushed aside in order to affront the threatening presence of Islam. Intellectuals and feminists on the right and left are invested in the interrogation of the religious and conservative practices of immigrant communities. A certain conception of Islam, which takes into account a critical view of this religion, has become a *sine qua non* condition for all aspirants to the public sphere. New public figures have emerged from the ranks of Muslim immigrants and gained legitimacy by associating themselves with critics of Islam. The figurehead of this new alliance between secular Muslims and intellectuals critical of multiculturalism is Ayaan Hirsi Ali, who supports a 'zero tolerance' policy towards Islam and serves as a reference point for other women.

A decade after the first invalidation of multiculturalism initiated by the Dutch intellectual Paul Scheffer, German, British and even French political leaders – although France never adhered to multiculturalism – announced in unison the end of multiculturalism. For Chancellor Angela Merkel, the model of a multicultural Germany, where different cultures cohabitate peacefully, has 'utterly failed.'[15] Instead of cultural relativism, the Chancellor, in front of a youth congress from her party, defended the need to reinforce the Judeo-Christian tradition as a guide for German values. In light of these political developments, I assert that the invalidation of multiculturalism follows a trajectory and assumes an operating principle that engenders policies of national (re)affirmation and hegemonic Western values to the exclusion of Islam.

This turning point in public debates about Islam is an alarming indicator that Europe is 'sick with xenophobia,'[16] according to Jürgen Habermas' diagnosis. In his view, Germany is 'prey to fits of agitation and political confusion surrounding questions of integration, multiculturalism, and "national" culture as the "culture of reference" (*Leitkultur*), provoking debates that consequently aggravate xenophobic tendencies among the public.'[17] Habermas condemns the instrumentalization of Jewish heritage to define European culture which ignores memory and history: 'apologists for the "*culture of reference*" refer to the "*Judeo-Christian tradition*" which distinguishes "*us*" from others and, via an arrogant annexation of Judaism and with incredible hatred, ignore all the Jews suffered in Germany.'[18]

The French philosopher Jacques Rancière has spoken about the rise of a new form of racism that doesn't result from 'popular passions' but 'comes from above.' According to him, this 'racism from above' is 'primarily supported not by some backwards social groups, but by a significant portion of the intellectual elite [...], by an intelligentsia that considers itself a leftist, republican and secular intelligentsia.'[19] The intellectuals in question have adopted statist reasoning and have become accomplices in the legitimization of logics of prohibitions and inclusion.

Tariq Madood, a political scientist who works on multiculturalism in England, uses the term 'cultural racism' in order to include groups marked by their cultural and ethnic differences. This is a way of denouncing the xenophobia towards Islam, which is not limited solely to considerations like skin color, racial and ethnic difference, but which encompasses cultural traits and derogatory stereotypes.[20]

Xenophobia, cultural racism, racism 'from above,' these terms aim to condemn discriminatory policies and prejudice towards foreigners, immigrants and Muslims. These terms put the accent on the categories of race, ethnicity and culture. They signal the phenomenon of radicalization in the perception of Muslim immigrants in Europe. Can they also enable us to understand the current tension of European publics towards Islam? Don't these terms instead indicate problems with immigration more than with the presence of Islam?

CAN WE SPEAK OF ISLAMOPHOBIA?

Vincent Geisser's book, which describes the emergence of a new Islamophobia, was a significant milestone in France.[21] In it, he developed the idea that the notion of Islamophobia is key to understanding public debates. Geisser asserts that it is necessary to distinguish between Islamophobia and racism, and denounces the roles played by intellectuals and media figures in the production and dissemination of prejudices and stereotypes of Islam. He states, 'Islamophobia is not simply the transposition of anti-Arab, anti-Maghreb and anti-urban youth racism: it is also a *religiophobia*.'[22] It is no longer exclusively the symbols of immigration, but also visible religious symbols that are targeted in debates. In fact, debates about the veil, mosques and minarets are 'symptoms of Islam,' a religion perceived as a 'retrograde pathology' in the phantasmatic Western imaginary.[23]

Geisser distinguishes among several forms of Islamophobia. Media and intellectual Islamophobia contribute to the promotion and diffusion of stereotypes which mobilize prejudices towards an imaginary, fantasized and threatening Islam. The author denounces the role played by intellectuals, whom he calls 'new experts of fear,' who mobilize 'latent Islamophobia.' They lead the ideological fight against Islam with no interest in the 'lived Islam' of Muslims, who are to them only 'marginal characters and ghostly shadows.' They invite Muslims to participate in debates in order to support these ideas: 'The Arab intellectual struggling against Muslim fanaticism in his own country; the Algerian feminist who is a victim of the violence of "religious nuts"; the enlightened mufti who denounces obscurantist readings of the Koran; not to mention the young "liberated" Arab woman in France who alerts French opinion to the ravages of Islam in French inner cities.'[24] The media largely promotes these 'new Muslim heroes.' We can add to this list the new 'integrated' female immigrants battling 'Muslim fundamentalism.'[25]

According to Geisser, Islamophobia, unlike racism, leads to the reversal of relations between the majority and minorities by victimizing Europeans. The 'real victims' are not Muslims, who are stigmatized by the regard of the majoritarian other, but the 'ethnic' French, who are attacked at the depths of their identity by runaway Islamization and all forms of globalization and cosmopolitanism.[26] Islamophobia thus serves as a marker of identity between an 'us' threatened with becoming a minority, and a massive 'them,' who are imposing their cultural difference and religious belief.

Living this difference in close proximity evokes fear, a feeling of intrusion and a rejectionary reaction. Today, immigration in Europe arouses reactions that can be described in terms of xenophobia and anti-Arab racism, but these terms do not account for the religious dimension, which is dominant and which the term Islamophobia aims to take into account.

But Islamophobia does not have the same status as the terms mentioned above, which have acquired a legitimate status. It is a part of the battlefield; its usage is controversial. For some, its usage reveals a phobic aspect, the 'irrational' character of discourse, allowing for criticism of representations of a community equated with its Muslim 'identity' without singularities, a face, or a history.[27] For others, it is a term invented by 'Iranian mullahs,' used by Islamists in order to block any criticism of Islam. For them, the very usage of the term 'Islamophobia' signifies an impediment to freedom of expression.[28] Can we speak of Islamophobia? This question has two facets: one raises the question of political legitimacy, the other of heuristic power. Is the notion legitimate and can it be translated into the political field in the same way as the notions of racism, xenophobia and anti-Semitism? On the other hand, does this notion have a heuristic and scientific capacity that allows us to seize the nature of the exclusion, which is of a religious order? The notion of Islamophobia has the merit of bringing to light the religious dimension, in other words the question that focuses on Islam in new social and political divisions. However, the term does not easily enter into the agenda of the French left, which remains blind to the question of religion even though it has long taken up the cause of the fight against racism and xenophobia. This question does not figure on the secular left's agenda, which remains faithful to the political tradition of denouncing racism and xenophobia but which is prey to accusations of political correctness, good intentions and passivity in the face of Islam, according to the spokespeople for neo-populism.

As much as European intellectuals from the left move to spontaneously denounce racially discriminatory practices and xenophobic acts towards immigrants, they remain reluctant to criticize policies that aim to prohibit Islam. On the contrary, they adhere to the principles of secularism, freedom of expression and the right to criticize Islam. Women on the left, feminists, anti-conformists, atheists, the majority of whom are inheritors of the counterculture of the 1960s, defend the 'courage' it takes to confront 'taboos' from the well-meaning left, feeding a sense of guilt that curbs criticisms of Islam. And yet, they have long expressed themselves widely in the European media, including in their most radical forms, as for example demonstrated by the echo that the hateful statements of the French author Michel Houellebecq and the Italian journalist Oriana Fallaci have had since the 2000s.

THE HOUELLEBECQ AND FALLACI AFFAIRS, OR THE SEDUCTION OF HATRED OF THE OTHER

No longer considered racist by the mainstream media, the widely publicized statements by these authors opened a new path for the most extremist Islamophobic speech. They deployed their sacrosanct freedom of expression, taking provocative positions against Islam, and their intervention in the subject was characterized by an outrageous tone that bordered on insult. These representatives of the 'nonconformist' or even atheist intelligentsia made themselves the defenders of respect for norms and values. They showed their attachment to the Western way of life and established order, affirming that they took a certain comfort in the Christian religion.

Michel Houellebecq, winner of the Goncourt Prize in 2010, is a 'new wave' writer known for his anti-conformist writings and his critiques of the inheritance of May '68. Despite his public disdain for political convictions and a retreat from public life bordering on nihilism, he stirred a polemic with his violent attacks against Islam. His novel *Platform*, published just before the attacks of September 11 2001, contained several passages hostile to the Muslim religion.

In *Platform*, Islam and its sacred text – the Koran – are the targets of repeated insult. The judgments presented of the Muslim world's major figures are all critical of Islam: the young Maghrebi housewife, an Egyptian biochemist, and a Jordanian banker. Each of them adopts the values of modern liberalism: work, science, and finance. In this book, there is a binary opposition between the Western world, depicted as superior and modern, and Muslim culture, which is backward and retrograde. The main character doesn't mince his words: he considers Islam 'the most stupid religion.' Even more than this injurious argument, it was the character's barbed remarks that provoked the astonishment of literary critics. In the story, after the character's girlfriend is killed in an Islamist attack, he unscrupulously describes his joy at the announcement of Palestinian deaths: 'Each time that I heard that a Palestinian terrorist, or a Palestinian child or a pregnant Palestinian woman had been gunned down in the Gaza strip, I felt a quiver of enthusiasm.'[29]

In the book, the author repeated several of the anti-Islamic tirades that the novel attributed to the characters.[30] Playing on this ambiguity of stating opinions similar to those of his characters, he erased the traditional distinction between author and narrator.[31] The porosity between the work of fiction and the author's personal opinions weakened the immunity of literature and its fictional world.

It is notable that freedom of expression, founded on the convention of the autonomy of the literary and public fields and on the immunity of the work of fiction, has been transformed in our societies, where a premium is put on communication. According to sociologist Jérôme Mezioz, the young generation of writers born in the era of mass culture has embraced the author's public role and his involvement in frequent polemics. The boundaries between the author and his work, the autonomy of the work and the author's public persona, fiction and reality are being blurred.[32] This phenomenon is not limited to literature, but equally characterizes the arts. Freedom of expression, as a cultural value, returns with force in the confrontation of European publics with Islam. Provocation characterizes public confrontations. Writers, artists and politicians celebrate it as the supreme act of freedom of expression.

If the Houellebecq affair, circumscribed to the French literary world, has remained relatively discreet, the fight against Islam by Oriana Fallaci, a renowned Italian journalist, has resounded in the media far beyond Italy's borders.

Oriana Fallaci earned international public acclaim as a war correspondent in Vietnam, Libya and Mexico and shaped Italian journalism with her memorable interviews. After the attacks of September 11, she published the book *The Rage and the Pride.*[33] In this anti-Islam manifesto, Fallaci revisits Samuel P. Huntington's thesis in *The Clash of Civilizations*, which considers Islam the

West's new enemy. In her previous book *Inshallah*,[34] she described Islamist 'kamikazes,' portrayed as characters full of hate and violence against whom one must react with rage and courage, ignoring intellectuals' 'chant' and their so-called tolerance. In Fallaci's point of view, an anti-intellectual rhetoric, 'a virile and crude anti-Islamism'[35] has emerged and will be adopted by all those who wish to bring down 'antiracist taboos' and systematically refer to Muslims in a derogatory manner.

Fallaci sees no issue with multiplying insults against Islam and Muslims, who she calls 'the fucking sons of Allah.' For her, this is a badge of courage. It is necessary to react and mobilize against Islam, which is invading and threatening Western civilization from the inside: 'there is no place for muezzins, minarets, fake teetotalers, their fucking middle ages, and their fucking chadors.'[36] This assault on the Muslim religion is not motivated simply by a secular mindset that rejects all religious beliefs, but is characterized by a new penchant for Catholicism. Thus, she distinguishes between the Christian God and Allah, the Muslim God: 'Allah has nothing in common with the God of Christianity. With God the Father, the Good Lord, the God who preaches love and forgiveness. The God who sees in men his children. Allah is a master God, a tyrant God. […] How can you put Jesus and Mohammed on the same plane?!'[37]

This penchant for Christianity is noticeable among European intellectuals, inheritors and defenders of the universalist, atheist left. Michel Houellebecq's remarks illustrate this point. He claims to be very critical of all monotheist religions, but he nonetheless admits that he has a certain affection for Catholicism. Unlike the Koran, 'the Bible, at least, is very beautiful, because Jews have a real literary talent […]. I have a residual sympathy for Catholicism, because of its polytheistic aspect and all its churches, stained glass, paintings and sculptures.'[38]

Values, heritage, patrimony and the Christian God are defended in opposition to Islam in order to distinguish a national and 'civilizational' 'amongst us' which we prize, or, as in the title of Fallaci's book, which gives us 'pride.' We must not have an inferiority complex or become intimidated by intellectuals and their accusations of colonialism and racism. Instead, we must have the courage to express our rage against Muslims, without scruple, in order to defend the cultural patrimony. Rage and courage, that is Oriana Fallaci's formula, which has been adopted by other European writers, thinkers and journalists, and all those who believe that in the battle against Islam, it is vital to tear down taboos in public life against racism and xenophobia. In public debates, the divide between left and right is becoming less clear. Leftist intellectuals who are secular and resist religion remain at best perplexed when they are not themselves seduced by this simplistic emotional formula: rage and courage in the face of Islam. Despite differences in style and posture, in the cases of Fallaci and Houellebecq, the boundaries between the private and the public, emotions and facts, feelings and ideas are confused.

'Why do Italians read Oriana Fallaci?'[39] This is the title of an article that suggests the way this question should be asked. The Italian journalist Giancarlo Bosetti addressed this question, seeking to explain Fallaci's popularity among the Italian public.[40] According to him, these books should not be considered an isolated phenomenon because their success makes evident the existence of an endemic form of rejection.

Remarks and admissions are seen, with some ambivalence, as characterized by 'a revealing straightforwardness': 'Fallaci is positively frightening and touches within the reader something profound and unconfessed that he never allowed himself to think, but which these pages, weighted with hatred and contempt, risk to brutally reveal: the repugnance that the Other inspires in all good Westerners, God forgive me. Luckily, this allergy is not fatal. But Oriana Fallaci, with the violence of a woman who sees a certain world order crumbling and who rises up within her pride and her flesh. There is a straightforwardness here – "You don't have any balls", she yells at us – verging on the odious but, not lacking in arrogance.'[41] These are the comments of Françoise Giroud, an exceptional figure in the French intellectual field. Born into a Jewish family from Turkey and a pioneer of feminine political journalism, her success incarnates 'French ambition.' As a young woman, Françoise Giroud protested against the Algerian war. Later, as secrétaire d'État à la Condition féminine, she defended the feminist cause; a journalist, author, scriptwriter and a firm atheist, she had an exceptionally rich life, professional career and political experience.[42] She figures among those who, while they are neither in the right wing nor racist, do not remain indifferent to Oriana Fallaci's statements.

Such remarks find support in their simplistic formula – rage and pride – playing on affect, spreading through a contagion and finding an echo among those who, in their intellectual and personal trajectories, appear immunized to a binary representation of the world. Many people have said they recognize themselves in this type of book and that they discovered their deep feelings and reasoning which they had not previously recognized. This is what accounts for their success. The unspoken is the element that facilitates thinking in terms of enemies; according to Bosetti, it is a 'negative' form of thought and a way of reasoning solely in the framework of a strong polarization, which asks people to choose, either 'us' or 'them.'

This 'way-of-thinking-based-on-enemies' and the importance given to the friend–enemy pair have been responsible for creating a political, moral and identity gap in Italy and more broadly in Europe. This contagious way of thinking has been propagated among intellectuals who seek to free themselves from the alleged yoke of multiculturalism, antiracism and pacifism. The Fallaci affair made this vice public.[43]

This 'negative' way of thinking based on the Other as an enemy seeks to tear down taboos in the public sphere. 'Freedom of expression' and 'courage' are the tools it uses to spread. This negative way of thinking denounces those who heed the siren call of a multicultural society and are lax in the face of cultural relativism. Muslim voices, preferably those of Muslim women, are enlisted in this fight. The negative framing of Islam's particular traits calls for the production, but also the legitimization and circulation, of this account. Writers, journalists and even researchers devote themselves to this task, sometimes actively, like Fallaci, sometimes through their contentment to acquiesce to it. Among a number of intellectuals, we can observe a progressive slippage from the criticism of multiculturalism to a repressive secular position, or an alignment with Catholic values and the defense of the Christian roots of Europe.

Europe, with its three monotheistic religions, is evolving towards a Judeo-Christian identity. In the process, Islam is marginalized.

It is no longer treated as an equal to the other monotheisms. As a religion, it is notably charged via mosques and prayer. Places and acts of faith common to the three great religions cease to be points of convergence among believers and are becoming points of division instead. Even in discourse by Catholic religious figures, there is a desire to push Islam aside and align with Judaism. The mayor of Treviso, president of the Lega de Venetia – a branch of the Northern League – involved in opposition movements against the construction of mosques in Italy, affirmed in the interview he granted us that 'the mosque is not a place of worship like the church for Catholics or the synagogue for Jews.' For him, 'Europe's roots are its Judeo-Christian origins.'[44]

NEW FACES 'FROM FAR-RIGHT BACKGROUNDS'

The political scene has not been spared these changes to the public sphere. These identity debates based on a confrontation with Islam have created fertile ground for the emergence of a movement that can be considered as neo-populism. It is less a new assault by the far right than a populist force that is riding the wave formed by the 'fall of taboos,' the displacement of boundaries and barriers separating the far right from the right and even the left. The political manipulation of fear in the face of Islam has caused movements, ideologies and people who once found themselves in opposing political camps to converge, and blurs the traditional left–right political division.

The 2009 European elections set the tone: the most liberal countries were surprised at the increase in votes for far-right political parties. In the United Kingdom, the British National

Party entered the European Parliament for the first time, winning two seats. In the Netherlands, the rich multicultural heritage was jeopardized by the victory of Geert Wilders' Party for Freedom (PPV). Republican France, which thought itself safe from the rise of far-right political parties, did not break with this pattern. The arrival of Marine Le Pen as head of the National Front and her growing popularity in polls show that France has been equally affected by the anti-Islamic wave that is sweeping Europe. New dynamics explain the return of the far-right movement: it is changing its face, ceasing to be marginal, hijacking the heritage of May '68, defending national values and introducing a new political repertory by taking Islam as its target. This movement is in the process of gaining a new legitimacy by adopting identity themes which have been gaining new ground in European public opinion in the past decade. The spokespeople of these movements have earned a new and particular public audibility. They have made their way into public life by capitalizing on the fear of Islam. They distinguish themselves in these debates by their combativeness against Islam, their irreverence towards the ideas of the 'politically correct' and 'conformist left.' Republicans on the right and intellectuals on the left remain perplexed in the face of the rise of these movements. They find themselves especially handicapped by the consequences of their own political ideas, which paved the way for the emergence of these new public actors and complacent populism.

Marine Le Pen represents the new feminine figure from the far right who has joined the other rising figures in Europe. These faces distinguish themselves from the previous conservative generation; sometimes they display a habitus close to the European counterculture and find themselves distanced from their predecessors. The leader of the Austrian far-right party, Heinz-Christian Strache, with his T-shirts with the effigy of Che, and Oscar Freysinger, the originator of the referendum against minarets in Switzerland, with his long ponytail, do not hesitate to borrow the emblems of cultural revolt. Both present themselves as partisans of sexual equality, feminism, freedom of expression, and the fights against homophobia and anti-Semitism. From this point of view, Marine Le Pen is representative of this break with paternalistic culture, the values of workers and Catholics from '*la France profonde*.' If her father made himself the spokesperson for the '*petit peuple*' against established elites educated in the *Grandes écoles*, his daughter, a lawyer and European deputy, has not sought to distinguish herself from the republican elite. On the contrary, she lends her face to Marianne, drapes herself in republican ideals and defends secularism. In a male party, while profiting from her lineage, she adopts a feminist posture; it is the posture of republican and secular 'feminism from above,' from where the Islamic veil of young Muslim women is fought.

These new figures enter the public sphere by provoking controversies over Islam in Europe. By stirring a lively debate about the construction of minarets in Switzerland, Oscar Freysinger, till then unknown in the political landscape, became popular on the European level. In France, Marine Le Pen exploits the theme of the Islamic threat, condemning Muslim prayers in the street and focusing public attention on it. She caused a polemic by comparing Friday prayers in the rue Myrha, in Paris's 18th arrondissement, to the 'German Occupation.' This comparison between Muslims and Nazis spurred several antiracist associations to file a complaint for inciting racial hatred.

Marine Le Pen pursues her advancement in the public sphere by speaking out on a number of controversies surrounding Islam. She denounces the full veil, calling for a 'full' law; she speaks out against 'mosque-cathedrals'; she lashes out against polygamy and denounces the 'ban on pork in cafeterias.' All these Muslim religious practices appear to her as a manifestation of Islam. Any tolerance towards Muslims leads, according to her, to discrimination against the 'ethnic' French.

It is becoming increasingly difficult to name these far-right movements. This difficulty in naming indicates the changed agenda and face of the far right in Europe. They cannot simply be understood in the tradition and continuity of 1970s xenophobia and anti-immigration policies. The category of race has assumed religious aspects. The actors in these movements no longer come from the extremities of the political landscape, but seek legitimacy from majority public, or 'national,' opinion. They defend their outspokenness and pride themselves on 'saying aloud what others think to themselves.' The public debate has taken on the emotional tinge of fear, echoing the sensational shock images and finding its rhythm in the circulation of stereotyped representations.

Like Muslims 'from immigrant backgrounds' who have escaped the immigrant condition and aim to experience citizenship in the post-immigration phase, these new faces of populism, 'from far-right backgrounds,' are no longer targets of ostracism but usher in a new populist era in Europe. These new political formations appoint themselves the defenders of the national community against 'the Islamic invasion' and converge at the European level in the name of partisan homogeneity. They combat the signs of Islam's public visibility in Europe, such as the headscarf, the construction of mosques and minarets, prayers in the street, ritual slaughter and the commerce of halal food. In their offensive against Islam, they are earning popularity among European publics.

They position themselves as guarantors of national values and promise to preserve the national 'amongst us' by fighting the 'Islamic invasion.' In their representations, Muslims are objectified in one monolithic category, without faces, history or voices.

In the course of these debates, we have also witnessed the constitution of the identity of a European 'us' against Muslims. Islamophobic policies have freed xenophobic inhibitions by calling for courage to speak freely about feelings, 'rage' and hatred for others, breaking with Europe's pluralistic and progressive tradition. The subject no longer holds back hatred and anger for the Other, an anger that imperils the democratic process but which also runs the risk of turning against 'its own,' as tragically illustrated in the case of the killer Breivik in Norway in 2011.

Murderous violence perpetrated against Norwegian youth is symptomatic of the ambient ideological climate in Europe with its 'murderous' threats for European democracy. The killer, Anders Behring Breivik, thirty-two years old, a graduate of the Oslo business school and a 'native Norwegian,' described himself as a 'conservative Christian.' His *Manifesto* shows that he accumulated disparate images, assembling a rhetoric based on the defense of identity against the Islamic malady. He denounces 'the softness and feminization of European culture' and deplores 'the lack of virility of the emasculated Western male.' The promotion of multiculturalism, the fight against racism, sexism and homophobia form what he depicts as 'an ideology whose goal is to *destroy* Western civilization.' According to him, multiculturalist elites – European institutions, government parties, the media and intellectuals – are principally responsible for this state of affairs. They 'betrayed' Europe. This is whom Breivik sought to punish by raising arms against innocent, young Norwegian Social Democrats. He reproached them for enabling a culture of tolerance that opened Europe's doors to Islam.

We are observing the retrograde transition of public life in Europe under the sway of destructive forces. The presence of Muslims in Europe, the manifestation of their difference in the public sphere, their religious visibility, all this, as we have seen, provokes the contraction of identity and anti-Islam political reactions which find a great deal of legitimacy in European public opinion. Each new controversy accelerates and amplifies this movement that is spreading across Europe. The entire intellectual and political arsenal, which enabled thoughts of the public sphere and Islam's cultural and religious difference, has fallen by the wayside. Thus, inexorably, multiculturalism, the rights of religious minorities and freedom of religion are losing their discursive force. Muslim migrants have found themselves dispossessed of a political language that could allow them to defend their presence in the life of the city. They are not welcome, except for those who adhere to the ideas of the secular intelligentsia, respond to the imperatives of feminism from above and to the values of the dominant culture of reference, the *Leitkultur*.

What do these controversies unveil? Is the European public sphere in the process of becoming a place where a conflict between civilizations plays out? A place for confrontation between Islam and the West? Can Europe escape these exclusionary spirals of violence and reciprocal policies of intolerance? Is there another way for the public sphere to again become a place for coming together, favorable to democratic pluralism? In order to respond to these questions, I chose to go into the field in different European cities and lead an inquiry among ordinary citizens, giving 'ordinary Muslims,' those who are implicated in and concerned by these controversies, the chance to speak.

2

Ordinary Muslims

> Investigation in the social sciences is as much about the need to document reality as the necessity to think in a new way.[1]

As we just saw, controversies surrounding Islam in Europe have led to the rise of neo-populist and even Islamophobic movements. But in parallel to these controversies, Muslim voices are making themselves heard. In debates on Islam, new figures are emerging: men and women, theologians and politicians, representatives of a new generation, engaged in a post-migratory phase and a process of integration. Their mastery of European languages and knowledge of codes of communication and social etiquette allow them to gain access to public debates. Some, like their opponents, have proved that they are skilled in the consummate art of polemics.

MEDIA FIGURES OF ISLAM

Among them are intellectuals, theologians and political figures known as 'liberated women.' They are the faces of European Islam in that their public statements concern the subjects European

Muslims are constantly questioned on: equality of the sexes, freedom of expression, wearing the veil, intolerance and terrorism. Their knowledge of the principles of Islam and European values gives them audibility both among Muslims and European publics. Their popularity with one group is sometimes a handicap in the eyes of the other. Facing rival or even antagonistic publics calls their credibility and statements into question. Their participation in debates for and against Islam raises a number of concerns, criticism and outright rejection. In the heart of Western countries, each one of these figures is controversial; some are suspected of falling under the influence of Islamists and are refused residence permits and entry visas, while others, those who are reproached for rejecting Islam, are intimidated or even receive death threats from Islamist radicals.[2]

We can observe a difference between these men and women in their public positions. The Muslim women who emerge in these debates most often make themselves the defenders of secular values and formulate criticisms of Islam. Unlike men who draw on their knowledge of Islamic theology, these feminine voices bring their life story and 'intimate' experience with Islam to the forefront.

By drawing on her experience as a Somali Muslim woman, Ayaan Hirsi Ali presents hers as an authentic voice from inside the community in order to denounce Islam's oppression of women. Evoking her forced marriage and the death threats she received, she has become the spokesperson for feminism and the value of freedom. She draws public attention to taboo subjects dealing with the condition of Muslim migrant women. She positions herself in debates as a Muslim woman liberated from Islamic laws and from the Muslim community itself. Her personal story as an

'Ex-Muslim woman' reinforces her aura as a free female 'Infidel' (and the title of one of her bestsellers)[3] and legitimizes her public interventions in the Netherlands. She has gained popularity among the French intelligentsia by advocating secularism without concessions to Muslim demands.[4] European feminists also admire Ayaan Hirsi Ali; in 2008 they awarded her the Simone de Beauvoir prize for Women's Freedom.

As a 'Muslim and European,' Ayaan Hirsi Ali positions herself in favor of European supremacy, occupying a position that can be described as 'one versus the other.' She has made herself the defender of secularism and individual freedoms she deems irreconcilable with Islam. She has aligned herself with right-wing neo-populist policies, notably with those of Geert Wilders in the Netherlands, against Islam in Europe.

These spokespeople who reject or defend Islam all straddle several countries and nations. Ayaan Hirsi Ali, a woman of Somali origin and a refugee in the Netherlands, was elected deputy in the parliament of The Hague before traveling to the USA, where she joined the American Enterprise Institute (AEI), home of the neo-conservative think tank. If Ayaan Hirsi Ali represents the voice of secular Muslims, Tariq Ramadan – the most famous of Muslim intellectuals – has begun to make himself known in European debates as the defender of European Islam. A Swiss citizen and French speaker, he teaches at Oxford University in England and heads a specialized center for Islamic legislation and ethics in Doha, Qatar.[5] Ramadan aims to link philosophical and theological reasoning. He has distinguished himself not only from secular intellectuals, but also from more classic theologians such as the sheikh Yusuf Al-Qaradawi, a Qatari of Egyptian descent and president of the European Council for Fatwa and Research, as well as a regular on the TV station Al-Jazeera. The fatwas issued by this transnational preacher have authority in both Muslim societies and among European Muslims. They are broadcast in English and Arabic on the website 'Islamonline,' founded in 1999.

All these actors use different media, participate in televised debates, publish articles in newspapers, write books translated into several languages, and have their own websites; they are not confined to one particular national space, but instead circulate between several countries and institutions. They have several 'homelands' and use information and communication technologies to defend their vision and propagate their ideas. As denationalized figures of European Islam who are nonetheless mediatized on a global scale, these thinkers, preachers, philosophers, theologians – men and women – participate in the establishment of new norms for Islam in Europe, principally concerning questions related to sexuality and equality between men and women.

TARIQ RAMADAN, CONTROVERSIAL MUSLIM INTELLECTUAL AND PROMOTER OF A EUROPE OF 'SHARED UNIVERSALS'

If Tariq Ramadan is undoubtedly the public figure the most representative of Muslims living in Europe, he is also the most controversial. The fact that he is the grandson of Hassan al-Banna, founder of the Muslim Brotherhood, gives him a special aura and makes him a charismatic figure among some Muslims, but also excites suspicion in the eyes of European publics. He is accused of 'doublespeak' and spreading Islamist propaganda.[6] Although he is fluent in French language and culture, it is in France in particular that he faces the most obstacles in participating in public life. His plea in favor of Islamic belief in Europe clashes with the fundamental principles of the French Republic, namely the principle of secularism and citizenship, which requires the renunciation of difference and community affiliation, whether ethnic or religious – the *sine qua non* condition of the integration of the individual. Far from adhering to the idea of republican universalism, Tariq Ramadan criticizes the West's pretension to hold the monopoly on the universal and has developed the notion of a 'shared universal.' For him, the universal must be a common space where several paths, several voices and several religions come together. This shared universal is forged in the intersections of commonality rather than in the integration of differences.[7] Drawing inspiration from Hinduism and the three monotheisms, he promotes the necessity of spiritual work and surpassing ego through self-reform, considering interior liberation the condition for sharing and pluralism; according to him, only introspective work allows us to meet others halfway.[8] For the political scientist Alain Roussillon, Tariq Ramadan has contributed to

> the emergence of a new Islamic positivity by engaging in a contextual reading of Text. His position sheds light on the terms and stakes of compromise, which condition any actualization of the interpretation of religious norms, searching for consensus in which Ulemas emerge as necessary partners. We can see how this dialectic works in the emergence of the Islamic feminism Ramadan encourages: on one hand, Muslims must move away from the patriarchal power that is imposed

> on them in Muslim societies, including in emigrant ones, and defend their right to education, work and autonomy; on the other hand, this must not be interpreted as blind imitation of the model of the Western 'emancipated' woman.[9]

In the course of our research, we observed Tariq Ramadan's popularity among young Muslims. In the interviews we conducted in different European cities, the interviewees spontaneously evoked his writings and conferences. In particular, young Muslims refer to his thinking when they broach the issue of how to live their faith in Europe. In fact, Tariq Ramadan is the first theologian who allows believers to see how they can live their faith as European citizens, and that being Muslim and living in Europe are not incompatible. The statements of a twenty-five-year-old inhabitant of Toulouse of Moroccan origin reveals Ramadan's influence on young Muslims who seek to reconcile their faith with their daily lives in Europe. Tariq Ramadan is someone who helped this young man understand and interpret his religion in the European context:

> I asked myself a lot of questions when I was younger and I always had the feeling that I was caught between two cultures because I was always led to believe that I couldn't be a Muslim who respected Islamic principles and a French citizen at the same time. I thank Tariq Ramadan. He helped me a lot in constructing an identity, taking into account my faith and my identity as a citizen. Today, things are a lot better. I am a French citizen of Muslim faith and for me, there's no problem with that.[10]

Tariq Ramadan's impact on European Muslims is not limited to the francophone context or to Arabic-speaking Muslims. Many, independent of their ethnic origins, 'recognize themselves in Tariq Ramadan's statements' – which they see as 'very reflective of the context' in which they live. A Danish woman with a Finnish mother and a Syrian father and founder of the association Critical Muslims has been inspired by Ramadan's work in constructing an identity in between two cultures – a Christian and a Muslim one. She regrets the absence of an intellectual Muslim like him in Denmark.[11] According to a young Italian woman of Moroccan origin, Ramadan 'touches on Muslim problems in Europe.'[12] A young Dutch man of Turkish origin also expressed interest in Tariq Ramadan's works and public statements in response to the question 'How do you live Islam in Europe?'[13] Tariq Ramadan seeks to give Muslims a new consciousness of their European citizenship by going beyond the prevailing discourse on immigration and the failure of integration. Most Muslims who responded to our inquiry appreciated the fact that Ramadan's analyses take the European reality of Islam into account.

Everywhere in Europe, whether they criticize or defend Islam, these public personalities are inaugurating a new phase: the post-migratory phase; they incarnate the a priori paradoxical appellation 'European Muslim.' That these figures are controversial is a sign that they are coming up against an obstacle and creating a collision effect; they reveal the difficulty in normalizing relations between dual members of the Muslim faith and European citizens. They crystallize the constraints and digressions in the process of the 'indigenization' of Islam in Europe. However, by their very presence, they are the instigators of the transformation of European public spaces. Intervening as they do as political actors, public intellectuals, theologians and experts, it is difficult to put them into one category. They are moving the divide between intellectuals and Islam and participating in making Islam the religion of reference in public debates.

THE NEW ISLAMIC HABITUS OF EUROPEAN MUSLIMS

We conducted our inquiry among ordinary Muslims who were interested in expressing their views on public affairs. We above all looked for ordinary citizens of Muslim faith who are not involved in media debates. Among them, we found practicing as well as non-practicing Muslims, immigrants and converts, feminists as well as imams from different ethnic origins – Pakistanis, Turks, Algerians … – but also young people from interreligious marriages. There were women who wore headscarves, others who didn't and who still considered themselves Muslim, consumers who prefer eating halal and organic, faithful people who wanted to see the construction of a new mosque in their city and converts who defended the Islamic patrimony in Europe. Our inquiry allowed 'ordinary Muslims' to speak, those representative of European Muslims today who find themselves at the heart of public controversies surrounding Islam while remaining absent from media or political debates. This research aims to make them audible and visible by inverting the unequal geometry of the media field.

In the course of our research project, *EuroPublicIslam: Islam in the Making of a European Public Sphere*, we spoke to more than four hundred people of all ages and backgrounds in twenty-one

European cities. Our fieldwork was conducted on two fronts: through individual interviews as well as group discussions. The research was conducted in French and English as well as German, Italian, Spanish, Dutch, Austrian, Turkish and Bosnian. The transcripts of the individual interviews and group discussions filled around three thousand pages. The material gathered over the course of this research was not limited to written documents. A documentary film[14] was produced using the video recordings of group discussion sessions. Two-thirds of those interviewed considered themselves Muslims, and one third were Christian, Jewish, secular or had no religious affiliation.

The semi-directive interviews, conducted individually, attest to the singularity of personal experiences and the personal way in which each person interprets living his or her faith in the course of everyday life in Europe. Priority was given to understanding the subjectivity and the piety of Muslims in everyday European life. In each interview, most of the interviewees expressed their satisfaction in simply explaining themselves. For once, they were not asked to comment on problems of integration or discrimination or their position on radical Islam. We asked them about different notions in Islam, on the boundary between the permitted and the forbidden, on what is sacred and blasphemous for them, on what has to do with their personal choices or with Islamic prescriptions.

The notion of sharia, which defines the ensemble of tenets that a Muslim must submit him- or herself to in terms of religion, social relations and juridical questions, occupies a central place in the Islamic universe of reference. Our interviews allowed us to see that this notion has little influence in the imaginary of the European Muslims interviewed and that it does not have a place in the definition of their beliefs. For European Muslims, living their faith in the European context implies adapting to secular laws as well as re-examining Islamic laws and tenets. Most Muslims do not recognize themselves in this notion, which they immediately associate with the application of corporeal punishments in Islamic states. They seize on discussions on the theme of sharia to reaffirm their affiliation to Europe.

Salima, a twenty-eight-year-old woman from a large Algerian family, was born in Valenciennes, in northern France. She is the oldest of six children and the most academically successful, holding a business degree. When we interviewed her, she was working in Geneva, Switzerland, in finance, and was single. In the portrait of a modern businesswoman was superposed the figure of a woman who made her own choices in her private and professional life while remaining faithful to her religious faith. At the end of her studies, she left for Pakistan and Afghanistan for six months on a humanitarian mission. When she returned, following the advice of headhunters, she moved to Geneva. She explains her decision as a professional opportunity, but also in terms of religious convictions: in effect, Geneva is known for its courses in Islamic theology. Salima is an athletic woman and likes hiking and skiing, sports that allow her to dress in a way that conforms to Muslim clothing standards. When asked what she thinks of the application of sharia law in cases of adultery, Salima hesitates an instant before responding: 'As a woman, and someone born here, the practices of stoning and whipping are especially shocking to me. It's true that for me, today, it would be impossible to subject myself to that.' As someone 'born here,' she finds punitive aspects of sharia, corporeal punishment, notably of women, 'shocking.'

She affirms her adherence to the European cultural area in an uncomplexed way.[15]

This portrait of Salima is not an exception. Her trajectory is traced both by her aspiration to professional success and her desire to live, learn and interpret her faith. Her belief implies personal engagement in all aspects of life. Living her faith means learning about Islam both in seminars and through personal techniques. Her professional, humanitarian and even athletic life choices are oriented by her adherence to Islam. The way she lives her faith is not automatic, but rather the object of constant attention and surveillance; she maintains a self-consciousness that constitutes her person and her professional path. In Salima, a new profile of the Muslim woman is appearing, a woman who does not hesitate in expressing her nonconformity with certain Islamic laws and prescriptions, especially as they relate to the condition of women, and who affirms with a touch of pride her critical spirit and independence, which she identifies as her European characteristics.

This profile reveals that 'ordinary Muslims' does not mean Muslims who live their faith in a 'habitual' way, transmitted by family tradition from their country of origin. Immigration opens a rupture with authorities of religious knowledge and breaks the classical chain of transmission. European Muslims find themselves in a social context where their relationship to religion is not preset. They readapt religion in a conscious manner. In this work in progress, they distinguish themselves from the preceding generation, characterized by the oral transmission of religion, and favor an intellectual apprenticeship of Islam. They thus master canonical texts by going to seminars and conferences and frequenting Islamic institutes and associations. This apprenticeship is at once personal and collective.

Exercising faith calls for memorizing surahs, hadiths and legends, but also for a daily repetition of practices and a mastery of body and mind. This process outlines the contours of a new Islamic habitus specific to European Muslims.

The notion of ordinary Muslims suggests the profile of Muslims who are fully invested in social life and actively engaged in this Islamic habitus, without this automatically implying Islamist militancy. The majority occupies the middle classes in European countries. They make up the nineteen- to forty-five-year-old age group, a young and active population. They are in the heart of society and social life and occupy positions in varied professions. During our inquiry, the Muslims we met worked in education – as teachers in primary and secondary schools, professors and researchers; in the medical field – as nurses, psychiatrists, psychotherapists, and doctors; in liberal professions – as lawyers, engineers and architects; in commerce – as owners of restaurants, bookstores, hair salons and textile studios; in artistic and cultural production – as graphic designers, rappers, hip-hop singers, web designers, sound engineers, film directors and fashion illustrators. They are also involved in associations and politics as directors of NGOs and public relation firms, city council representatives and directors of local and international organizations.

WHAT VISIBILITY FOR ISLAM IN THE PUBLIC SPACE?

Following Islamic prescriptions, Muslims make their presence felt in a visible and active way. The qualification 'ordinary' here does not evoke being invisible and passive. The expression of faith is a form of action. Faith as a belief, but also as a performance, calls for a personal and public mode of action. The act of veiling oneself or praying proves this religious form of a mode of action: it is at once interior and personal, performative and public. However, Muslim citizens present a troubling visibility, or 'strangeness,' because they aspire to be ordinary citizens while demonstrating a religiosity with distinctive traits. They become visible and make themselves noticed instead of blending in with the majoritarian society. This ambivalence between the manifestation of a visible difference and the aspiration to be ordinary citizens can best be captured in Hannah Arendt's approach to public space as a place for appearing.[16] According to the philosopher, those who have the courage to leave their shelter and to unveil themselves, to show their presence and their singularity in public, perform an act of citizenship: it is in action and appearing in public that they become citizens. Arendt invites us to reflect, as Étienne Tassin writes, about 'the heroism of action,' the conquest of 'ordinary glories' in the public democratic space.[17] Muslims contest their place in daily life and follow Islamic prescriptions which single them out. It is by seeking to be good Muslims and ordinary believers that they become visible citizens.

Thus the two fronts of our inquiry focus on the subjective aspect of faith in the private sphere and on its visible and controversial aspect in the public sphere. Religious faith is an intimate and personal thing. Faith displaced into public life by practices and symbols of piety acquires a new dimension and becomes visible in the eyes of other citizens. In our interviews with European Muslims, we sought to understand how they construct their religious subjectivity in 'private' in introspective practices, while in our group discussions we observed them in 'public,' in an interactive situation with other citizens, in order to study the relations between Muslim and non-Muslim citizens.

The two facets of our fieldwork – interviews and group discussions – are complementary and even interdependent. The interviews allowed us to understand the subjective aspect of religion and personal interpretations of controversies. The group discussions created the necessary conditions for the actors to position themselves in relation to one another and confront their differences by engaging in debates. The semi-directive interviews told us what happens in the 'wings,' while the group discussions allowed us to observe what happens on the public stage. Following Erving Goffman's distinction, public space, like the stage in a theater, is made up of a 'front stage' and a 'backstage'; the actors cross the boundary that separates the wings from the performance onstage.[18] In other words, it is when Muslims move their faith across the boundary of the private sphere that Islam becomes visible. The question of the visibility of religion is closely linked to the construction of faith in the private sphere. This visibility is not simply a media affair; it is in part inherent to Muslim actors and the manner in which they display their faith in public.

Thus it is Muslims themselves, those who attempt to live their faith and follow religious tenets in their daily lives in Europe, who give Islam visibility in the public sphere. Media coverage is not the only party involved in these affairs. We see Muslims of European nationality in the countries in which they live who dispute their place in the city and show their singularity. The demands they make about Islam are proof in themselves of their level of integration because calling for the construction of mosques, wearing the veil or consuming halal food shows Muslims' engagement in European life. They are active citizens in the social and political terrain of their respective countries; through their demands, they familiarize themselves with juridical and administrative rules and with economic and political actors.

European publics are not indifferent about the rise of Muslim presence and visibility. Controversies attest to the discord in public opinion caused by the expression of faith in public. There is a whole repertoire of polemics about Islam. Among those we studied, these included collective prayer in the street, the construction of mosques in city centers, wearing the veil in schools, the availability of halal food in businesses and the banning of sacrilegious representations in the arts. Not every Islamic tenet is a source of controversy. Not every controversy is linked to the expression of Islamic faith. The religious practices subject to controversy mentioned above are not all equal from the point of view of Islamic theology. Prayer – *'ibâdât* in Arabic[19] – is one of the five major obligations that constitute the pillars of Islam. Wearing the veil and eating halal food, considered as the social obligations of religion – *mu'*âmalât in Arabic[20] –are open to interpretation. There is a general consensus on the prohibition of pork and slaughtering animals according to prescribed rules, while the obligation to wear the veil is a subject of debate among theologians. The meaning of the sacred – banning blasphemy of the Prophet – is a value that Muslims have very much interiorized. The expression of faith among Muslims is not limited to these practices or orthopraxy that we generically term Islamic tenets, and which refer to rituals and religious practices. It is these practices which are contested and have become objects of controversy among European publics.

In one way or another, these controversies disrupt, disturb and rattle the universe of European Muslims, practicing and not. Their personal stories about Islam intersect with the conduct of these debates. There is no airtight seal separating the public perception of Islam and the subjective stories of European Muslims. Muslims feel that they are perpetually questioned and interrogated about their relationship to their religion.[21] Their stories are traversed by these controversies and media representations of Islam. Even those who are not in the media space are spectators in that they are part of the public. This implication affects and transforms their discourse. These controversies question all Muslims independently of their relationship to the Islamic faith. We integrated into our research the voices of these Muslims, those who are not plaintiffs on behalf of Islam but who are nonetheless affected by these controversies. These are citizens of the Muslim faith, no less ordinary than others, but who have not necessarily actively sought to adopt the distinctive symbols of religion.

With the emergence of these controversies, Islam has left the community of believers, ceasing to be an affair among Muslim believers, and instead becoming an affair for all. The common thread of these controversies guided our choices in selecting participants for our discussion groups: city dwellers who were opposed to the construction of a mosque in their neighborhood, teachers who wrestled with the demands of young Muslim girls who wished to wear the veil, citizens involved in fighting the social battle against racism, as well as progressive Catholics and Jews interested in interreligious dialogue … All are implicated in controversies surrounding Islam.

Our approach favors the notion of public space, which is not reducible to media space. From one space to the other there are pathways and sometimes overlaps, but they are not superimposed on one another. Before the media arrives, each one of these controversies arises in a specific place and is initiated by citizens. We favored this spatial and contentious dimension between social actors without ignoring the media dimension of controversies. We conducted our inquiry in public space around the actors and with them, in concrete and physical spaces in the cities where these controversies emerged.

RESEARCH ITINERARIES IN A EUROPE OF CONTROVERSIES SURROUNDING ISLAM

Our research itinerary was launched according to the emergence of controversies. Of the twenty-one European cities where we conducted our inquiry, Toulouse was our first stop. Two new affairs linked to the wearing of the headscarf led us to this city in February 2009: the first was known as 'Sabrina' after the young woman in question; the second 'Tisséo' after the name of the public transportation service in Toulouse. The French context was marked by the 2004 legislation that banned religious symbols from schools, known as 'the law against wearing the veil.' The law, which aimed to end the veil affair, caused a new rift. There was a 'before' and 'after' the 2004 law. It is 'after' the vote on this law that the two new affairs arose in Toulouse. They were the consequence of the attempt to apply this law to new places, notably the university and public transportation. Although they appear to be isolated cases, these affairs show how the grounds of confrontation expanded and how the arguments, which have been used in other controversies since then, changed.

Sabrina, a PhD student and research assistant at Toulouse's Paul Sabatier University, was asked to leave school after refusing to remove her veil, and was accused of threatening her colleagues' freedom of conscience. She was banned from accessing her place of work for 'disturbing public order.' The second affair concerned a woman in Toulouse who was barred from renewing her monthly Tisséo pass because her hair was covered by a scarf in her identity photo. Passengers were required to show their 'bare heads' in photos in order to respect the need to identify them. The woman's face was not covered. She was thus identifiable. The law was nonetheless applied: she was refused access to public transportation.

Once it came to be seen as a cause of disturbance to public order, the veil has since been banned in public places, universities, buses and on the street, and not only in public schools, as the 2004 law initially intended. In such a context, equating the principle of secularism and the interest of public order has become more and more evident in France.

The controversies we studied in Toulouse did not spread to the national or European level. They remained discrete. They nonetheless allowed us to observe an extension of the ban on wearing the headscarf in places that were not initially covered by this law. The ban on the veil no longer applies only to public schools and students who are minors, but began to spread to other spaces: universities, public transportation, school grounds and even the street. The kinds of women targeted by this ban also expanded: students, women going to pick up their children after school, childcare assistants in preschools, women in burkas or full veils.

Controversies have a spatial dimension. They do not emerge in the public sphere in an abstract way, but in concrete spaces and specific physical places: school, bus, pool, street, parliament, hospital, prison, tribunal, theater, art gallery, cafeteria, cemetery, etc.

Muslims, like all other citizens, visit these public spaces on a daily basis as users and consumers. The Tisséo affair in Toulouse illustrates how controversies surrounding the veil, even if they primarily concern schools, can also gain new ground, spreading to new spaces, such as the bus.

The bus as a mode of transport assures the mobility of citizens; it is also a symbolic place of equality among them in accessing public space. The bus is an example of a physical space that at the micro-sociological level makes public norms and laws appear, and reflects policies of segregation and exclusion. It is a public space where power and discriminatory relationships play out in terms of race, sex and religion. In our collective memory there is Rosa Parks, the African-American woman who made the bus a symbolic space for antiracist campaigns. In 1955, she refused to give her seat to a white passenger and sat in a seat where African-Americans were not allowed. By this performative act, she transgressed the forbidden and norms imposed by racial segregation. By making the difference in treatment of blacks and whites visible, she made everyone aware of racial segregation in public spaces.

The bus also occupies a preponderant role in the division between conservatives and modernists in Muslim societies. Conservatives have used the bus as a space to lead their battle and require the separation of men and women according to Islamic norms. On this note, we can't help but wonder, with some irony, if this desire to impose secular norms in public places in Europe is not in fact opposed to its own intentions. In the name of women's rights, don't we end up excluding a segment of women by blocking their access to public space? Thus it appears that, despite profound differences, feminist demands and Islamic norms intersect. Both are favorable to the marginalization of women to certain places, away from the male 'gaze.' Controversies about pools and hours reserved for women illustrate this point. Feminism in 1970s Europe, which called for the construction of a female identity away from the male gaze, would have supported this type of demand. At present, European feminists fighting against 'Islamization' of norms prefer mixing the sexes and seek to impose secular norms in these spaces.

Our inquiry was not restricted to only one country or only one question, the veil affair. The emergence of controversies on different themes indicated our research itinerary. This itinerary led us from Toulouse to Sarajevo, passing through Istanbul, Milan, Bologna, Cologne, Berlin, London, Lyons, Birmingham, Brussels, Geneva, Paris, Cordoba, Amsterdam, Copenhagen, Madrid, Oslo, Rotterdam, Treviso and Vienna. We didn't follow a map of European nations or the countries in the European Union. Instead, we chose to denationalize the inquiry and follow a European cartography sketched by a series of controversies wherever they appeared. Controversies don't stop at national boundaries and they led us to places where Muslims are not always migrants – for example, Sarajevo, which is different from other cities in our study in this way. Sarajevo has a unique status in our inquiry in that it gave us the opportunity to note the endogenous character of Islam in Europe. Leading our inquiry in Sarajevo required us to reverse our perspective on a migrant Islam that is exogenous to Europe – Muslims from the outside.

The position of this inquiry is to deconstruct sociological categories in terms of 'Muslims' and 'Europeans.' It differs from sociological studies that focus on a group of Muslims, an immigrant quarter, a community of the faithful or neo-fundamentalist militants. It seeks to render the faces of Muslims and Europeans in the singularity of their experience, the diversity of their personal trajectories and the plurality of their convictions. The core of this research is the deconstruction of binary and collective categories for Muslims as well as Europeans. The recent turn to identity in Europe aims to give a voice and a face back to the people, notably through the far right's discourse. Pierre Rosanvallon, a historian of Western democracy, shows how the rise of populist politics is linked to this turn to identity in Europe. According to him, public opinion, which is indispensable to the life of democracy, has turned into the figure of a 'people-opinion.' This personification of collectivity calls for the permanent figure of the interior enemy who is liable to threaten the identity of the European people.[22]

We aimed to overcome the opposition between binary categories through a double process. First, our research denationalizes Europe and seeks to go beyond the idea of a unity, a people and an opinion of the Other; it decollectivizes Muslims who are always represented in terms of communities, ethnicities or radical groups. In order to explore the horizon of possibility, we used an experimental approach on the ground with individuals, to test for the possibility of another link.

THE ROLE OF THE EXPERIMENTAL PUBLIC SPHERE (EPS) IN OUR RESEARCH

The appearance of a controversy in a city has the effect of reconfiguring the public field. Associations, community spokespeople, religious figures and politicians intervene. First, we accounted for the public field that was constituted in its relation to the event that led to the controversy. We prepared a field document describing this field as it took shape around the controversy, with the appearance of diverse actors, their interventions and their respective positions. Once we were in the place of inquiry, we invited the actors, both those involved in the controversy and those simply affected by it, to participate in interviews and group discussions. The experimental aspect of our research is primarily in the constructed character of our groups.

We conducted our inquiry on the ground around an event-controversy in a specific place. This was an active decision to distance ourselves from the media sphere and instead anchor our inquiry in the social context. The discussion groups allowed us to see the actors in their multiplicity, making them irreducible to binary categories such as 'Muslims' and 'Europeans.' Bringing ordinary people together and opening up a free space for debate, the discussion groups were organized as 'Experimental Public Spheres.'

The groups we brought together in the course of our research don't exist as such in reality. We were not in a natural group, 'between us,' but in a group formed by researchers. Like public space, site of the emancipation of the self, where private gives way to public in meetings with others, our experimental research space invited participants to break away from their multiple affiliations, without however renouncing them, and interact with other actors. The course of the research was conceived as an Experimental Public Sphere because we sought to find out whether around these interactions and confrontations links, ideas and unheard-of forms would emerge, capable of configuring an alternative public space.

This Experimental Public Sphere allowed those who felt unheard, misrepresented or even stigmatized to speak out. It functioned like the Theater of the Oppressed, founded in Brazil by Augusto Boal. It favored a form of 'theater of attempt,' different from 'theater of spectacle,' in which spectators become actors. His theater is based on important contemporary subjects in society. Augusto Boal invented a dispositive approach for teaching individuals, the 'oppressed,' to make their voices heard, to confront a situation and to learn to analyze it. It is by improvization rather than dramaturgy that citizens find themselves onstage discussing their wishes, needs and desires. If for Boal the theater is a form of knowledge, it must also be a means for transforming society. In his vision, 'the theater can help us construct our future instead of simply waiting for it.'[23]

In the manner of the Theater of the Oppressed, the Experimental Public Sphere allows participants in the frame of the research not to remain confined to the role of simple 'informers' who remain passive spectators to the story, but to enter into the social game. The dispositive approach of the research in fact creates a 'space' conceived as the 'stage' of a theater. This is as valuable for participants as it is for the team of researchers. Each member of the team – moderator, multimedia operator and analyst – has a defined role to play. There was also an interpreter present as we led our research in different European cities and thus in different languages. The researcher that formed the group played the role of mediator. He or she was the closest to the participants, about fifteen in each group. The multimedia operator who filmed the sessions, which lasted for a minimum of four hours, was also responsible for visual supports used during the sessions. By his or her material presence – camera, sound recording devices, film projector, computer – the multimedia operator reminded participants of the constructed aspect and the research protocol. As an analyst, I listened to what was said individually but also looked at what was going on collectively onstage. My role was to accompany the group in its search for meaning and connections, and to intervene at key moments: changes in register, turning points in the course of discussions, or reversals in the situation. I also shared my interpretation with participants during the session's proceedings. I gave them my interpretation of what appeared to be (im)possible. For each group, the horizon of an alternative public space was explored.

Group discussions were not led as collective interviews aimed at establishing each person's opinion, but instead were meant to create a situation in which participants could move beyond their own opinions and examine preconceived notions that each person had about the others. In order to make this possible, the scenography of each session was divided into three acts. The chosen controversy was projected during the first act by visual supports – images, photomontages, documentaries … Thus we began by eliciting the participants' engagement as they grappled with current events. During the first act, positioning, interactions and new configurations appeared within the group. The second act was devoted to questions relative to the daily experience of

Muslims, the Islamic habitus and their accommodations to Islam in their daily lives in a European context. It was a special moment for exposing the divergences between the subjectivity of the Muslim actors and the public perception of Islam. The third act explored the necessary conditions for surpassing reciprocal rejection and moving towards mutual recognition. In this way, revealing the possibility for the formation of an alternative public space underlies this third and final act.

The Experimental Public Sphere places social actors in an experimental situation that contains an imaginary aspect and a performative dimension through which they put themselves onstage and enact a different social choreography. The participants can in this way deepen their perception of the world and their perception of others, causing stereotypes to fall away. The experimental space for research, like the theater, transforms ways of thinking and constructing the social. In this way, the experimentation is an imaginary experimentation, designed to reveal the possibility of a new social organization or lack thereof. As with any research in the social sciences, we aimed to introduce a rift with common sense, criticize unquestioned beliefs and go beyond notions of what is self-evident. 'Investigation in the social sciences is as much the need to document reality as the necessity to think in a new way.'[24]

3

Controversies Surrounding Muslim Prayer

According to a saying linked to the Prophet Mohammed,[1] if the space is appropriate and suitable for meditation, Muslims can perform prayers anywhere on Earth: 'The entire world a place for prayer.' Prayer is one of the five pillars of Islam (the other four being the profession of faith, fasting, charity, and pilgrimage to Mecca). It is an act of faith that all Muslims must respect – according to one hadith, the first work that the faithful will be asked to account for on Judgment Day is prayer.

AN IMPORTANT RITUAL, CHALLENGING TO RESPECT IN THE EUROPEAN CONTEXT

Muslim prayer, or *Salaat*, which must be completed five times a day, is a sacred moment when Muslims take a break from their worldly activities in order to concentrate their attention on Allah and show their adoration. Prayer aims to consolidate faith and follows specific rules. It is an act codified in Muslim law. Believers must stand before God with a heart sincere in its devotion. They prepare themselves for this ritual with ablutions to purify the body. In order to purify their hearts as well, believers repeat a chant that expresses their intention to perform their prayers – in the name of Allah and the recommendation of his Prophet Mohammed.

Prayer is a spiritual process that requires bodily discipline.[2] It is at once an act of humility and an act of submission to divine will; this ritual must not be improvised or performed in an absent-minded way. The believer's posture – standing with hands crossed, eyes cast downward in humility, bowing, prostrating, kneeling – and the suras from the Koran recited during each prayer, aim to reinforce the intimate bond between the believer and God without any intermediaries. Prayers must be performed alone, although collective prayer in mosques is recommended particularly for men. The Friday midday prayer is the most important of the week. Believers are closely assembled in the straightest rows possible to show the equality of all men in front of the Lord.

To perform their prayers, all Muslims around the world turn towards the Qibla – the direction of Mecca. Media images of Muslim prayer in Europe are thus focused on the prostration of the faithful, all turning in the same direction. This vision, seen as representative of the collective submission of a community of shared faith, is highlighted and compared to the individualism of secular society in the West.

To be a good Muslim, one must always fight against the routine nature of prayer, and submit oneself to constant watchfulness;

rigor is a guarantee of authenticity and of perfecting the self. In the European context, following Islamic dictates and maintaining faith require constant effort on the part of the faithful: faith is never attained once and for all. Faith is constantly tended to and cultivated. Muslims' daily lives put it to the test.[3] In Western societies, respecting Islamic dictates in daily life is often a challenge and at the very least an exercise that demands repeated effort (*jihad al-nafs*).[4] In a secular context, Muslims' acts of piety are the objects of continual recall, particular attention, and permanent monitoring. Believers must overcome all kinds of obstacles in respecting prayer times, completing ritual purifications of the body and heart, concentrating and finding spaces for prayer. Their daily lives are full of invisible tactics and efforts at accommodation that require a keen awareness of Islamic practices.

From a religious vantage point, Muslims do not see anything inappropriate in praying outside mosques, unfolding their rugs on the ground on street corners, in the hallways of schools, in town squares, or outside cathedrals. These practices make Islamic prayer more visible in European societies, and in that these practices transgress the boundaries between places of worship and secular spaces, they are perceived as a disruptive intrusion by a foreign religion in public life. The manifestation of religion in an emblematic way, in public, leads to virulent debates. A series of controversies proves the difficulty of treating Muslims' religious practices within existing political and juridical frameworks, such as freedom of conscience and religious freedom or minority rights. Public prayers have taken different forms, both individual and collective. Streets, schools, and city centers have become unusual spaces for prayer, raising controversies in several European cities, such as Paris, Berlin, Milan and Bologna. Controversies that we sought to make explicit in our inquiry.

IN FRANCE AND IN GERMANY, THE SAME POLEMIC OVER PRAYERS IN PUBLIC

In the 2000s in France, the controversy linked to this phenomenon was named for the street in which it occurred, 'prayer in Myrha Street.' Myrha Street is located in Paris's 18th arrondissement, in the Goutte d'Or neighborhood, which has a majority immigrant population. During Friday prayers, the Khalid Ibn Walid Mosque attracts many believers. Without sufficient space inside the mosque, those praying often spill outside. The rector of the mosque, Hamza Salah, expresses his distress: 'I cannot forbid entry to a believer who has come to pray because there is no room. This is not a museum or a movie theater.'[5] Every Friday at noon, rugs appear on sidewalks as men spread them out one after another, blocking the street for the duration of prayers; when prayers are over, rugs are quickly rolled up again, and the crowd of believers disperses as everyone returns to his usual activities. This weekly adaptation of space has occurred progressively, with the help of local powers to ensure the safety of all participants.

Nonetheless, these accommodations on the local scale draw the attention of politicians at the national level. Marine Le Pen, president of the National Front, was the first to bring these prayers on Myrha Street to the center of a national debate. She compared prayers in the street to an 'occupation,' thus likening the Muslim who prays in the street to the German occupier during the Second World War. During the internal campaign for the presidency of her party, she declared at a public meeting in Lyons: 'This is an occupation of portions of territory, of neighborhoods where religious law is applied; it is an occupation. Of course there are no tanks, there are no soldiers, but it is an occupation all the same.'[6] Her remarks have drawn indignant reactions from the political class, but street prayers have become a source of tension. The implementation of a ban has become an important part of the French political agenda. The then interior minister, Claude Guéant (UMP, Union for a Popular Movement), included the prohibition of street prayers in his agenda. 'Street prayers must cease,' he declared, adding that his compatriots were not 'against one religion or another; but the fact that public space is appropriated in this way does not conform to the principle of secularism.'[7]

In Germany, the controversy over prayers in public places was launched by the story of a young Berliner who performed his prayers at school. Yunus Mitschele, whose mother is Turkish and whose German father converted to Islam, is a student at Diesterweg Gymnasium in the Wedding neighborhood in Berlin, largely made up of immigrants. Yunus began praying at school at age fourteen during recess. He used his jacket as a prayer rug in the school hallway; sometimes a small group of classmates joined him in prayer. The school's administration forbade this 'prayer in the hallway.' The case was brought before a court and led to a public debate. In the name of the constitutional right to religious freedom, some opted for a pragmatic solution: designating a room for those who wish to pray in school. For their opponents, such a decision would mean granting a privilege to one particular religion and would risk jeopardizing the principle of neutrality in schools. In 2011, after four years of legal battles, the Leipzig federal court decided in favor of a ban on prayer in school and reaffirmed that schools must be the guarantors of religious neutrality.

In these two cases, we can identify the characteristics of European Islam. Two forms of public prayer, in Paris and Berlin, collective and individual, in different spaces – the street in an immigrant neighborhood and the hallways of a school – represent different facets of Islam's visibility. We can distinguish in them two different generations, an Islam with two faces: the Islam of workers and that of schoolchildren.

We can also see how in both France and Germany, the foundation of space – its so-called neutrality and secularism – are used to frame this debate and to prohibit public prayers, at the expense of principles of freedom of conscience and freedom of religion. We find that Islam's visibility in public space is at the heart of these debates. In terms of immigration and the organization of religion in public life, France and Germany have different historical and political trajectories. French secularism, defined by the principle of neutrality in public space, forbids all religious symbols in schools. In Germany, the public manifestation of religion is authorized, as is proved by the presence of crosses on classroom walls. If in France the question of Muslim immigration is linked to the colonial past in Algeria, Germany's relationship to Turkish immigrants follows an altogether different trajectory. Despite these differences, we can nevertheless recognize a growing proximity between two countries which seek to reaffirm the 'neutrality' of public space in order to prohibit religious practices associated with Islam.

In Italy, where public prayers have fed even more virulent controversies, it is not the principles of neutrality and secularism that are invoked to combat Islam's visibility, but the Catholic influence on public space, giving these debates an entirely different dimension.

THE 2009 BOLOGNA CONTROVERSY

In Bologna, home to the fifth-largest church in the world, the Basilica of San Petronio, built in the fourteenth century, Muslim residents are fighting for their place. An artistic hub of northern Italy, the city is home to a university attended by the most illustrious figures of the Middle Ages – Irnerius, Dante, Boccaccio, Petrarch – and is considered the oldest university in the West. In Bologna, nicknamed 'Bologna, the learned one' ('*Bologna la dotta*'), but also 'Bologna, the red one,' in reference to its communist past as well as the color of its terracotta tiles, Islam is gaining ground despite the power of the Catholic Church and Christian images which offer evidence of hostility to Islam. The famous fresco in the gothic Basilica of San Petronio, dating back to the early Renaissance, proves this: in it, we see the Prophet Mohammed destined for Hell, next to Lucifer.

A rally in support of the population of Gaza under the threat of Israeli attacks took place in Bologna on 3 January 2009 in the Piazza Maggiore, a central destination for visitors and residents. At the end of the rally, Muslim participants began collective prayers. The rest of the demonstrators, including pacifists, anti-globalization and left-wing activists, formed a line of curious spectators around them. The Muslims dedicated their prayers, punctuated by supplications (*du'a*), to the residents of Gaza. Photographers quickly immortalized this collective prayer, Muslims bowing towards Mecca in Bologna's Piazza Maggiore, with the Basilica of San Petronio in the background.

This event sparked the anger of the city's politicians and Bolognese. Representatives from the Catholic and Muslim faiths, politicians of all stripes, including trade unionists and representatives from City Hall and shopkeepers from the neighborhood, intervened in the debate, alongside other leading figures: writers, academics, intellectuals and polemicists. Some accused Muslims of planning their collective prayer in advance, because they came to the demonstration with their prayer rugs. They thus denounced the political instrumentalization of an act of faith, proof, if any was needed, of the radicalization of Islam. For their part, Muslims defended the authenticity of their act of faith. They reminded their adversaries that it is their duty to perform five prayers per day, and that the end of the demonstration coincided with the prayers they perform at dusk. As an example, they cited the hadith according to which, 'Wherever you are at the time for prayer, perform the *salaat* there, for that is a *masdjid* for you.'[8]

The Muslims we interviewed insisted that prayers are above all a message of peace. For the Bolognese, Muslim prayer in front of a cathedral was seen as a transgression, the invasion of a sacred space and the mark of a lack of respect for the Catholic faith. Some Muslim associations publicly apologized for having unintentionally offended Christian sensibilities.

Unlike the Catholic Church in Milan, which invites ecumenism and interreligious dialogue, the Bolognese clergy remained firm in its positions. Uninterested in interreligious dialogue, the Bishop of Bologna interpreted Muslim prayer in front of the Basilica of San Petronio as a political act, the sign of the 'Islamization of Europe.'

He referred to the statements made by his predecessor, who in 2000 warned of the 'Islamic peril in Europe and Italy.' Giacomo Biffi, the Cardinal-Archbishop Emeritus of Bologna, in fact called for a return to Christianity in order to save Europe. Against Islam's assaults, he saw one choice: 'Europe must be Christian again, or it will end up Muslim!'[9]

Adopting a pragmatic position, some saw this act of public prayer as evidence of a need to build mosques and regulate religious spaces for Islam, as was done with churches. Muslim associations take this position as well, repeating their call for the construction of mosques.

This collective prayer resurrected previous debates about the project to build a mosque in Bologna's San Donato neighborhood. The city initiated this project in 2007 in order to respond to the demands of its Muslim residents. This project was the object of massive resistance and led to a 'citizens' movement against the mosque,' a movement supported by the Northern League, the neo-populist political party. The Northern League, founded in 1989 by Umberto Bossi as a regional movement to protect the independence of northern Italy, became by the 1990s a national political movement that led a crusade against the 'Islamist plot against Christendom.'[10]

In Bologna, the controversy took a new turn on 10 January 2009, when activists with the Northern League occupied the Piazza Maggiore after starting a petition aimed at getting enough signatures to close the Islamic Center's Nour Mosque. Those who called themselves 'real Bolognese' intended this action as 'retaking the Piazza' after what they considered the Muslims' 'offensive' action. They thus began a battle to mark their hold on urban territory.

The events in Bologna seem to have had as an effect the accentuation of a spiral of identity politics and the rise of neo-populist movements in the face of Islam in public space, which was perceived as a threat.

The visibility of Islam was at the heart of these debates. Public prayers were perceived as an ostentatious symbol. This visibility was disturbing. Unlike Christians, who live their faith within spaces reserved for this function, Muslims display it publicly. In Muslim societies, during Friday prayers, the faithful spill outside mosques into the surrounding streets. This does not shock anyone. Prayer is not 'visible' and it is not the object of public debate. But in European societies steeped in Christian tradition, where prayer occurs inside churches, around the family table, in monasteries and sites of pilgrimage, collectively displaying faith outside mosques, in profane places – streets and town squares – creates a sense of dissonance in Europeans' imaginary. Some saw the collective prayer in Bologna as a pre-monotheist, pagan act.

This prayer was also seen as a social transgression, a disregard for the spatial codes of demarcation between natives and migrants. The latter, far from remaining in the industrial parts of the city, on its periphery, impose their presence in the city center. Despite Bologna's communist past, the visibility of Islam in the Piazza Maggiore was intolerable. This public square, a place for political gatherings, was defended as a stronghold of Catholicism, reserved for the city's natives. The emergence of Islam and its difference and the visibility of Islamic prayer revealed the sacred character of this piazza. The preponderant role Catholicism plays in Italy gives public space a particular dimension. Unlike France, where secularism calls for neutrality in public spaces, in Italy, Islam found itself in confrontation with Christian symbolism.

Finally, opponents of Islam questioned the authenticity of this act of faith. They decided that it was a political tactic. The fact that prayer was dedicated to the Palestinian cause only fed fears of Muslims' loyalty to Italy, legitimizing their marginalization and exclusion. Thus the public sphere was reorganized around the controversy surrounding Islamic prayer: the anti-mosque rhetoric was resumed with greater intensity, divisions shifted, courses of action came into conflict and initiatives for banning the construction of mosques multiplied.

THE GROUP DEBATES IN AN 'EXPERIMENTAL PUBLIC SPHERE' IN BOLOGNA

It was in this context that we arrived in Bologna in June 2009 to interview inhabitants, both Muslims and native residents, about this controversy, and create the conditions for a debate, allowing us to see whether the dynamics of public space were representative of the social reality. In order to conduct a group discussion, we chose Bolognese residents, actors in the controversy or those who felt they were concerned. Among the eleven members of our group, there were three second-generation young Muslim women who grew up in Italy, wear the headscarf, and are active in the Association of Young Italian Muslims (GMI).[11] The two Muslim men in the group were converts to Islam. The first is an imam who directs the Islamic cultural center of Bologna; the second, a young researcher on the Muslim world, married to a Moroccan woman. Facing off against them are voters from the Northern League who came in a large group which included the founder of the 'citizens' movement' against the construction of mosques. They were all actively involved in the controversies in Bologna surrounding Islam and members of the committee against the construction of the San Donato Mosque. There were also Italian representatives open to other cultures: a young leftist shopkeeper, a student of Eastern languages, and a woman who lived in England and was sympathetic to multiculturalism.

The group is characterized by a strong polarization between, on the one hand, the young Muslims, and on the other the Northern League voters. Norma, the founder of the 'citizens' movement,' quickly begins to speak. First, she argues against the construction of the San Donato Mosque and for the closing of existing prayer rooms. This sixty-year-old Northern League activist, close to conservative Catholics, complains that Muslims are too favored in her opinion: 'We cannot give the authorization to build a mosque when a lady next door has all the trouble in the world getting a shed built, even though she has all the necessary permits. It's reverse racism. They are turning the majority into the minority.' Another Northern League voter agrees: 'If one day, I decide to build a Catholic church where I want, I don't think the mayor's office would give me the green light.' The League members express the anger they feel at the idea of losing their rights, privileges and place in society and commerce: 'Our stores close and their businesses prosper. How is it that immigrants sell their fruits and vegetables next to big stores? Why are there all these kebab stands? I'll say what I think: to us, they are clearly recycling dirty money … it's a territorial occupation because they buy back everything little by little. Everything will be Muslim land.'

We quickly passed from the opposition to the construction of mosques to fears about dirty money, occupied territory, conspiracies – in short to a representation of Muslims as invaders. According to these participants, the Vatican itself is giving in to this invasion: 'There is a clear political project favored by the Vatican: bringing Islam to Italy.' The Muslims in the group try to bring the debate back to a legal basis and remind the group of the right to religious freedom. Behija, a twenty-three-year-old Muslim woman of Moroccan origin, came to Italy when she was eight years old. Today, she wears a headscarf and is a law student. In the group, she defends Italian constitutional principles. Talk of a conspiracy does not move the debate forward, she says; instead, they should concentrate on what really matters and discuss the religion in relation to Italian constitutional law: 'The idea that the Vatican wants to bring Islam to Italy makes no sense. Let's discuss the Constitution of the Italian Republic that has been in effect since 1948. According to legal provisions, everyone has the right to live his faith and perform the rites associated with it in private or public. In order to really feel like a citizen, you have to respect the rules and laws. If a Muslim Italian citizen respects Italian laws and Italian principles, then there is no more to say. If a mosque asked for authorization, it is following the rules; that is what matters.' According to Behija, the most important thing is respecting a country's laws. Behija considers Italian law applicable to her.

The League's voters refuse to engage in a constitutional debate. They do not allow Muslims the opportunity to adopt a legal discourse to defend their rights. They question Muslims about Christians' rights in Middle Eastern countries. By using this reciprocal tactic, they symbolically send the Muslims in the group back to their suspected countries of origin. 'I would like to have churches built in Cairo, Syria ... your countries,' one of them says in a sarcastic tone. Another goes further, ironically proposing that the Muslims ask 'your king of Morocco' for the money to construct mosques. Muslims are not accepted as Italian citizens, and are marginalized.

Stefano, a young Italian man, 'Bolognese by origin' and a convert to Islam four years prior, steps in and tries to find common ground. He reminds everyone that Muslims, like himself, are Italian citizens, and that they are from here and not from somewhere else. He responds to the reciprocity argument between European Muslims and Eastern Christians by defending democratic values: 'I think a state that calls itself secular and democratic must apply the principle of secularism and the values of democracy regardless of what is going on in other less secular and less democratic countries.' But for the opponents, the goal was not to debate with the Muslims, but to fight Islam, which in their eyes is a threatening exteriority. It is through mosques that foreign powers will gain a foothold in their country: 'We consider mosques as states within the state.'

In a small city like Bologna, rapid and widespread immigration and the distinctive signs of Islam elicited fears and gave inhabitants the feeling of having lost social peace. Norma describes her anxiety in the face of these sudden changes: 'We are in the middle of a too-fast transformation of our society and community. It is not easy, that is why we feel all this anxiety.' Her description of sudden changes to their universe is echoed by the other members of the group. Giuliano, who calls himself a secular, progressive, and anticlerical Bolognese profoundly attached to his city, and the owner of one of the oldest shops on the Piazza Maggiore, seems very moved by the discussion of fear and the threat of invasion. 'I feel similarly to what Norma said. Anxiety and fear are entirely understandable to someone who grew up here … it is true that the size of the city isn't growing while its population is. It's all about space and power … I understand that she feels "invaded" by people she doesn't know. I understand that. "Anxiety" and "fear" are words that come from the deepest human feelings.' Giuliano adds that he stopped voting for the left because he sees it as crippled, paralyzed by the reality of the situation.

MUSLIMS IN ITALY, FAKE ITALIANS?

What is striking in these discussions of fear is not the failure of integration, but on the contrary the social ascension of immigrants in this city. What stirs the Bolognese's anger is the fact that they are forced to share the same space, the same rights, and the same privileges with new immigrants. The closer Muslims are, speaking the same language, growing up in the same communities, and living near by while expressing their religious and cultural differences, the more worrisome they become. The discussants do not focus on the figure of the immigrant, the foreign worker who lives in the city's industrial zones. Instead, they worry about the members of the new generation of Muslims, those who have achieved linguistic proficiency, professional qualifications, mastery of legal language and who have experienced social mobility, all while claiming to be followers of Islam.

These politics of rejection are fed by the fear of losing privileges to those whose social ascension in the city is imminent. Muslims are described as 'favored' and 'haughty,' as taking the place of Italians in commerce, constructing mosques next to the old Catholic lady's house, laundering dirty money, and are suspected of terrorist acts. The discourse surrounding the immigrant minority is reversed by the autochthones' discourse of the fear of finding themselves in the minority when faced with the ascendance of new Muslim migrant groups' social mobility. It is when we lose the comfort of established hierarchies and boundaries of separation that we see the figure of the Other as a close and imminent threat. We are in a phase in European history when Muslims are transgressing spatial boundaries, stepping into spaces which are not reserved for them and making their religious difference visible.

In every exclusionary rhetoric, the problem is not those who stay in their corner, confined to the spaces reserved for them, but those who transgress established boundaries and show their presence in the city by climbing the social ladder through education and commerce. In interwar France, Hervé le Bras was evidence of the hostility towards Jews, accused of rising in social status without taking the route used by French peasants, who occupied the lowest rung of the social ladder. Jews were accused of cheating in order to succeed, of disloyalty towards the nation, of not being from here, of being falsely French-born. They were called cosmopolitan.

Today it is Muslims, citizens of European countries who have difficulty proving that they are not foreigners, that they are not from 'somewhere else' and that their ties are now to Europe, just like our discussants who said they grew up 'here' and thus feel Italian. Souad, a twenty-something Muslim woman who wears a headscarf, studies Eastern languages and works in police headquarters as a translator between Italian and Arabic, addresses the group. She reminds everyone that she was born in Italy, and her ties are here, in the Bolognese region. Muslims are not 'foreigners,' she says, and she doesn't feel like an 'immigrant.' She feels 'one hundred percent Italian.'

Sarah, a high school student, shares the feeling that she is fully part of Italian society: 'I wear a headscarf, which is rather visible. That might make people think that I am not integrated. But that is not true. I feel more Italian than Algerian. I feel like an Italian Muslim.' This definition of integration does not contradict religion. As Daniele, an Italian convert to Islam eleven years prior and a manager at an Islamic center, puts it: 'integration shouldn't mean renouncing your faith or rejecting someone else's. This realization should be a part of dialogues with the other.' But it is in fact this display of difference that unleashes others' resentment. The recognition of Islam as it appears in Italian public life, with its material forms of visibility like headscarves and mosques, is a problem.

Muslims tend to use a conciliatory discourse, insisting on commonalities and shared interests: 'Even now, we share many things.' There is just this conflict between 'for the mosque' and 'against the mosque.' They seek to destroy 'these walls.' This call is not echoed by their counterparts. On the contrary, the debate deteriorates in a rapid and aggressive manner and descends into stereotypes about Islam: the headscarf as a symbol of polygamy, the mosque as a hotbed of violence and criminality. Acts of intolerance and violence are cited as evidence of Islam as backward and obscurantist. There is no shortage of local examples: The Basilica of San Petronio is under police surveillance to protect the medieval fresco depicting the Prophet Mohammed in Hell. The

Egyptian-born journalist Maghdi Allam, who chose to convert to Catholicism and was baptized by Pope Benedict XVI in 2008 at the Vatican, lives under police protection in Bologna owing to the death threats he received.

The Muslims in the group deplore the fact that they are held responsible for these acts of intolerance, acts which, in fact, they denounce. They complain that they have a hard time getting their personal views across, even in a group such as this. 'Even here, among the Muslims present, there are five very different people from different cultures. But afterwards, they will still say, "They're all the same".' Souad finds it regrettable that the dialogue was not more productive, that no real debate took place: 'the fact that we came here and are leaving with the same points of view we had before, for me that's a big mistake. We agreed to this meeting to understand one another a little better, to understand what others think.' She gives up. 'Being nice to people who aren't nice to me, that's how I act every day.' She is resigned to maintaining this behavior in spite of it all.

WHEN ISLAMOPHOBIC DISCOURSE SUBVERTS DEMOCRATIC EUROPEAN PUBLIC SPACE

Attributing reason to Europeans and fanaticism to Muslims is a notion shared on a subliminal, if not hegemonic, level present in debates about Islam. And yet, our inquiry in Bologna signaled a reversal of affects. We met Muslims with different faces, voices and life experiences, young women, converts and professionals who aspire to be 'ordinary citizens' without having to disguise their Islamic difference. Despite our expectations of finding

Muslims who spoke of their stigmatization and marginalization and expressed anger, we found Muslims who displayed patience. The binary representation opposing the potentially threatening, radical Muslim and the inoffensive and reasonable European citizen was reversed in the course of our research.

Faith as a form of patience was mentioned several times as a shared and valued virtue among the Muslims in the group, despite their youth. It was contrasted by the aggression and impatience of the League members, all of whom were older. We observed the contrast between these two attitudes in both verbal and corporeal language: the Muslims were calm, poised and very attentive to what others were saying, taking notes, trying to articulate their ideas, make themselves heard, and communicate. The members of the League were hostile, frequently interrupting others and not letting them speak, including the researchers, and showing that they were irritated by the Muslims' presence by grimacing and snickering. They acted as if they were teaching the others a lesson, pointing their fingers at them and making accusations. Their arguments did not always follow a logical path, and were often incoherent and abrupt, which made understanding them difficult. The Muslims' arguments were clear and their voices were distinct. The League members formed an almost indistinct bloc. The group's 'moderates' were individuals without a political agenda or shared opinions. The young leftist shopkeeper, the student of Eastern history and culture and the woman who supported multiculturalism were silent, diffident spectators. The contrast between the Muslims, who wanted to start a dialogue, and the members of the League, who sought to poison the proceedings, weighed heavily on the research atmosphere. The moderates did not step in. In this way, they gave free rein to the League members. Through their silence, they acquiesced and lent them their voices, allowing them to proceed and ruin the exchange. The invaders are not Muslims, but members of the League who literally invaded this space of discussion and debate.

The voters from the League showed their determination to not participate in our group or follow its rules. They did not respect the rules of communication or group dynamics; they interfered in others' statements, rejecting all social interaction and finally sabotaging the very functioning of the discussion group. They imposed a power structure just like the one that exists in current public space. They gave us the means to understand the reasoning behind their course of action. The League, like all those who boast about their combativeness towards Islam, has become popular. They owe their influence among participants and moderates to their attacks on Islam. Thus, they became entrenched in their position against the Muslim women in the group, discussing reverse racism, using the Catholic faith as a tactic, mentioning conspiracies and the Muslim invasion of Europe; they repeated themes and stereotypes about Islam and responded to Oriana Fallaci's call to express their 'rage' and their 'courage' in the fight against Islam. Their attitude cannot be reduced to intolerance, but rather reflects the voluntary adoption of an offensive attitude, a pursuit of the Other, an attitude which we can qualify as uncivil, and which leads to the poisoning of public space. We see how Islam, or rather 'Islamophobia,' enters the rhetorical and political agenda of neo-populist groups and finds credence among 'moderates,' 'autochthones' and the 'silent masses' who bar entry to new arrivals who come in the spirit of integration.

The research we conducted in Bologna gave us insight into the lives of its residents and actors, and helped us understand the role played by neo-populist groups' 'Islamophobic' discourses in the (dys)function of contemporary public space. It showed us how public space has been poisoned, sabotaged, and violated by some of the members of groups affiliated with neo-populist parties. Incivility is one of these groups' political strategies, and they disrupt the norms governing social interaction and engagement with others. Those who equate these offensive acts with freedom of expression do not respect the norms of social interaction and the role of civility in public life. By adopting offensive, even vulgar language, and proclaiming the audacity of 'saying aloud what everyone really thinks,' facilitators of Islamophobia, including intellectuals from the right and left and spokespeople for neo-populism, aren't breaking taboos, but rather the norms of civility in public life. This is not a conflicted relationship with others, but a total rejection of them and of shared space. Thus the movement 'against the mosque' simply represents the exclusion of Muslims.

At the end of our four-hour meeting, which was more a row than a real discussion, we were left with a sense of shock and disappointment. The League members left right away, satisfied in their combativeness. The Muslims in the group remained in the conference room, bowed and quiet. It had not been a surprise for them. They experience this hostility every day. The other researchers and I were not only disappointed by the dysfunction of the discussion, but also felt responsible for not having been able to avoid the aggression in the group. Afterwards, I spoke to Simone Maddanu, a member of my research team, to discuss the meeting. Sitting at an outdoor café on the Piazza Maggiore, we shared our disappointment. Our research had revealed the brute force of those who engage in anti-Islamic debates. We were shocked by the way they had sabotaged our discussion group. What were the reasons for this dysfunction? Was our group representative? Were we wrong in our choice of participants? We had a difficult time accepting what had happened before our eyes.

Simone Maddanu studied the Islam of young Muslims in Italy. His doctoral thesis showed how, by means of religious associations, these young Muslims follow a peculiar path towards integration.[12] In his research, Maddanu sheds light on the emergence of a double Muslim and Italian identity among these young people, quite similar to those in our group. This surge of racism, legitimized by false representations of Muslims, seems to him unfounded and unacceptable. I myself was not expecting to hear this vulgar and xenophobic discourse in Bologna, particularly coming from people who appeared to be respectable representatives of the middle class. The city, with its historic university and architectural beauty, represented the quintessence of the European culture I learned to idealize during my Turkish education. I had to readjust my view of European culture in light of the realities before my eyes. I had to face the task of writing about what I saw in my research. In fact, during the group session, I tried to do so in conclusion. I asked the moderates: 'Is your silence acquiescence to this discourse which sees Muslims as enemies? Do you accept representation by these neo-populist movements?' Faced with their continued silence, I said to myself, 'maybe this is really Europe after all.'

The group discussion doesn't invalidate the current dynamics which close off public space. On the contrary, it proves the destructive force of anti-Islamic rhetoric and neo-populist action, which are no longer limited to political groups, but are developing among local populations and the residents of different cities. A growing sense of failure characterizes the inclusionary capacity of public space in Europe. Nonetheless, street prayers reveal the presence of Muslims in the heart of European cities. Unlike the first generation of migrant workers who were happy to discreetly confine their faith to their homes and places of work, to the factories on the urban periphery, today, new Muslim citizens display their religiousness publicly.

4

Mute Minarets, Transparent Mosques

Mosques are religious monuments dedicated to the practice of the Muslim religion. Strictly speaking, they are not sanctuaries. In Islam, only the Kaaba sanctuary, located in Mecca, is a holy place. Unlike in churches, there is no altar in the mosque. It is a space where the faithful come together to pray under the direction of a prayer guide, the imam. Because Islam is 'strictly monotheist, and divinity is conceived as one and immaterial [*tawhid*], the religion contains no images; to the extent that the representation of animate beings is proscribed by tradition and this proscription seems to have always been practiced, at least in religious edifices.'[1]

The Arab term *jâmi'* denotes 'mosque' and comes from *jama'a*, which originally designated that which brings together or reunites the community of believers. In the Islamic tradition, the mosque plays a role in the organization of urban space. It is part of an architectural complex which generally includes an interior court, a covered market, a religious school [*madrasa*], a library, a clock shop, a fountain, a clinic, a cafeteria, etc. In medieval Islam, there was an autonomous public sphere that was quite dynamic and separate from political power, in which theologians [*oulemas*], Sufi brotherhoods, and the members of pious foundations [*waafs*] debated the moral foundation of society around sharia.[2] In the name of the community of believers, the religious elite guaranteed the moral order and permitted the existence of a public arena independent from sovereign control. The community of believers constituted the center of gravity around which norms and Islamic activities in public space were organized. In contemporary societies where public space follows the rhythm of activities based on secular norms, religious figures and mosques have been relegated to a secondary role. Nonetheless, with the religious revival and Muslim immigration in Europe, mosques are again playing an important and unexpected role in public space.

In Europe, a large number of Islamic centers and prayer rooms were constructed ad hoc to respond to the needs of migrant populations.[3] There are many of these improvised mosques, lacking distinct signs, hidden in workers' quarters, inside nondescript buildings, in old abandoned industrial zones, on the periphery of large cities. As long as these places for prayer are not identifiable as mosques and remain hidden from citizens' view, their presence does not bother anyone. In contrast, when the characteristic form of the dome and minarets are visible in the skies of European cities, they stir societal debates. The visibility of mosques is subject to controversy because it makes cultural and religious otherness apparent.

THE FOUNDING CONTROVERSY: THE 2009 SWISS REFERENDUM

Before the referendum on minarets in Switzerland, I could never have imagined that these architectural elements would one day become the symbol of the troubling visibility of Islam and that they would weigh heavily in the debate about the construction of mosques in Europe. The minaret – the tower from which the muezzin delivers the call to prayer – symbolizes the spiritual elevation of man towards God. Minarets are a part of the unchangeable and familiar patrimony of Muslims. How can you imagine Istanbul without its minarets? Every time I cross Galata Bridge, I am amazed by these willowy lines, the heritage of the great Ottoman architect Mimar Sinan, which gives the old city its singular silhouette. When and under what circumstances did the esthetic aspect of one culture's religious symbol become the mark of an unbearable ostentation and the source of a controversy for Europeans?

In Switzerland, a 'neutral' and pacifist country where the proportion of Muslim immigrants is among the lowest in Europe (400,000 people), there are only three minarets – one in Zurich, constructed in 1953, one in Geneva, constructed in 1978, and one in Winterthur, constructed in 2005; yet the Swiss widely supported a referendum on 29 November 2009 banning minarets.[4] A permit application for the construction of a minaret above a building used as a prayer space in Wangen was submitted in 2005 by the Turkish Cultural Association. This application, which elicited strong opposition among residents, was rejected several times by local associations and committees. After a long legal battle, the Swiss

Federal Supreme Court authorized the construction of a minaret under the condition that it not be used for the call to prayer and that it would not alter the building. A mute minaret, isolated from view, of around four meters tall, was built in January 2009.

Despite its small dimensions, this minaret became known under the name 'The Wangen minaret affair.' The local debate about its construction quickly spread throughout the country, occupying the center of public controversies. What emerged in these debates was, as always, the feeling of being invaded by Islam and the fear of losing the sense of being 'at home.' In the media discourse, Muslims were considered foreigners and were told to go build their minarets in *their* native homes. The Federal Democratic Union of Switzerland, a right-wing party, became very active in this affair, developing, for example, 'citizens' initiatives' against the construction of mosques and minarets, which was likened to a manifestation of the rampant Islamization of Swiss society. A committee composed of members of right-wing parties created the popular initiative 'against the construction of minarets.' According to the Swiss legislative proposal, a 'popular initiative' supported by 100,000 signatures is sufficient for proposing a revision of the Constitution. This initiative necessarily led to a referendum. The number of signatories far surpassed the necessary threshold. Unlike a referendum introduced by the executive branch, Swiss referenda can only be initiated by the people. On 29 November 2009, a large majority of Swiss voters, 57.7 percent, voted to add a ban on the construction of minarets to the Swiss Constitution. Against all expectations, the Swiss people chose to say 'no' to minarets. This result, which was a surprise to Swiss society itself, radically modified the tone of debates about minarets and mosques in Europe. Oskar Freysinger, the spokesperson for this 'popular initiative' and a relative unknown in the European political field, saw his popularity rise. With his longish hair pulled back in a ponytail, he joined the gallery of the new public figures of European neo-populist groups. In their fight against Islam, these figures do not hesitate to borrow the symbols of cultural revolt and defend equality of the sexes, feminism, freedom of expression and the fight against homophobia, blurring the left–right political divide.

Ironically, this vote banning minarets pushed Switzerland, which is not a member of the EU, to the front of the European stage. We went to Geneva in December 2009, one week after the vote. The members of our discussion group, dismayed by this result, expressed their distress. They stressed that this legal proposition had not been proposed by the state, but initiated by civil associations, by the people; according to them, this would have negative repercussions for the Swiss democratic tradition. The statements made by David, a Franco-Swiss convert to Islam and the founder of the Ligue musulmane genevoise (Geneva Muslim League), make evident this democratic reversal: 'Usually in Switzerland, we have a superiority complex in relation to other European countries. With our system of direct democracy, we see ourselves as an example. This time, we find ourselves in a peculiar situation, because a popular initiative conceived by the Swiss people chose to deny the most fundamental rights.' According to the participants' analysis, Switzerland risked becoming the 'black sheep' of Europe by providing an example of intolerance. Far from remaining confined to the Swiss context, this vote resounded in other national contexts, giving the public debate a transnational

European dimension. Some lamented the Swiss error and called for vigilance in not recreating it elsewhere, while others applauded 'the courage for saying aloud what everyone thinks to himself.' Polls conducted in several European countries showed that opinion favored banning the construction of mosques and minarets. Even in France, where the construction of mosques had not been a source of hostility up to this point, 41 percent of French people pronounced themselves against further construction.[5] This was not to be outdone by public opinion in other countries: 78 percent of Czechs, 70 percent of Slovaks, 59.3 percent of Belgians, 51 percent of Danes and 60 percent of Italians did not want to see minarets.[6] The poster supporting the Swiss popular initiative became the European emblem of the opposition to mosques. This poster shows black minarets resembling pointed rockets against a background of the red and white Swiss national flag, with a woman in a black burka, her face obscured, occupying the foreground. This dramatic image was accompanied by the slogan: 'Stop! Yes to the ban on minarets, stop Islamization.' This poster was reused by all the far-right European parties and adapted to the colors of their respective national flags. Next to the minarets and the veiled woman, the far-right British National Party (BNP) started a new round of attacks against Islam by directly targeting Turkey just as it was submitting its application for membership in the European Union. On their poster, they added the verses recited by Tayyip Erdogan, leader of the AKP party and the Turkish head of state, interpreted as an avowal of the 'militant' intentions of Islam: 'The mosques are our barracks, the domes our helmets, the minarets our bayonets and the faithful our soldiers.'

IN ISTANBUL, TWO MOSQUES REVEAL POLITICAL AND ESTHETIC STAKES

The poem from which the quotation above was taken was written in the 1920s in the context of the war of independence and Turkish national mobilization. The author remains anonymous. Tayyip Erdogan recited these verses at a meeting at a side event at his electoral victory party in the municipal elections of 1997. By comparing minarets and mosques to the arms of war, he stirred fears of radical Islam in Turkey and was sentenced to ten months in prison for inciting hatred. According to the Turkish media, this condemnation marked the end of his political career that he began in 1994 as mayor of Istanbul. However, as soon as he was released from prison, he founded the Justice and Development Party (AKP), which won the legislative elections of 2002. During the decade 2002–12, Tayyip Erdogan led the government and his popularity grew steadily. In order to commemorate his time in office, he hoped to have a mosque built in the heart of Istanbul.

The new mosque would be built on the highest of the seven hills in Istanbul, Çamlıca Hill, on the Asian side, so that it would benefit from the greatest possible visibility in the city. This mosque is meant to rival the Suleymaniye Mosque, built by the famous Ottoman architect Mimar Sinan, and situated on the facing hill, on the European bank of the Bosporus. The imposing size of this future mosque, the dimensions of its domes and the height of its minarets, make it an especially ambitious project. Ever since this project was made public in December 2012, it has provoked strong criticism and opposition. Besides its ostentatious visibility, this project is critiqued for its bad taste in attempting to imitate the Suleymaniye Mosque and lack of architectural creativity or harmony with its environment. For some believers, the mosque in Çamlıca appears as a symbol of the arrogance of Islamic power and Erdogan's influence in the lives of residents.

In contemporary Turkey, mosques as places of worship are generally built in a utilitarian way at the initiative of the residents of certain neighborhoods by Anatolian developers. Today, they are at the center of public attention in that they are becoming an indicator of national Islamic power, thus acquiring a new form of visibility. Their architecture and esthetic choices have acquired real importance. Thus in controversies surrounding mosques, the political aspect and the esthetic aspect are closely linked. If the project of a grandiose mosque in Çamlıca represents the desire of a political power to mark its dominance, another controversial mosque in Istanbul, the modestly sized Şakirin Mosque, responds to other more esthetic and social imperatives.

The Şakirin Mosque, constructed in 2009 and designed by a woman belonging to the secular elite of Istanbul, represents a first in Turkey. We interviewed a believer finishing his prayers, who declared that this modestly sized mosque was a 'revolution' because its architect 'took away walls everywhere'; for him, this made it 'a symbol against the imposition of a single and unique way of being a Muslim.' With its modern and innovative architecture, this mosque brings together contemporary art and traditional know-how. The museum in its courtyard reveals the esthetic and cultural positions taken by the architects on this site of worship, commissioned by the rich Turko-Saudi Şakir family, known for their charitable actions. The family constructed this mosque in memory of their mother, Semiha Şakir, from where the name Şakirin derives. The structure is the work of the reknowned architect Hüsrev Tayla and the interior designer Zeynep Fadıllıoğlu. Yet media attention has centered on Fadıllıoğlu, the owner of chic brasseries in Istanbul. By referencing the worldly life of this designer, some have nicknamed this mosque the 'prayer club' (*Club Bes Vakit*). The mosque made headlines in Europe in articles with evocative titles such as 'Istanbul skyline gets a feminine touch'[7] or '*Mosquée féminine*.'[8]

Zeynep Fadıllıoğlu justifies and defends this resolutely feminine touch. In contemporary mosques, the space reserved for women is most often somber, inhospitable and difficult to access. Starting with this observation, Zeynep Fadıllıoğlu attempted to give women a central place. This is why in the Şakirin Mosque, men and women enter through the same door. Moreover, the space dedicated to women is spacious, luminous and situated on a balcony from which there is an unobstructed view of the *mihrab*, which shows the direction to Mecca and next to which the imam directs the group prayer of the faithful. This turquoise *mihrab* in the form of a shell is emblematic of the feminine imprint in this unconventional mosque. It favors transparency: three glass façades catch the daytime light and allow a glimpse of the silhouettes of cypress trees in the oldest cemetery in town, Karaca Ahmet. The calligraphic style used in the mosque's façade recalls the inscriptions on ancient tombstones. The glassmaker Orhan Kocan conceived the glass façades as the pages of an illuminated Koran. The sacred character of the space is evident in the reproduction of verses, while the play of shadow and light protects the faithful from outside view.

The different liturgical elements of the mosque were conceived and decorated by contemporary artists from Turkey and abroad.

The *mihrab* was designed by Tayfun Erdoğmuş, an artist and the director of the Fine Arts Department at the University of Marmara; the interior fountain was created by William Pye, a British artist known for his water sculptures.[9] Some have remarked, with some humor, that this mosque's high artistic interest makes them think of an installation at the Istanbul Biennial of contemporary art.

The Şakirin mosque represents the new face of Turkey, where the divisions between social classes are less rigid, and the walls between religious and secular are foundering. The polarization between 'two' Turkeys, Muslim and secular, is giving way to intersections that are not without conflict. During our interview, Zeynep Fadıllıoğlu admitted that she had been the object of fierce criticism by secular Turks from her milieu, representative of the European side of Istanbul, for agreeing to construct a mosque rather than a school. The construction of a mosque was perceived as the betrayal of the secular values of the Turkish Republic.

However, this mosque is becoming a place where the faithful from modest backgrounds or from the new middle classes are coming into contact with artistic and intellectual milieus. While situated in the conservative neighborhood on the Anatolian side of the city, the mosque welcomes the population of the European side. In our investigation on the ground just after its inauguration, the mosque was already not only a place for worship appreciated by neighborhood residents, but also a tourist attraction for people from all over the country. A procession of tour buses from Bolu, Bursa, Kocaeli and other regions deposited a constant flow of visitors in front of the mosque – young women along with men and women of all ages. 'Ataturkist' women, among them the spouses of retired military, mixed with the young veiled women from the new middle classes. Emine and Zeynep, two veiled women, took a half-hour-long bus ride with their friends from the Istanbul suburb of Ümraniye. These young women were 'curious to see a mosque built by a woman.' The prayer space reserved for women particularly delighted them.

It may be observed that the esthetic innovations and architectural work in the construction of mosques go hand in hand with a respect for religious tradition associated with contemporary art while taking account of new social demands. The Şakirin mosque, characterized by its feminine and esthetic conception, is equally pleasing to religious and to secular people. This mosque goes beyond the old divide between religious and secular and materializes a new alliance between traditional know-how and contemporary art.

Mosques of this kind are thus becoming an interface between different actors, both religious and secular, as well as architects, donors, municipal authorities and residents. Mosques have high stakes in reconfiguring the relationship between power and Islam. For example, the project for a mosque in Çamlıca plays the role of marking national Islam's presence in the city. But not all mosques have national stakes. In Bosnia, unlike in Turkey, Islamic world powers are attempting to impose themselves throughout the territory.

IN SARAJEVO, GLOBAL ISLAM AGAINST LOCAL ISLAM?

In 2008 in Sarajevo, nicknamed the 'European Jerusalem,' the project of constructing a new mosque in a secular neighborhood raised fears of the Islamization of the city, formerly a multiethnic and multi-religious place. The Islamic renaissance, called 'muslimania' by secular people, is perceived as a threat to Bosnian 'cosmopolitanism' whereby mosques, synagogues and Catholic and Orthodox churches stand alongside one another. The painful memory remains of a war during which thousands of mosques were destroyed. Bosnians use the expression '*warchitecture*' – a war against edifices – to designate the systematic attacks against mosques.

After the 1992–96 war, transnational Islamic powers sought to establish themselves in Sarajevo and shape the local Islam of Bosnians. The financing from humanitarian organizations in the Middle East and Gulf made the local Muslim population fear the arrival of a foreign strain of Islam. Controversies around the construction of 'new mosques' developed against the background of a multicultural and cosmopolitan heritage, vivid memories of the destruction of mosques during the war and the current foreign influences of global Islam.

In the EPS discussion that we held in Sarajevo, Bosnians debated the new mosques established by Saudis, Malaysians and Indonesians. Sanela is a young woman who wears the veil and has a Muslim father and a Croat mother. She says that she feels much better in local or 'Bosnian' mosques. She feels welcome and at home there. But like the majority of participants, she refrains from criticizing the new mosques. The memory of the war weighs on them. As Bosnians, they are appreciative of the Muslims from these other countries because, they say, 'The mujahedeen that came to help us were ready to die with us.' But if for the participants the construction of these mosques is a 'gift' that they cannot refuse, they also fear that it is a Trojan horse. These often imposing mosques frequently do not seem adapted to the Islam practiced by Bosnians. The implantation of an Islam which is foreign to their customs worries them. They do not recognize themselves in the purist and Salafist interpretation of Islam. The strict separation of men and women, the critique of the commemoration of the Prophet's birth, Mevlit Kandili, a Bosnian national holiday, and the overly minimalist interior of these mosques trouble them. From their standpoint, Bosnian Islam is tolerant of women, close to local and festive traditions, and concerned with the esthetic of places of worship.

We were able to experience for ourselves the differences between local Islam and the Islam of global powers. We were welcomed in the Bosnian Ali Pasha's Mosque, while in the new Saudi King Fahd's Mosque, controlled by Salafists, we were turned away, despite our headscarves. There, the full veil is required.[10]

These mosques from different countries and cultures are nonetheless appreciated by some Sarajevans. Azra, a Muslim theologian, does not see the downside in the multiplication of Saudi, Kuwaiti, Indonesian, Malaysian, etc. mosques. She takes pleasure in seeing the mosques' architectural and cultural diversity without having to travel. She sees it more as a source of cultural enrichment for Bosnians that allows for the expression of differences in the heart of Islam.

If, for some, Sarajevo is experiencing a new cosmopolitanism internal to Islam, others deplore the loss of the multi-confessional heritage. Vildana, a Muslim journalist with secular inclinations, draws attention to the Islamic standardization of the city: 'What message are we giving to non-Muslim Sarajevans with these mosques that are cropping up all over? If we want to defend the idea that Sarajevo is a multicultural city of Serbs and Croats, they have to feel at home here and be able to build their own places of worship.' She regrets the fact that 'for the last ten years or so, a Catholic church in the Grbavica region has been waiting for a building permit.' At the end of our meeting, the participants in our group decided to create a petition in favor of the construction of this church. This made us the direct witnesses of the instantaneous results of our research: a group reflection led to a real capacity for action and intervention in real public space.

The field of research in Bosnia showed how mosques play a decisive role in the diversity of definitions of Islam and religious beliefs. Controversies surrounding Islam emerge largely in countries in western Europe which are touched by the phenomenon of migration. But, as we just showed, mosques are also becoming political stakes in majority-Muslim countries. The thread of controversies surrounding mosques led us to places, cities and countries on the margins of Europe. In Turkey as in Bosnia, two majority-Muslim countries, whose place in Europe is called into question time and again, there are social debates surrounding mosques. These debates draw a different cartography of Europe to the one delimited by its boundaries, nations and member states. Switzerland, which is not a member of the EU; Turkey, whose membership of the EU is not desired; and Bosnia, whose European identity is denied, enter into the European field by means of Islamic controversies. These examples provide a counter-field that allows us to shed light on and supplement different contours of European Islam. Different faces of Islam emerge around the theme of mosques. The Islam of migrants, national Islam and world Islam face off over various interpretations of religion.

IN COLOGNE, THE FUTURE GREAT MOSQUE ACCEPTED NEXT TO THE OLD CATHEDRAL

Islam, as it exists today in European nations, is exacerbating tensions between visibility and invisibility and between the traditions of migrants and the cultural environment of each country. Unlike what is happening in Islamic lands, minarets are mute[11] and mosques are made discreet. Given worries about security and a desire for transparency, European democracies are demanding the visibility of places of worship instead of confining them to basements and garages. But giving mosques back their visibility is not an obvious process; what forms and spaces should be given to them and via what concept should they be conceived? Must a mosque always have a dome and a minaret? Can you build a mosque without distinctive signs? Can we imagine, like the Swiss, minarets without mosques? Can we replace the word 'mosque,' which troubles some people, with 'prayer space' or 'cultural center'? How can a mosque – a place for the faithful to gather – welcome members of different ethnic groups? For example, do the Turkish communities visit the Pakistani mosques in Birmingham? Are the Turkish mosques in Berlin used by Maghrebi or other minority Muslim German groups? How can mosques be recognized as shared spaces where all European Muslims can mix? What criteria should determine the language for preaching? How can we rethink spaces in the mosque for women, young people, children and all inhabitants? All of these questions are important in light of the lived daily experiences of Muslims in Europe.

The mosque is an interface between the urban environment, Muslim citizens and religious pluralism. Accepting the visibility of mosques leads to a series of negotiations and regulations on esthetic, cultural, financial, architectural and spatial levels, so that places of worship can become an element of shared patrimony in the future. Debates about the construction of mosques accompany the process of the indigenization of Islam and its reterritorialization of Europe. According to Stefano Allievi, one of the first researchers of controversies surrounding mosques in Europe, debates about mosques, like a barometer measuring atmospheric pressure, indicate the intensity of conflicts over symbolic power in European territory.[12]

The project for the construction of the Cologne Central Mosque in Germany characterizes a new step in the encounter of Europe with its Muslims and the stakes of post-immigration. This project began in 2008 under the initiative of the Turkish migrant community in Germany. The Turkish Islamic Union, the DITIB,[13] provided all the financing. An advisory council was created, bringing together the city's different local, political and religious interlocutors to follow the evolution of the project. Despite this participative and consensual process, the 'Pro Köln [pro-Cologne] Citizen's Movement' opposed the construction of this mosque. The choice of the prefix 'pro' signaled a change in communication strategy that we can also see in other neo-populist mobilizations. By adopting a mode of expression that stresses the 'for' and not the 'against,' these militants attempted to rid themselves of racist and reactionary connotations and neutralize the political ostracism they faced. However, they used the politics of fear in the face of an invading Islam to build popular support on the European level.

The 'Pro Köln' movement invited far-right and anti-Islam European groups to a 2008 congress meeting in Cologne. However, unlike a majority of the Swiss, residents of Cologne strongly expressed their opposition by refusing to extend hospitality to the participants of the 'Pro Köln' movement: blocking the airport, having cab drivers refuse to pick them up, and making it impossible for them to find a hotel or other lodging. The anti-mosque rally was finally canceled and construction of the mosque continued.

We created an EPS group in Cologne surrounding this controversy. Our group was made up of residents of Turkish origin, among them a female theologian, a secular feminist, three veiled women, and a convert, as well as representatives of Jewish and Protestant interreligious movements. Unlike in the Bologna group, there were no members of neo-populist parties. Along with the presence of 'antifa' – antifascist – militants, and the founders of the resistance against the 'Pro Köln' meeting, there was a strong left-wing component. For this reason, there was not a strong sense of polarization in this group, but rather a shared interest in exchange by all members. However, the denunciation of the media construction of Islamophobia did not play a large role. This can no doubt be explained by the victory of civil society in the face of the politics of fear. Despite their victory, the participants from the left repeated the dangers of anti-immigration politics and the rising Islamophobia in Europe that they saw in local and national elections. They sought an alliance with the Turkish participants against the neo-populists. The Muslim Turks remained very reserved. As the objects of discriminatory acts, they are well aware of rising Islamophobia, but they remain reticent in aligning themselves with the left and engaging in a political confrontation with the far right. Serkan, a student of Islamic theology, reproaches the left for not adopting a better tactic against neo-populism. For him, they should have taken seriously and debated some of the subjects brought up by sympathizers of the 'Pro Köln' movement: 'The far right put their finger on real problems. A debate would have been beneficial. Remaining silent on these questions helped the "Pro Köln" movement.' In other groups, we saw the same distancing by Muslims with regard to confrontational politics. Since patience was a virtue we discovered among the members of the Bologna group, a non-confrontational approach appeared as a shared public virtue for European Muslims.

The city of Cologne is practically a counter-example, as most residents were welcoming of the mosque. They were even impatient to see a new building in their city's landscape. This welcome is all the more significant when we consider the defining emblem in this city's landscape is its cathedral. In fact, the city of Cologne is home to the third-largest cathedral in Europe after those in Seville and Milan. Considered a gem of Gothic architecture, it is a UNESCO world heritage site. For sympathizers of the 'Pro Köln' movement, the construction of a mosque next to the cathedral would signify not only the disappearance of the city's emblem, but especially the invasion of the city by Islam.

Francis is a young German man born in Cologne. He runs a bookstore and is active in a pacifist group, 'Kein Blut für Oil': No Blood for Oil. He is one of the Cologne residents who are enthusiastic about the project of constructing a mosque near the cathedral. In a group discussion, he said he was convinced that the mosque would add to the beauty of a city whose only major trait was a cathedral.

While the young German man claimed ties to the mosque, the young Turks born in Germany professed their attachment to the cathedral. They expressed their pride in having the Dome as their patrimony. Miyesser, president of a Muslim women's association, told us that when she sees the Dome upon returning from her trips, she says to herself: 'Now I am home.' Şeyda, the other young Muslim woman in the group, is a theologian who wears the veil. She states with pride that she likes to play the tour guide when her friends come from Turkey. The Dome is the first place she takes them. The mosque and the cathedral are thought of as an ensemble, and not in an exclusive way as one versus the other.

WHEN MOSQUES CREATE A NEW PUBLIC CULTURE

The case of Cologne marked a turning point in the representation of mosques, which are generally seen as objects of suspicion, as hotbeds of communitarianism or networks of radical Islam. In Cologne, the mosque is perceived as a shared space for the cohabitation of all residents. The esthetics of mosques play a central role in the acceptance of their image. Contrary to preconceived notions about the 'over-visibility' of Muslims, the Cologne mosque reassures by the esthetic choice of 'transparency' that was made in its construction.

The esthetic of transparency harks back to a desire for opening towards the outside, towards all citizens. The mosque's dome is made of aluminum composite, and its glass façades aim to capture natural light. The architecture claims to reflect the spiritual esthetic as well as ecological criteria. Resolutely avant-garde, the Cologne mosque has a rounded dome with slender minarets that evoke the light and elegant forms of the great Ottoman architect Mimar

Sinan. The German architect of this mosque, Paul Böhm, known for designing churches, defends the mosque's visibility through its distinctive signs, which signal the presence of Muslims without forcing them to hide.

Transparency is a political response that the members of our group also support. Hasan, from the Centre for Research on Religion and a representative of DITIB, thinks that the esthetic choices of the Cologne mosque correspond not only to the expectations of the Muslim community, but also to those of German society. The esthetic of transparency reassures that there is nothing to hide and opposes the negative perception of Muslims as closed in to themselves. On the other hand, despite the Turkish Muslim community's acceptance of modern architecture, a certain continuity with tradition must be preserved so as not to alienate the faithful. The Muslim members of our group said they were curious and impatient to see the new mosque finished, and hoped that they wouldn't feel too disoriented by it. Şeyda, the theologian who visited the Şakirin mosque in Istanbul, finds it too modern for her taste. She doesn't doubt that the Cologne mosque will be in harmony with the Ehrenfeld neighborhood.

European mosques mark the territorialization of Muslims in Europe; their esthetic can only be imagined in a process of interaction with the environment. The choice of a German architect contributed to this process of exchange, intercultural learning and mutual transformation. Some German residents of Cologne even congratulate the Muslim community for using a non-Muslim architect, and mention in passing that only a Catholic architect can lead the construction of a church. The innovation in architectural forms responds to the multiple exigencies of traditional know-how, both social and religious. According to the architect Paul Böhm, the dome of the Cologne mosque, in the form of joined hands, symbolizes the dialogue between and joining of religions. Without abandoning the centrality of the prayer room, and in keeping with the priority of an atmosphere suited to the spiritual quest of the faithful, the mosque also contains non-religious zones open to all inhabitants, such as a hammam, shops, restaurants, etc. The Cologne mosque promises to be a space that welcomes all cultures, and not only a place of worship reserved for the faithful.

The participatory process that accompanies this mosque project, which includes diverse actors – politicians, architects, urban planners, believers, and local authorities – and its architectural creativity should make it the symbol of a desire to surpass political polarization, religious and secular divides and binary oppositions between populations.

The quest for an architectural vernacular continues in other European countries, but is not always realized. In Rotterdam, for example, the name 'Polder mosque' refers to a native and typically Dutch mosque. The term 'polder' means a land taken over by irrigation. In popular language, 'polder' also refers to a Dutch specificity. Thus the 'Polder mosque' shows the desire to create a Dutch Islam. Unlike the mosques imported from Muslim countries, known as 'homesick' mosques, the 'Polder mosque' promises an alternative esthetic that is anchored in the local. The architect, Ergün Erkoçu, born in The Hague to a Turkish father and a Dutch mother, a 'native' Muslim, is one of the creators of the concept of the 'Polder mosque.' During our interview with him, he explained his vision of mosques to us, which according to him are meant to welcome all of society, not exclusively Muslims. As the architect of the 'Polder mosque' project, he designed a mosque in Feijenoord, a neighborhood in Rotterdam that is home to a variety of cultures, as a place to bring together different groups: 'black and white, poor and rich.' But this mosque will never be built; instead, the project of an 'ethnic' mosque was chosen.

Some residents lament this, such as a woman who explained to me that every day when she passes the stadium to go to work, she sees an unaesthetic, impenetrable and communitarian mosque. She recognizes that the 'Polder mosque' would probably have been more visually attractive and welcoming.

Through the case of Cologne, we see how a mosque can constitute a new public space. The elaboration of a participative process in its construction and architectural language allowed the project to surpass a series of polarizations and confrontations between Islam and Europe. In fact, public space is currently characterized by the insistence on putting incommensurable differences with Islam at the forefront and banning various forms of its manifestations. New laws impose majoritarian national norms that dominate public life; in this way, they put an end to the process of interaction and accommodation to the religious needs of Muslims. On a micro-sociological level, the case of Cologne shows that there is an alternative to the vicious circle of identity politics, fear and legal exclusion. If the ban on minarets in Switzerland occupies the realm of non-negotiable and implies the closing of public space and experimentation, the construction of the Cologne mosque, in contrast, opens the public field to the horizon of possibility by playing the role of an interface between the alignment of actors, the exploration of new esthetic norms and the transformation of mutual perceptions.

Reversing the current political dynamics of opposition will not happen on its own. Residents of Cologne express and organize their resistance to the politics of fear and the populist right in a thoughtful and collective manner. Cologne made itself known for its hostility and resistance to Nazism. One of the founding fathers of Europe, Chancellor Konrad Adenauer, was originally from this city. As mayor of Cologne between 1917 and 1933, he openly opposed fascism and refused to fly the Nazi flag during Hitler's visit. He signed the Élysée treaty with Charles de Gaulle on 22 January 1963, which had as an objective the reconciliation of the two countries and which marked the beginning of European unification. Residents of Cologne remember with pride these great moments from history that still remain in their collective imaginary. We might surmise that the sedimentation of history gives the people of Cologne a democratic force capable of guarding against the rise of the xenophobic and Islamophobic populist right. Past experience can favor democratic vigilance, but it is not sufficient for contending with new problems. Envisioning the construction of mosques calls for a process of reflection on the meaning of Islamic visibility in European territory. The visibility of a new place of worship is a notification of the presence of new arrivals and their stake in the territory and in public space. This visibility requires the input and intervention of all the city's residents. It is through controversies that opinions can emerge. An attempt at democratic and esthetic imagination is necessary so that controversies surrounding mosques no longer become a source of discord or a factor of alienation, but instead the means for all parties involved to achieve consensus.

Mosques favor the opening of public space to the exploration of new religious norms and new esthetic forms. They create a new public culture in Europe. The architectural revival of mosques seeks to articulate esthetics and spirituality with new environmental norms, marrying traditional craftsmanship with contemporary art. The Cologne mosque thus represents a successful encounter between Islam and Europe, and symbolizes a European Islam.

It is not legislative politics that encourages the invention of new esthetic forms, but a new public cultural politics. From this perspective, it is not about adapting to Islamic difference, but creating commonality by sharing the tangible. Mosques thus participate in the process of 'making the public.' Constructing a mosque implies putting in contact members of different communities and social classes who don't usually intermix. A project for constructing a mosque requires learning each other's respective cultural codes and becoming more acquainted. This encourages creativity and innovation, unlike the imposition of so-called ethnic or imported mosques that imitate already existing mosques. On the other hand, opposing all the distinctive signs of mosques and trying to assimilate Islam implies renouncing the richness of religious traditions and architectural forms, and threatens to lead to a cultural impoverishment – an orientation that religious fundamentalists and Salafists share with European modernists.

Which Islam? Which Europe? These are the questions that controversies surrounding the construction of mosques raise. The Cologne mosque and the Swiss vote provide two different answers. The first reveals the possibilities of bypassing binary oppositions; the second puts an end to the process of interaction and mutual transformation. But it is the Swiss referendum that changed the course of debates on mosques in Europe. This referendum acquired the status of a founding controversy in that it is through the act of voting that this controversy led to a normative and legal form. The Swiss example constitutes a model of reference on the European scale, while the case of the Cologne mosque remains limited to the city scale. Nonetheless, the city of Cologne allows us to observe the microcosm of an alternative public space. The architectural innovation that links the esthetic of transparency with traditional know-how can allow us to no longer see mosques as places for withdrawal into communitarianism or a means of propaganda for radical Islam.

5

Art, Sacredness and Violence

In Islam, the notion of sacredness, linked to the prophetic tradition, finds its source in the Revelation. The sacred world of Islam finds its meaning in the Koran and the Prophet. The Koran is a sacred text because Muslims consider it as the word of God descended through the Prophet's heart.[1] This proximity between Mohammed and God, and the descent of the holy Word through him, makes him the most sacred of men. As a receptacle of God's word and thus of divine Presence, the Prophet's body is made sacred and venerated by believers.[2] The Prophet occupies a unique place in Muslims' conscience and life. The encounter with the Prophet Mohammed is a special way of accessing Islam's spiritual universe. It is the Prophet who received and transmitted the Koran, a revealed text that emphasizes the eminent place of God's Messenger, at once Prophet, model and guide.[3] The Koran emphasizes Mohammed's humanity and makes him a model for the faithful. For this reason, holiness in Islam is primarily an imitation of the Prophet. Muslims maintain a real closeness to the Prophet figure. In Islamic tradition or *Sunna*, Islam values mimetic learning and the spirit of emulation of the words and actions of the Prophet. *Sunna* provides a common matrix to Muslims that allows them to remain in contact with the genesis of Islam and the prophetic tradition.[4]

LOVE OF THE SACRED AND SECULARIZATION

The relationship with the sacred assures the intemporal nature of the Muslim religion and maintains the unity of the community of believers beyond denominational and ethnic differences. But religion is inseparable from the intimate experience of the believer, his way of life and interpretation of his faith, which depend on time and space.

Muslims reinforce their ties to the sacred universe of Islam by following the rituals of Islamic faith. They pray five times a day facing the Sacred House – Kaaba – the cubic edifice found in the center of the Masjid al Haram mosque in Mecca. The pilgrimage to Mecca (haj) is one of the pillars of Islam. All Muslims must go at least once in their lives. The daily life of believers is oriented by these holy sites and punctuated by sacred moments like the *al-Qadr* night or 'Night of Destiny' during Ramadan, the night when God sent the Holy Koran down to the Prophet. This night of Revelation is the most sacred of all, when Muslims try to bring themselves a bit closer to God.

The term 'sacred' corresponds to the Arab word *muqaddas*, which designated everything that bears traces of the divine. Haram designates all that is forbidden or taboo. In order to enter the world of the sacred, the believer must purify his body and soul. The separation between the sacred and the profane is based on the opposition between pure and impure. Muslims adapt their relationship to sexuality, food practices and funereal rituals based on this rich material that codifies their corporeal practices. In daily life, the body occupies a central place in the celebration of the sacred as a vector of expression of the pure and impure.

Representations of living beings with a vital breath (*ruh*) – human beings and animals – are impure, and thus incompatible with the practice of prayer. In Islam, the presence of images in prayer spaces makes access to the sacred impossible. The ban on images turns on three juridical principles: the ban on worshipping idols, the notion of impurity and the idea that one must not create in God's place.[5] The *Sunna* describes how the Prophet had all the idols in the Kaaba destroyed before performing his prayer in order to impose the belief in one God on a polytheist world.

During the process of secularization that has occurred in the West, the sacred is no longer an organizing force in social and moral life, although it has retained its appeal to Muslim populations. In fact, in the re-Islamization movements that have gained ground in the past thirty years, the collective Muslim conscience has invested even more in the relationship to the sacred. Muslims maintain a reverential relationship to the sacred in a Europe where renouncing the sacred is considered the entryway into secular modernity. This asymmetry in the relationship to the sacred creates worries on both sides, and feeds a reciprocal feeling of rejection in Europe. The philosopher Abdennour Bidar, a convert to Islam and author of *Self Islam*, describes this division in revealing terms when he mentions that in the West, the notion of sacredness has undergone a dissolution, while for Muslims it has in contrast undergone a 'solidification':

> […] I have the impression in the West today of finding myself in a world where there is no sacredness. […] On the Muslim side, the sacred is in an exactly inverse situation than that in the West: one where the sacred is entirely fixed, rigidified, solidified and has taken on extremely hard forms and has returned to its most archaic forms because it is considered completely intangible and outside human reach. […] Speaking with Muslims, one realizes that as soon as the Koran or the Prophet Muhammad is mentioned, the strictest sort of veneration is required. There is no place for irony or any form of humor or distance, never mind any kind of criticism. […] And the West, which no longer knows anything about the sacred, finds itself faced with this archaic, hypertrophied rigidified form of the sacred, which can only repulse it.[6]

This asymmetry in the relationship to the sacred feeds a reciprocal distrust between Muslims and Europeans and breeds tension. Just as Christians had to grow accustomed to images that offended their religious convictions, Muslims' tolerance is being severely tested. Faced with disrespectful representations of Islam and their Prophet, Muslims feel offended and respond with acts of intimidation and violence. Thus in Europe, the hegemony of secular values is imposed by some and contested by others.

Muslims who live in Europe must become accustomed to caricatural representations of their Prophet, which date back to a period well before the present. Modern Western attitudes towards Islam and its Prophet have medieval roots. In the seventh century, faced with Muslim civilization in full expansion, Christians saw Islam as a religious and military threat. Islam's influence began to be felt in large parts of the Christian Roman Empire, from Syria to Spain. Society was slowly Arabized in areas ranging from language to social and cultural customs.[7] In medieval Christian texts on Islam, we find descriptions that echo the situation we are experiencing today: 'insults of the Prophet, crude caricatures of Muslim rituals, the deliberate deformation of passages from the Koran, degrading paintings of Muslims as libidinous barbarians, gluttons and semi-humans.'[8] In the twelfth century, Mohammed was the object of virulent attacks by Christian authors. Judged as a 'heretic,' he deserved an 'ignominious death.' It was said that he would be attacked and devoured by hogs: 'he was often struck without warning by attacks of epilepsy [...]; one day, as he was walking alone, he had an episode and fell to the ground; hogs discovered him convulsing and ripped him to pieces so that only his heels were recovered.'[9]

While the era of Great Invasions is long since passed, the fear of a conquering Islam ready to take over Europe remains very much alive. Of course, it would be absurd to establish a direct continuity between the medieval perception of Islam and ours today. But behind the fears of Europeans faced with Muslim presence, there is one constant: the negative perception of Islam. Some complain that they no longer feel at home. At a time when churches are being deserted and Christian conversions to Islam are steadily increasing, Muslim customs are perceived as a threat. In this context, satirical and degrading images and representations of Islam have inundated literary and artistic production in Europe once more, colliding with the sensitivity of Muslim migrants, new European citizens.

Representations of the Prophet in the medieval era remain part of the agenda of Muslims in Europe today. We have an example in the fresco of the Basilica San Petronio in Bologna, which attracted the attention of Muslim inhabitants and elicited their discontent: the *Last Judgement*, a work by the Renaissance painter Giovanni di Modena. In this scene, drawn from Dante's *Divine Comedy*, the Prophet Mohammed can be seen in the lower portion of the fresco that corresponds to the depths of Hell. In the middle of the terrifying spectacle of slashed bodies and limbs being mutilated by demons, the Prophet, who is nude, is being dragged by the devil into the part of Hell reserved for those who instigated scandals and schisms.

In 2006, when I visited the Basilica of San Petronio for the first time, some Muslim associations had already discovered this fresco and manifested their anger at this representation, which they saw as defaming Islam and its Prophet.[10] That day, I attentively observed the fresco. Without the inscription 'Muhammad' in Gothic letters, if was hard at first glance to spot the Prophet. Immobile in the crowd in front of the fresco, faced with irrepressible emotions, I could not feign indifference. As I was leaving the basilica, I asked myself about the discomfort I had felt. The artistic dimension did not protect me against this ferocious representation of the Prophet in the interior of a basilica. Maybe I was myself unconsciously attached to the intimate and sacred relationship that Muslims have with the Prophet? Besides the violence of the image, which appeared to me in this visual confrontation, was the asymmetric relationship to the experience of the tangible in religious culture. Coming from a Muslim culture, I did not have many figural images of the Prophet. My imagination was not populated with artistic and/or deprecatorty representations of other prophets.

The ban on divine representations and even on all images in Islam is often evoked without reflection as to whether this is equally true for the prophets of other monotheist religions. In the Islamic tradition, the prophets of the other religions of the Book – Abraham, Moses, Jesus … – are also considered sacred and thus it is equally blasphemous to offend them through representations. In the discourse of European Muslims today, they note with some pride the recognition in Islam of all the prophets of monotheist religions.[11]

Attacks on the Prophet are regarded by the majority of Muslims not only as insulting and blasphemous, but also as non-recognition of their religion on a theological level. These accusations create the feeling of an injustice, an absence of reciprocity between Islam and Christianity. In Muslims' eyes, all acts of violence perpetrated against them translate into a sort of religious hostility that we can consider as 'Islamopobia,' which underlies current cultural discord. In this contemporary historical conjecture, the discourse on the ban of images in Islam is presented as proof of its incompatibility with the secular modernity of the West,[12] while at the same time hiding the religious character of the conflict.

THE FOUNDING CONTROVERSY: THE FACES OF MOHAMMED

The encounter of Islam and Europe[13] entered a new stage with the publication on 30 September 2005 of twelve satirical drawings of the Prophet Mohammed in *Jyllands-Posten*, a major Danish daily newspaper. This 'Danish cartoon affair' clearly developped on the basis of a cultural and religious confrontation. It is a founding controversy because, by inscribing itself in the European collective memory, it became a reference point, raising the question of iconoclasm and of sacred in the encounter with Islam. It arose where it was least expected, in Denmark, a Nordic country where the question of Muslim immigration has not occupied a central place in public debates and where Islamist extremism is little feared.[14] As Jytte Klausen wrote, it is paradoxical that Danish Muslims were characterized as 'Mad Mullahs,' as the largest group of Muslim immigrant workers, who came from Turkey in the 1970s, have lived there peacefully and are not inclined to support radical Islamist groups. These satirical drawings circulated a certain contemporary perception of Islam in Europe, one with terrorist, violent and misogynist tendencies.

The twelve caricatures were published in the cultural section of the Danish newspaper under the title 'The Faces of Muhammad.' Under the pretext that Kåre Bluitgen, the author of children's books, lamented the fact that she could not find anyone who dared to illustrate her book on Mohammed, the journalists decided to present Danish cartoonists with a challenge and break the taboo on representing the Prophet. In its editorial, the newspaper explained that this was meant as a response to the intolerance of Islamists towards freedom of expression and self-censorship by the media, influenced by 'political correctness.' Here we see a European leitmotiv of wanting to bring down Islam's sacred taboos: according to the journalists, the use of satire and blasphemy allowed them to test the limits of freedom of expression supposedly threatened by Islamists, and indeed by all Muslims. The title chosen by the paper, 'The Faces of Muhammad,' was unambiguous: it was about transgressing the boundary of a figural representation of the

Prophet. It was a way of provoking the Other, in this case Muslims, starting with their own values and forcing them to conform and submit to a satirical representation of Islam in a one-directional model of humor.

The drawing of Mohammed with a turban shaped like a bomb, with the fuse lit and ready to explode, had the greatest effect on the collective conscience of Muslims because, already blasphemous in and of itself, it also suggested that terrorism is inherent to the Muslim religion. This caricature introduced a new 'cliché' that characterizes the perception of Islam in the post-9/11 world. It has nothing in common with the stereotyped vision of Mohammed with a sword in hand. This cliché differs from the offensive representations of the Middle Ages, in which the Prophet was associated with impure animals, such as dogs and hogs. What is slanderous and sacrilegious in this case is the depiction of the Prophet carrying a bomb, and associating him with suicide bombings. There is semantic slippage from the image of a warrior to that of a terrorist martyr. Like all martyrs, Mohammed is ready to die; the bomb's fuse hidden in his turban, already lit, captures the very moment of his imminent demise. In this image, the artist transmits his perception of Islam. He gives the Prophet a terrorist's face, but his sketch reveals his hidden desire to get rid of Islam by killing its Prophet.

It is not only the representation of Mohammed that was shocking, but the supposedly moralistic aim of the artist. For all Muslims, it is less the drawing itself – the insult against the Prophet's person – than the implicit message that was experienced as a form of symbolic violence. Focusing on the ban on images in Islam hides the provocative power of the artist and his perception and intention. The caricatures draw Muslims' attention in a provocative manner, stirring a public controversy and moving beyond the question of the sacred in the Muslim community. The Danish cartoon affair favored the emergence of a new mode of interpellation of Muslims by Europeans. A new public agenda was established around the question of images and the sacred, humor and faith. The vocabulary of blasphemy in Western usage came into opposition with the notion of the sacred in Islam.

With this controversy, the rhetoric of blasphemy and the response of certain acts of murderous violence exacerbated the antagonism between 'us Westerners' and 'those Muslims.' This controversy mobilized an entire semantic arsenal in the disproportionate clash between ethical and cultural codes. The circulation of clichés and the discursive resonance in other European public spheres brought about a transversal dynamic. Until then a peripheral country in northern Europe, Denmark entered the European public stage via its caricaturists, who made themselves the spokespeople, or rather scribes, in the confrontation with the forbidden in Islam by opposing the notion of 'blasphemy' with a defense of freedom of expression.

WHEN ART CREATES VIOLENCE

Since the 1990s, art has become an indicator of controversies on representations of Islam. The sacred symbols of this religion, Mohammed, its Prophet, and its holy book, the Koran (*Qur'an*), as well as the emblematic figures of contemporary Islam, veiled women and Islamist jihadists, occupy an increasingly predominant place in European art. Artistic manifestations of Islam in Europe focus on the veil and the burka, minarets and prayer rugs. These 'master symbols' of Islamic difference lend themselves to the representational game in the works of artists who have found in them a treasure trove of graphic richness and a performative dimension. The themes of Islam appear in contemporary artistic forms as well as in non-conventional forms, from installations, collages, videos and caricatural performances to posters and graffiti. The themes of Islam penetrate into spaces dedicated to art – galleries, foundations, international fairs – but also into non-institutional spaces of artistic creation, such as bus shelters, the subway and the street.

Spaces dedicated to art and public spaces intersect. The power of images strikes hard without spatial mediation between spaces where art is exposed to quotidian spaces and where provocation and communication mix. The art world contributes to the visibilization of Islam in Europe, but at the same time creating antagonism between Europe and Islam. Art has become a battlefield where scandals and polemics arise, leading to threats, acts of intimidation and violence against authors, cartoonists and artists; all those who question Islam based on secular European values, thus seeking to transgress boundaries of the forbidden and the sacred. Salman Rushdie's *The Satanic Verses*, Ayaan Hirsi Ali's screenplay for *Submission*, and *The Faces of Muhammad* by the Danish cartoonists, all these titles target what is sacred in Islam: verses described as satanic; submission as an allusion to the fact that, in Arabic, the word Islam has this meaning, making this a characteristic of the religion; the representation of Mohammed. In these works in different fields – literature, cinema, caricature – there is a common satirical representation and disrespectful attitude towards the Prophet and the Koran. It is also worth mentioning the central role that sexuality and the bodies of Muslim women play in transgressing religious and sacred taboos.

Salman Rushdie drew on the founding events of Islam to write a fictional story in a farcical register. Muslims felt offended: he gave Mohammed's companions and wives, venerated by Muslims for their intimacy with the sacred body of the Prophet, the names of prostitutes in a brothel. He denigrated the sacredness of the Prophet by calling him 'Mahound,' which comes from the term used by Christians in the Middle Ages to refer to the Devil.

Submission is the title of the ten-minute short film made in 2004 by Ayaan Hirsi Ali and Theo van Gogh. The action takes place in a fictional place, 'Islamistan,' just as the term 'Londonistan' is used to refer to the Islamized city. Islamistan is 'an imaginary country where most people are Muslims and Sharia law is in place.' Neither entirely a documentary nor a work of fiction, this short film shows veiled women forced to marry, beaten by their husbands, raped, whipped for the crime of adultery, all acts which, according to Ayaan Hirsi Ali, are justified in verses of the Koran, and enacted on the naked bodies of these female victims of Islam. It is the juxtaposition and collage of Koranic verses and female nudity – the defilement of the sacred through sexuality – that constitutes symbolic violence and offense for Muslims.

In the countries where they were created – England, the Netherlands and Denmark – these three works sparked fierce polemics that developed and spread far beyond national boundaries, like a contagious epidemic. These polemics are nonetheless inscribed in an indelible way in the collective European conscience. The fatwah issued by Ayatollah Khomeini against the author Salman Rushdie in England, the assassination in Amsterdam of the intellectual Theo van Gogh, the producer of the film *Submission*, and the death threats against the Danish caricaturists are evidence of the overlapping of violence and the values of the sacred and art. A rhetoric of confrontation has converged in a binary mode around these events, between those who defend freedom of artistic expression and those who are attached to the sacred values of Islam, between those who want to test the tolerance of others and those who do not hesitate to resort to violence and intimidation.

During these debates, the values of liberty and equality sometimes seem to preclude Muslims. Subjected to the principles of tolerance, humor and satire, they are expected, as Christians have over time, to renounce their ties to the sacred and submit to the process of secularization in order to conform to the rules of modern secularism.

What offends Muslims? Is it the violation of religious law, the ban on figural representation of the Prophet? The notion of blasphemy, which in the past represented a means of religious repression at the expense of individual liberty in Europe, came to the surface in the caricature affair under the impetus of those dedicated to freedom of expression. Does this notion tap into the affective universe of Muslims today?[15]

Over the course of our research, we did not meet any Muslim who referred to blasphemy. The spokespeople for Islamic associations did not use this term. In his declaration on the caricature affair, Sheikh Yousouf Al-Qaradâwî – president of the International Union for Muslim Scholars (*oulemas*) and the European Council for Fatwa and Research (Dublin) – did not use the word blasphemy or any of its synonyms in Arabic. Instead, he firmly condemned the 'insults,' 'offenses,' 'hatred,' and 'contempt' of Islam and Muslims.[16]

In England, Sheikh Siddiqi, founder of Hijaz College Islamic University, started a campaign to denounce the humiliation of Muslims. Made up of five hundred Muslim scholars of all different backgrounds, the Muslim Action Committee, of which Sheikh Siddiqi is president, defends 'global civility.' A lawyer of Pakistani origin, Siddiqi believes that Islam's values can fill the ethical and spiritual void of British society. He himself incarnates accommodation between Islam and British culture. He wears a lawyer's robe in his profession and Islamic garments when he is acting as a sheikh. In order to make himself more accessible to his audience, he uses new technology, such as websites, along with more traditional means, such as holding a weekly spiritual consultation. In our interview with him at Hijaz College in Warwick,[17] he responded to the caricature affair. Unlike those who give the legal field priority in defending Muslims' rights and recognize the crime of blasphemy, in effect at the time of this controversy, Sheikh Siddiqi highlighted the virtue of civility as a foundation for public life. In the Muslim Action Committee, he took the initiative of drafting a declaration of global civility. He considers the Danish caricatures and Salman Rushdie's book as insults against Muslims as a whole, but he did not use the word blasphemy, which belongs to the religious register. According to him, insulting someone's mother and insulting the Prophet are the same thing: 'Knowing that I love my Prophet more than my mother, why would you insult him?' he asked. He does not refuse to discuss the Prophet or listen to criticisms of him. He simply hopes that a boundary will be established between insults and freedom of expression. He thus interprets the Danish cartoon affair as an interpersonal conflict and calls for the virtue of civility as a foundation for public life.

THE PRODUCTION OF AN ESSENTIALIZED AND DEHUMANIZED IMAGE OF THE MUSLIM

Describing the Danish cartoon affair, American anthropologist Saba Mahmood speaks of a 'moral injury.' The sensitivities of Muslims were offended not because religious 'law' was transgressed, but because the relationship to the self, experienced as a relationship of intimate dependence with the Prophet, was mistreated.[18] Thus the offense subjectively felt by a large number of Muslims who saw the caricatures does not come from the transgression of a moral taboo, but the *quantum effect* of a damaged habitus. The Danish caricatures reintroduced the role of affect into the public field: intentions count. The fact that the living relationship between Islam and its Prophet was targeted is a source of the feelings of offense and shock.

'Is critique secular?' With this question, Wendy Brown examines the equivalence between freedom of thought and secularism. She questions the premise that truth, objectivity, reality, rationality and science can only emerge by being freed from prejudice and religious authority. In the mental universe of liberal secularism, freedom of expression and blasphemy are positively linked to one another. The act of blasphemy seeks to break the limits imposed on it and create new freedoms. Blasphemy carries with it a potential critique of the established order, of what is allowed and forbidden. That said, not all blasphemous artistic expression signifies a break with the authority of tradition. Claiming that the blasphemous character of a work is the precognition of social creativity is one of the *doxas* of modernity that should be unpacked. Thus, in the case of the Danish caricatures, Talal Asad denounces the instrumentalization of the notion of blasphemy by secular humanism: 'blasphemy can simply be an act of violence that disguises itself as creative rupture.'[19]

The hegemonic discourse of secular modernity promotes disrespect for religious interdictions as a *sine qua non* condition of freedom of expression, thus allowing the use of offensive language. In certain political cultures, notably in northern European countries, the use of blasphemy is valued as a 'civil virtue' of democracy. Jytte Klausen affirms that 'in northern Europe, however, rudeness is sometimes regarded as authenticity and is even seen as a civic virtue when directed against pompous and arrogant figures of authority.'[20] However, the current offensive language targeted at Muslim foreigners, minorities and immigrants has gained new ground in public debates. This aggression is presented as proof of 'courage' in the fight for freedom against religious beliefs. As we saw in the first chapter, saying aloud what everyone really thinks, breaking down leftist taboos against racism, and criticizing politically correct ideas are what really characterize the shift in European public culture, which sees itself as combative towards Islam (see Chapter 1).

A reconfiguration of space/time is under way. Public controversies surrounding Islam prove that Muslims are present in the same space/time as other European citizens. At the same time, using the rhetoric of Muslims' alterity with secular values aims to symbolically expel them from European citizenship, or even literally expel them through national security policies. This is where the paradox lies. While offending Muslims' sensitivities, these polemics have produced a synchronic relationship between actors who do not see themselves as contemporaries or co-citizens. Public controversies create a new temporal tie between actors who discover that they are active in the same public sphere. Historical and theological arguments are often presented as a way of emphasizing that the Muslim religion, having never undergone a Reformation, prevented a hermeneutic reading of the Koran, fixing it in a sacred intemporality that has become anachronistic. The rhetoric around controversies focuses on the fact that the 'imagery problem' in Islam is a sign of an anachronistic and 'unyielding medievalism,' capable of threatening the advances of the Western world, of stopping or reversing them.[21]

The Danish cartoon controversy is symptomatic of the growing visibility of a proximate relationship. It 'becomes public' by making people who are foreign to one another interact and confronting their cultural codes by creating new alliances and new divisions. By juxtaposing cultural norms in a kind of collage, the cartoon affair produces the effect of an infraction of the cultural boundaries of the Other, leading to a process of interpenetration of Islam and Europe, which does not occur without provocation and violence. The visual character of the Danish caricatures brings the sensorial domain to the forefront of communication, stirring the emotional domain and evincing visceral and sensitive reactions. This controversy demonstrates the weakening of the rational and the capacity of dialogue in the public sphere to the benefit of predominantly sensorial and passionate communication. Images, which are easily reproduced, circulate more easily than words and books. Images, clichés, and caricatures are adapted to the speed of new communication networks to the detriment of the time needed for mediation, interpretation and exchange. Figurative and linguistic clichés produce an objectified image of the Muslim that is essentialized and dehumanized. The endogenous aspect of Islam in Europe is denied. Muslims are not considered citizens of the here and now whose faces are familiar. They are objectified as coming from 'over there,' from another time. The globalization of the caricature affair accelerated the circulation of these stereotypes and propagated the binary confrontation in other contexts. Controversies, scandals and polemics surrounding clichés of Islam have attained an unprecedented velocity and a global visibility through their circulation in all kinds of media.

Controversy is at once the confrontation of differences (in the French sense) and the confrontation of two parties (in the English sense). In a controversy, the possibility of disagreement emerges, and the agnostic aspect of the public sphere appears. However, instead of sparking a public debate and leading to a reflection on the respective norms of the secular and religious, this controversy led to a confrontation between two entities encapsulated in the terms 'the West' and 'Islam,' thus aiming to maintain the hegemony of the former over the latter. In a paradoxical way, the caricature controversy became a purely media event instead of making actors' voices heard or leading them to a debate that would open the possibility of another link and another policy. When it is confused with the media sphere, the public sphere's material capacity to present actors and have them engage in a discursive rapport diminishes. Consequently, actors' voices and their rootedness in a geographical space and the stakes of the controversy are eclipsed by the overrepresentation in the media of clichés and stereotypes. 'Ordinary Muslims' disappear from the public scene. Is another public field conceivable? Let's return to the field and our research. Let's return to a localized space with real actors who contested the meaning of a controversial work.

A FICTIONAL PRAYER ROOM IN BRUSSELS

In 2009 in Brussels, a prayer room shown in a window on the Passage Charles Rogier, bordering a Muslim neighborhood, triggered a controversy. This installation, by the artist Mehdi-Georges Lahlou, entitled *Cocktail, or Self-Portrait in Society*, showed a fictional prayer room, identifiable by the prayer rugs assembled on the floor. Among the men's shoes, arranged by pair in front of each prayer rug, a pair of red high heels stood on one rug, representing a transgression of Muslim rites, which are sensitive to the notion of desecration. The installation, visible from the street, sparked the anger of the Muslim inhabitants who saw in this display a deliberate provocation and a sign of hostility against Islam. After becoming the target of thrown stones and spit, the window was covered by a black panel before being definitively removed.

We brought together a group of Brussels residents in order to engage in a discussion about this controversy on 5 December 2009, in a room in the AutoWorld Museum. Mehdi-Georges Lahlou was among the participants. Our group was made up of twelve people, including a large proportion of second-generation Muslims in Brussels, believers who are also engaged in intercultural action. Some of them were acting leaders of associations, notably of the Circle of Arab-European Students from the Free University of Brussels, at the heart of the 'Green Door' Association, which fights poverty and exclusion, and the International Group of Study and Reflection on Women in Islam (GIERFI). Among the participants, there was also a young man who was a member of the Salafist movement, a secular Muslim woman who worked in antiracist movements and a progressive Belgian Catholic.

Mehdi-Georges Lahlou arrived at the meeting accompanied by a bodyguard. He is young, with black hair and a neatly trimmed beard. He explained that his work was an autobiographical investigation: 'My body is the primary tool in my work.' Mehdi-Georges Lahlou thus lent his face to the figure of a man wearing the headscarf, and directed an Eastern dance performance in a Paris exhibit where he was harassed by several young Muslims. As his name suggests, this artist has several ethnic and religious affiliations. He is Franco-Belgian, and has a Spanish Catholic mother and a Moroccan Muslim father. He himself says that he is from nowhere, that he comes from somewhere else. In his videos, both installations and performances, he uses his own body to question the forbidden in Islam, to play with taboos, values and sacred places. In one of his installations, he walks naked around the Kaaba, a sacred building and holy place in Islam. He looks for links between humor and Islam, especially where they seem to be uncertain or even impossible. He says you can laugh about Muslims. Not about Islam.

Sensitive subjects, such as homosexuality and transsexuality, are at the heart of his artistic preoccupations. In his artistic work, he questions and stages his own sexual orientation. Mehdi-Georges Lahlou cross-dresses to modify the appearance of his body and play with masculine and feminine identities. As a man, he keeps the attributes of virility, such as body hair and muscles, but from women he borrows high heels. By juxtaposing stereotypes that distinguish between masculine and feminine appearances and behavior, he maintains an in-between status that upends the social norms of sexual order and the distinction between genders. The term 'transvestite' specifically denotes a modification of the sexual order. As Judith Butler shows in *Gender Trouble*, cross-dressing is subversive in that it generates doubt and defies what seems to be fixed and stable in eternity – a masculine or feminine essence.[22]

In our discussion group, we projected photographs of Mehdi-Georges Lahlou's installation of the fictive prayer room, the source of fierce polemics in Brussels. This installation, which transgresses the forbidden in Islam and subverts spatial organization of interior and exterior, between men and women, is troubling. According to Islamic religious rites, one must take off one's shoes in order to enter a prayer room or a mosque. In front of each rug, a pair of men's shoes was placed, and on one of the rugs, a pair of women's high heels created a feeling of strangeness and troubled boundaries because, in the Muslim religion, women are not allowed to pray beside men. This pair of patent leather stilettos not only made women present among men, but their bright red color evoked transvestites. This installation in fact was a triple transgression – spatial, religious and sexual – inside a mosque: the separation between the exterior world and the prayer space is not respected; the rule of segregating men and women is transgressed; and the ban on homosexuality is raised. This was the infraction of a sacred space through the desecration caused by the exterior world and sexuality. The troubling effect of this installation is not understandable without a certain familiarity with rites and prohibitions in Islam. But the composition of this fictional prayer room is notable for its borrowing of European cultural codes that put sexuality at the heart of the questions of liberty and equality.

Lahlou explained his artistic choices to the members of the group, sitting in front of the screen where *Cocktail, or Self-Portrait in Society* was projected, presenting himself as a defender of freedom and humor. Mustapha was the first member of the group to be angered: 'God knows that I have a sense of humor; but quite frankly, you offended me.' Mustapha confided that he felt personally offended by the artist's choices: 'I admit that I saw the image of shoes on the rug in the subway at quarter past seven in the morning, so I wasn't really awake. You got the effect you were going for. "Another Islamophobe," I said to myself. I won't hide that from you.'

Mustapha's reaction is echoed by many Muslims, who complain that artists' works are imposed on them. They feel bombarded by these images on their way to work, when they walk through the neighborhood, or when they're watching television. These images constantly solicit them and test their capacity for tolerance. It is the imposition of these images, the interpolation forced on them, that they find intolerable. Mohsin, a student of political science and the president of the Arab-European Student's Circle at the Free University of Brussels, went further, noting the absence of free choice for spectators: 'We don't really have the freedom to go towards the image. The image imposes itself on us.' The work shown in the street belongs to everyone and thus the significance that the artist imbued in it is lost. When artistic space spills into the streets, works are exposed to everyone's gaze.

While some in the group complained of the forced interpolation of Muslims and expressed their resentment towards the artist, others, mostly women, were open to dialogue. They appreciated the artist's familiarity with Muslim culture, transmitted by his father, which in their eyes legitimized his process of ethical questioning. Karima, who works in the audiovisual sector, was happy that someone on the 'inside' was questioning the community: 'When I saw these photos and when I saw that the name was of Arab origin that interested me, precisely because it is someone from Muslim culture who is interrogating its codes.'

For them, questioning Islam's codes signifies moving away from monolithic visions of Muslims and liberating themselves from the limitation of 'giving a good image of Islam.' In the context of immigration, Muslims feel obligated to protect their identity, tighten the bonds of the community and to present an identical image to the welcoming society. The new generation of young Muslims has begun to criticize this conformism. Buoyed by their double belonging as Muslims and Europeans, they allow themselves to debate unresolved and troubling questions without a complex.

Fatima is one of the figures representative of this generation. A believer, she wears a headscarf and belongs to Tariq Ramadan's European Muslim network.[23] A PhD candidate in political science, she has studied at university for some time, like many young Muslims in this movement. For her, Lahlou's installation was in no way shocking and she laments the fact that it had to be removed following acts of vandalism against the gallery. She is openly critical of Muslims: 'I've had enough of this community that is overly sensitive over nothing!' The installation rightly questions women's place in mosques: 'Where is women's space in prayer rooms?' she asks. 'It bothers me that women in mosques are confined to a small separate room where they can barely find a space!' Reminding the others that, in the Prophet's time, women had access to the main prayer room, Fatima condemns the discrimination against women that occurs today in European mosques.

Najette, a thirty-two-year-old woman born in Brussels, defines her place in the discussion through the clarity of her statements. She works as a social assistant in an NGO that defends the rights of migrant workers. She has worn a headscarf since she was eighteen. She came to the group with her twin sister who does not wear the headscarf. Najette insists that, through art, one can question traditions. Bolstered by Fatima's intervention, she returns to the question of women's place in mosques, also asking about women's place in the heart of the Muslim community as a whole. 'Whether or not she is religious, what is a woman's place in society?' Seeing women's shoes among men's shoes made her think about the equality of men and women. Here, we see the expression of a feminist and egalitarian conscience with the desire to speak in the name of all women, without dividing between those who are religious and others.

The red high heels not only evoke women. For Rachida, born in Brussels, a trade unionist who has lived in the Molenbeek neighborhood for twenty years, the red shoes raise 'the question of homosexuality in Islam.' They are 'the symbol of these men who do not find their place among men.' Lahlou, the artist, recognizes himself in this interpretation as he notes his belonging to a tradition of European artists, such as the Spanish director Pedro Almodóvar, who situate their work 'at the crossroads of identities' between women, homosexuals, and transvestites.

The shoes are also the sign of defilement brought from the outside into a place of worship. For Muslims, placing shoes on a prayer rug is considered an impure act. Some instead insist on the fact that in Lahlou's installation, the men's shoes were placed alongside the rugs, where the feet would be placed, and not at the head, where Muslims bow down during their prayers. This theological nuance in interpretation makes this work credible in their eyes. Saida, a PhD candidate in political science who wears the veil and is a member of FEMYSO (the Forum of European Muslim Youth and Student Organizations), develops these theological arguments and notes that she appreciates art. It allows her to consider problematic subjects, such as religion, women, and sexuality.

The debate takes a different turn with regard to the symbolic presence of the shoes in the prayer space. The group 'experiments' with an intersubjective and gendered form of communication, with multicultural interpretations, and raises a new public inter-relation, an alternative to current public space. A plurality of points of view and multifaceted interpretations emerge in the discussion of this artistic installation, denoting that the rhetoric currently being heard in the public sphere has been surpassed. The initial perception of this installation, its provocative and offensive character, is inversed by the interpretive power of the actors and their singular and intercultural experience.

ART AND THE POWER OF INTERPRETATION

Art is a form of the perceptible, but works of art can be analyzed as works of 'public art.' They provoke reactions. Consequently, they also create a social link, presenting people with a sensorial and subjective, but also a public, experience. As Christiane Ruby notes: 'It is not for nothing that public art is also art in public, making public spaces and the street potential moments of the extension of relationships with others, in and through the mediation of the work of art.'[24] Art provokes, causes disagreements, and creates a disruptive effect in the consensual world: '[…] works of contemporary public art sometimes show that we can still create heterogeneity in the midst of the identicalness of the world, political commonplaces and media values.'[25]

In its capacity to represent and provoke, art participates in the agnostic dimension of the public sphere that allows artists and actors to publicly contest and break with the consensus of the established order. Islam, as a major symbol of the difference we have seen in this chapter, enters European artistic works, provoking waves of shock and series of scandals. The provocative effect is produced by the juxtaposition of the codes of the sacred and profane, of purity and defilement, of what is permitted and forbidden. Bringing together the Prophet and a terrorist, the veil and nudity, prayer and shoes, the believer and pork, all these are themes relative to Islam that are broadly used in contemporary public art. By making visible the symbols that refer to opposite codes, secular and religious, European and Muslim, a disruptive and transgressive effect is created in the collective imaginary. Some of these representations can be considered as many replies to ambient Islamophobia, reflecting the ideology of the majority. But independently of their artistic quality and the intention of artists, these works are a part of public space through the polemics they cause. They solicit the gaze and the interpretation of Muslims.

In any case, the binary system between Europe and Muslims is insufficient to an understanding of the process of interaction under way. Art is the privileged medium for studying these processes of interpenetration, mutation, the representation of the self and the Other, and the reciprocal use of the cultural codes of the Other. This allows us to trace, on the scale of micro-practices, the interweaving and co-penetrations of categories defined on the macro-historic level as 'Europe' and 'Islam.' Artists themselves, by their profiles and trajectories, illustrate the hybridization going on, sometimes intentionally. They follow the trajectories of immigration, diverse strategies of integration, and multiple modes of belonging to European societies; they question the identities involved, transgress the forbidden, mix cultural codes, borrow symbols from several cultural areas and interrogate the forbidden in Islam, thus embarking on a process of reciprocal adaptation. Independently of the intention of the artists, and whether or not they are 'blasphemous,' these works of art introduce the themes of Muslim difference and their presence in Europe to the public agenda. As reflections of the intersections of the codes of the sacred and the secular, of religion and sexuality, they make way for new esthetic and normative forms.

As we saw in the conversation surrounding Mehdi-Georges Lahlou's installation, Muslims seize the work as a mirror to interpret their personal experiences as European citizens of Muslim faith. They express the difficulty, even the impossibility, of living their faith while remaining indifferent to European secular and egalitarian norms. The fact that Lahlou's installation did not directly target the Prophet made a debate on the troubling questions concerning the body and sexuality possible.

Unlike what happens in current public space, where oppositions are reconfigured on the macro-historical level of cultures, we experimented with another interpretation of these norms in a micro-sociological approach, closer to the subjectivity of 'ordinary Muslims.' The public sphere, in its democratic and ideal functioning, allows for the emergence of a multiplicity of perspectives. Thus in experimental public space, the personal points of view of the actors – believers, women, homosexuals – unfold, rendering the uniformizing category of 'Muslims' and the opinions attributed to them null. By going beyond the face-off between clichés and stereotyped images of Muslims and Westerners, the particularities of each person and the originality of respective positions that defy all categorizations, even sociological ones, emerge. We discover personal experiences, each one singular. Thus, in the Brussels group, we noticed the change of level, from the macro to the micro, and the reversal of power dynamics between a majority and Muslim migrants. By engaging in intercommunity exchanges, Muslims gained the power to interpret clichés and images. In the Experimental Public Sphere, by their ability to interpret their own representations, Muslims began to denounce overly sensitive reactions. They rejected the use of violence by inverting social events. This demonstrates that it is possible to counter the current course of opposition and confrontation in order to create a new politics. A public sphere in which there is time and place for intercultural interpretation, away from the immediacy and voracity of media communication, would allow for democratic experimentation.

6

Veiling and Active Minorities

For the majority of Islamic theologians, wearing the veil is not a major prescription. The headscarf has nonetheless become a master symbol of contemporary Islam, a sign of the Islamic renewal. Since the 1990s, debates in Europe have focused on Muslims wearing the veil in public life. An emblem of the seclusion of Muslim women and the segregation of the sexes in a traditional universe, the veil is also a powerful image of Islam in public life.

THE VEIL: SIGN OF INVISIBILITY AND OVER-VISIBILITY

The contemporary figure of the veiled woman, in all its ambivalence, is thus inscribed in a paradoxical position of invisibility and over-visibility, torn between religious consent and the conquest of public life. The field of action open to veiled women can be traced by the tense relationships with both secular feminism and Islamic authority. As these veiled women break with established frameworks and explore norms in both their private and public lives, they transform their condition, from visible minorities to 'active minorities.'

Generally, the veil can be described as an object of piety and modesty that allows Muslim women to conceal their assets, covering their hair and the shape of their body. According to theologians, 'the Koran is not specific, but the exegetic tradition is unanimous in the consideration that women should cover their hair, their neck, their ears, their arms and their legs. Only older women, who no longer arouse men's desire, can ignore these prescriptions, under the condition that they refrain from highlighting their beauty.'[1] For some, this prescription is more about rules of propriety, discretion and modesty than the forbidden. This piece of cloth protects the feminine and intimate space from strangers' gaze. The term hijab reflects separation and protection from the male gaze. Muslim jurists confirm that wearing the veil is not a religious act (*'ibâdâte*), but a relational one (*mu'amalâte*) – in other words, an ethical consideration that integrates customs and traditions. According to them, these rules do not explicitly require women to cover their heads or faces. They explain that the Koran does not require wearing the veil, but rather calls for modesty, which is expressed differently in different Muslim societies.

In Europe, where Islamic customs are not dominant, motives for wearing the veil follow an entirely different logic. The women interviewed during our study explained their veiling practices as part of their personal religious progress, as a way of reinforcing their intimate relationship with their faith and bringing them closer to Allah. Salma was born in Denmark to Syrian parents.

Her father is an engineer and her mother a lab technician. She is pursuing her doctoral studies on the Near East at the University of Copenhagen. We met her at the Royal Library on 9 February 2010. For Salma, covering her hair is a natural extension of her religious faith: 'Before wearing the hijab, I was already saying prayers five times a day, so it came on naturally. Wearing the hijab is important to me because I want to do what Allah asks me to do. It's an act of devotion that brings me closer to God.'

The Islamic act of covering is not part of a cultural automatism that is transmitted from one generation to the next, nor is it a sign of communal belonging, shared with or imposed by others. Living conditions in immigration are characterized by a discontinuity with the religious customs of the family, with a breaking of the chains of transmission and learning faith. The living conditions of migrants in Europe encourage the individuation of beliefs. Tuba, born in Amsterdam to Turkish parents, is twenty-seven. We interviewed her at home, in northern Amsterdam, on 6 February 2010. She is an example of this individuation of religion:

> Because I live here, in Amsterdam, I did not start wearing the veil as a tradition. It's not by habit either. On the contrary, I wear it consciously, and it makes me happy. No one makes me wear it. My dad doesn't get involved and my husband would prefer seeing my head uncovered. But the veil is a part of me. If I take it off – Allah *muhafaza*! [God help me!] – it would feel like I was betraying myself. My headscarf is a part of me that I love. I don't think it is the only thing that represents Islam, but for me my headscarf is a part of my happiness living in Islam.

Most often, the choice to wear the headscarf is not simple allegiance to a religious prescription that aims to control the exterior appearance of Muslim women, but something that penetrates the deepest layers of the pious self: wearing the veil is a personal act of faith.

Muslim women who live in European countries where Islam is not part of collective customs are more keenly aware of their faith and of the public gaze directed at them. They say that it is impossible to forget that they are veiled. The veil in Europe is not as natural as it is in Muslim countries, neither for those who wear it nor in the eyes of society. In the secular European context, the veil is becoming visible, even 'ostentatious.' Public perception of the veil in Europe influences the consciousness that women have of their faith and their means of religious self-presentation.

In immigrant societies, a new profile of Muslims is emerging. Unlike women in the first generation, young veiled women master European languages better than their parents' languages. They are educated and socialized in a cultural environment of ethnic, religious and sexual diversity. They aspire to teach, enter professional life, and affirm their place in public life. They are breaking the linguistic and cultural boundaries of their parents' countries of origin while turning towards religion. Unlike their parents, who preferred to keep their religious beliefs discreet, the new generation does not hesitate to publicly demonstrate their faith. Contrary to what one might assume, it is not the parents who want to keep their daughters within their religious and customary traditions by making them wear the veil.

Yasmine's father did not hesitate to express his astonishment when his daughter covered her hair at eighteen: 'We are in the

Netherlands,' he said, 'think of your future, you cannot become a lawyer if you wear the veil. Think about it. Do you really want to?' After studying economics and law, Yasmine became the first female president of a new mosque in Europe, the Polder Mosque (see Chapter 4), located in west Amsterdam. Yasmine's success in bringing together her professional career and her religious convictions shows that the latter do not necessarily force people out of social life and away from the host country. In some cases, religious choices can encourage the adoption of strategies of original professional integration.

Our interview with Yasmine took place on 12 February 2010 in her office in the Polder Mosque. She told us that many people were surprised to learn that the presidency of the mosque was offered to a woman. Some older people were not happy with the imam; others challenged her with theological questions, while feminists congratulated her while expecting her to take off her headscarf. Proud to be the first woman to lead a mosque in Europe, Yasmine explained the multi-ethnic vocation of her Polder Mosque to us: 'We are the only mosque in Holland that is not a place for prayer for one specific ethnicity or community. The Polder Mosque rests on several pillars, like Islam. The first pillar is the Dutch language, the second, inter-ethnic relations, the third, a place for women. Here we are "female friendly".' Yasmine added that this mosque is admired by female Dutch converts who can listen to the *khutba* – the Friday prayer – in their language and pray in the common room with the men.

The veil is a sign of belonging to the Muslim religion. In Europe, there are also veiled female converts to Islam. Maryam is Norwegian, and converted to Islam four years before we met. She is divorced and lives alone with her eleven-year-old daughter. She works as a guard in a women's prison. She is active in communal life and is involved with the mosques in Oslo. She explains her conversion to Islam as a spiritual quest and wearing the headscarf as a sign of belonging to the Muslim community: 'I devote myself to Islam now and I am happy to wear the veil. Given that I am white and a new convert, I feel even more connected to the Muslim community by wearing the headscarf. I don't think I am a better Muslim with the headscarf, but I like feeling accepted and respected,' she confided to us at her home in Oslo on 23 May 2010.

Adopting the headscarf eases converts' rapprochement with the minority group, and helps them come into contact with other Muslims. For them, the headscarf is thus a marker of proximity with the Muslim community, just as it is a marker of distance from the host society for women of Muslim origin. Nonetheless, the fact that the veil is worn by both Muslim women and converts is leading to a new experience of commonality among citizens: the Islamic veil ceases to be a reference to a foreign culture or a phenomenon linked to immigration, and becomes the symbol of the here and there by becoming a part of the daily lives of European citizens. Classifying Muslims as immigrants and native Europeans as non-Muslims has lost its operating logic in this post-migratory phase when Islam is becoming an endogenous religion in Europe. The phenomenon of converts is ample proof.

In this context, the veil has acquired a new significance in the European context as the group of women who wear it is becoming more diverse, bringing peripheral zones to the nerve centers of society. The veil, once localized among immigrant workers, associated with the first generation of female migrants, who were often illiterate and of peasant origin, is now worn at school by young women born in a European country or by European converts to Islam. In this post-migratory phase, the veil is gaining new public visibility. This visibility is acquired through the social mobility of women in breaking the boundaries of their homes and accessing education. It is the veil worn by Muslim women, European citizens, in a process of integration that is troubling. However, the veil's visibility, which focuses the attention of the public gaze on Muslim women, breeds a contradiction with the very meaning of the veil and with Islamic norms of modesty. The veil in Islam, whose function is to protect modesty, reminds others that the Muslim woman is not available, and invites them to 'look away,' is becoming an object of curiosity in Europe.

Fatma, a young woman of eighteen born in Berlin to Turkish parents, is finishing her studies in one of the most prestigious high schools in Germany. Interviewed at her home in Kreutzberg on 25 September 2009, she confirmed the contradiction for us in these terms: 'The headscarf should not draw attention, it should not scream: "Look at me, I am Muslim." Because a woman covers herself to conceal her charms, her beauty [*ziynet*], to not attract attention when she is in the street. But us, we attract attention because we are veiled. As if we were more visible because we are veiled.' She adds, laughing at her own confession: 'We might go too far too, with our scarves with loud patterns in the latest colors …'

Wearing the veil, adopted to conceal feminine beauty like a curtain separating them from others' gaze, paradoxically exposes women even more to the eyes of the public, bringing Muslim women from a lack to an excess of visibility. This ambivalence in the veil makes it difficult to understand the status of the contemporary

Muslim woman. Often seen as the victim of patriarchal religious traditions or as an instrument of political Islam, the Muslim woman appears only with difficulty as the actress in her life and as sincere in her faith. The intellectual consensus dominant in secular societies is in fact founded on the belief that in order to act freely, the individual must be emancipated from all religious or communal constraints. The Muslim woman in public life and the freely chosen wearing of the veil fit neither the presuppositions of liberal individualism, nor those of secular feminism. Debates on Islam in Europe are developed around this blind spot, the denial that women who wear the veil have the capacity both to act and to believe. Erected as a 'master symbol' of Islam, its perception crushes the subjectivity of female believers and erases their personal histories. Their human faces are lost behind the symbol. Once again, the reification of Islam leads to the disappearance of 'ordinary Muslim (women).'

DIDACTIC SECULARISM AND THE 'OSTENTATIOUS' VEIL

In France, where the debate on the veil created a major controversy, the defense of secularism has been a central point. The first 'Headscarf Affair' broke in the fall of 1989 in Creil, in the Parisian region, when the principal of the Gabriel Havez Middle School, believing that covering of hair with a scarf was not compatible with the good functioning of an educational establishment, called for the expulsion of three girls, aged thirteen to fourteen. Since then, different theoretical interpretations of secular schools – secularism open to differences, inclusive secularism versus didactic secularism

– were contrasted in French public space. Fourteen years later, in 2003, the debate on the Islamic veil restarted: this time, no one called it the 'Headscarf Affair' but the 'Islamic Veil Affair.' This semantic slippage signals the amplification of the religious qualification of the scarf in order to affirm its incompatibility with French secularism. The debate on the headscarf succeeded in mobilizing French society's collective passion for secular values. Taking on a national scope, this debate led, according to Emmanuel Terray, to 'political hysteria.'[2] In debates, opinion converged in the same direction, blocking all other arguments: banning the headscarf at school became a majoritarian position.

It was in this atmosphere that the previously mentioned (see Chapter 1) 'Stasi Commission' was created in 2003 to lead an inquiry on the application of the principle of secularism. This commission was made up of intellectuals, specialists on Islam and immigration, historians of secularism, and representatives of the teaching profession and associations. Labeled the 'Commission of Sages' by the media, they recommended the adoption of a law that would respond to the expectations of public opinion and political power. Despite the multicultural proposals mentioned in the commission's report, only one proposition was retained: the banning of ostensible symbols of religious belonging, such as the Christian cross, the Muslim veil and the Jewish kippah. Although this law explicitly sought not to target only Muslims, in public space it was called the anti-veil law of 2004.

The commission not only played a mediating role between statist power and public opinion, it also contributed to defining 'the Islam problem' in France. The political scientist Nadia Marzouki showed how the object 'Islam' was built on public expertise, capable of orienting political decisions.[3] Members of this commission defined their criteria by making strategic use of argumentation and by building on the 'civilizing force of hypocrisy,' according to Jon Elster's formula.[4] Thus, we regularly hear the same formulas – for example, that the veil must be banned in order to protect young Muslim women from the oppression that they suffer in their community. As some have noted, the recourse to a commission of experts as a tool and public method of deliberation were problematic:[5] it inserted itself in the public debate, making itself solely responsible for vouching for republican principles to the detriment of the dissenting voices of citizens.

But beyond the establishment of a new law, aiming to regulate the presence of Islam in public secular space, a shift in the very definition of secularism in the 1905 law occurred on this occasion: Jean Baubérot, a historian of secularism,[6] spoke of a regression and even a 'falsification.' For him, with this law, secularism inclusive of differences was being renounced, and the principle of the state's neutrality towards religions was being replaced by the neutrality of citizens. From this point on, the state expected its citizens to conform to neutrality in the public sphere. Secularism, which became a fetish value, is today one of the techniques of governance that aims to produce Muslim subjects who conform to the values of the French Republic. Secularism, which now has a prescriptive role and a didactic function, aims to impose its norms on Muslims and teach them to conform, beginning with equality of the sexes. Faced with the Muslim presence, or more particularly faced with the presence of headscarves in public schools, French secularism has taken on a new orientation. It has acquired a prescriptive role, and endowed itself with a didactic and emancipating mission towards young Muslim women. It expects citizens of the Muslim faith to conform to secular values on questions of sexuality, established as common norms of the nation. Feminism and the Republic converge in this didactic function of secularism.

The new inflexion in secularism is different from a purely political approach that fights Islam. It was established by experts and scientists, like a normative framework for governing citizens, notably those of the Muslim faith. The installation of the first secularism charter in schools in the fall of 2003 illustrated this normative role in governing citizens. The mission of this charter, according to public authorities, is to remind everyone of the mission of the republican school, to make its values shared and 'to help form students into citizens without harming anyone's conscience.'[7] The charter proclaims that secularism is a condition of citizenship and guarantees the values of freedom and sexual equality. It imposes a normative model to which students, implying specifically Muslims, must imperatively conform. The charter completed the work of the Stasi Commission and the two laws that banned, respectively, the veil in public schools (2004) and the full-body veil in public places (2010). The legal corpus gave a new normative and didactic form to secularism by moving it from the domain of liberty of conscience to the domain of public norms. As a consequence, the Veil Affair cannot be understood as a purely media affair. It is inseparable from the very transformation of the public field with the support of new legislation. Controversies around wearing the veil thus contribute to the redefinition of normative frames of action in the public sphere. The entry of ordinary Muslims into the public sphere depends on the renegotiation of their conformity to the norms of public life.

Secularism is often referred to as a 'French exception' in contrast with Anglo-Saxon multiculturalism as a means of explaining French fervor against the headscarf. According to the American historian Joan Scott, appealing to secularism is the affirmation of the republican model of citizenship with cultural assimilation as the only possible route. Invoking 'French' secularism in the face of Islam appears to her an ideological tool to justify the exclusion of Muslim students in public school. The 2004 law thus proves, according to her, the difficulty in France of 'being both Muslim and French.'[8] Asking the question, 'Why don't the French like the headscarf?' the American anthropologist John Bowen describes how French secularism, beyond the principle of the law, offers actors a narrative framework and responds to certain social anxieties, notably the fear of communitarianism, political Islam and violence against women.[9]

Yet these anxieties can be found all over Europe. France, with its republican model and attachment to secularism, is not an exception. We thus have to move outside national frameworks, leave behind 'methodological nationalism,'[10] and account for the fact that despite differences in historical heritage and national particularities, we are observing today in Europe a convergence in ways of trying to frame of Islam. Thus France and Germany, two very distinct countries in their relationship to religion in the public sphere, nonetheless come together in their ways of debating Islam and attempting to govern it, as we saw in terms of 'street prayers' (see Chapter 3). These two countries put into place techniques of governance in order to prescribe, with the help of intellectual experts, the norms relative to freedoms and sexual equality to which all citizens must conform. This is why managing the 'Islam problem' cannot be reduced to national policies of social and economic integration: unlike the 'immigration problem,' Islam is a factor in transforming established frameworks. As the organization of public life, the production of norms of citizenship and the self-presentation of European societies are interrogated in the name of the Muslim presence, Islam, once an exogenous factor, is becoming a systemic force.

THE STASI COMMISSION AND THE GERMAN 'CONFERENCE ON ISLAM,' OR THE PARADOXICAL NORMALIZATION OF EUROPEAN ISLAM

Like the Stasi Commission in France, the Conference on Islam (Deutsche Islamkonferenz – DIK) in Germany, launched in 2006, illustrates the efforts made to create a framework of identity in relation to Islam. In these two countries, political powers created a 'forum for semi-public debate.' The members of the Stasi Commission and the Conference on Islam – politicians, experts, invited actors – debated the necessary conditions for the emergence of Islamic actors in the framework of liberal and secular values. These two forums were interposed in the public sphere as an intermediary body.

In Germany, the organization of the Conference on Islam marked a turning point in relations between the state and Muslims. Through this conference, those in power wished to promote dialogue between representatives of the government and Muslims living in Germany, combining all groups.[11] Where the Stasi Commission aimed to account for obstacles in the application of secularism in public institutions, the German

Conference on Islam explicitly aimed to start a dialogue between Muslims and public powers. Both functioned as techniques of governance, institutes of the state for the controlled integration of Muslims.[12] As Schirin Amir-Moazami observed, the German Conference on Islam defined the normative framework in particular concerning lifestyle, the status of women and sexual norms to which Muslims must conform to transform themselves into secular subjects.[13] Although the German Conference on Islam did not make rhetorical use of secularism, it rested on the same secular presuppositions in the notion of citizenship as we found in France.

In the 2000s, the German Conference on Islam and the Stasi Commission in France played a determinant role in remodeling the discursive lines in the public sphere relative to secular and sexual norms. These two commissions participated in the reproduction of prevalent norms, but during the process of repetition and reaffirmation, the norms underwent a new interpretation. From the multiplicity of repetitions sprung forth something new. As Jacques Derrida writes, reiteration is the emergence of the Other, of the singular. Between repetition and newness, there is no incompatibility.[14] In European controversies linked to Islam, the repetition of secular norms is reiteration in that repetition is never a simple replica of the original. Thus the process of secularization towards Christianity, under way in Europe for centuries, is today engaged in a controversial dialogue with another religion.[15] The new meaning of secular is defined in tandem with Islam. The act of opposing secularism and Islam thus puts them in relation. In other words, in this process of reiteration, secularism tinted with the Christian religion takes on Muslim characteristics.

The 2004 law in France proves, in the most explicit manner, the interpenetration of secularism and Islam.[16] The law links the act of wearing the veil to the political experience of the French and in reality creates a profound transformation by introducing the conditions for a new perception of this object both by those who wear it and their opponents.[17] In effect, according to Sidi Mohammad Barkat, the law constitutes the institutional framework of a possible subjective transformation of the implicated parties,[18] and of an eventual renewal of the exegesis of the founding texts of Islam.

A decade after the 2004 law on secularism, Muslim actors are beginning to intervene and dispute Islam's place and its signification, not based on an ideal Islam, but as it has been configured in the European public sphere in which they live. Tareq Oubrou, a theologian and imam in the Bordeaux Mosque, went back to the polemic in the new normative and institutional framework. Instead of relying on the Koranic text or a religious 'elsewhere' like Islamic thinkers, Oubrou anchors his statements in the French context and ties them to the terms of the law. Himself a product of Moroccan immigration and an involved member of Muslim communities, he defends integration and participates in defining a 'French Islam.' Pleading for 'a discreet Muslim visibility,'[19] he acquiesces to the public perception of the veil in France as the ostentatious visibility of Islam. He denounces the 2004 law as political intervention into religious affairs, but at the same time he recommends to women that they take off their headscarves. Thus he addresses two parties: women who wear the veil and the writers of the March 2004 law. He criticizes the fact that the law conflates the kippah, the cross and the veil.

According to Oubrou, covering one's hair is an 'equivocal and minor prescription' in the Muslim religion. The veil, he affirms, cannot be considered a religious object, because it is not a religious symbol. There are no religious symbols in Islam, he reiterates. Without stating that he is in favor of the law or of secular norms, the imam of the Bordeaux Mosque affirms that the headscarf is not part of a major prescription in Islam and invites Muslims to display discretion in the expression of their faith. Relying on his religious authority, he feels free to make a judgment on wearing the veil and he takes part in the production of norms in French society that characterize 'good Muslims.'

More generally, the arrival of veiled Muslim women in European public space is the object of multiple negotiations, not only within the family unit, but also among theologians of Islam, public powers and the feminist and gay movements.

THE FAILURE OF THE POLITICAL CANDIDACY OF A DANISH MUSLIM WOMAN

On the European political scene, women candidates wearing the headscarf have begun to appear. They come from different ethnic origins and can be found on the left as well as among conservative parties. These candidacies elicit lively controversies and do not always lead to electoral participation. Mahinur Özdemir, the daughter of Turkish merchants who settled in Schaerbeek, a Brussels neighborhood with a large immigrant population, was elected in 2009 to the regional parliament despite criticisms of her candidacy in the centrist-conservative party. In France, Ilham Moussaïd, of Moroccan origin, ran in regional elections in the Vaucluse in 2010, at the age of twenty-two, for the New Anti-Capitalist Party (NPA). After a polemic surrounding her candidacy, which was deemed contradictory with the orientation of this leftist party, she was forced to leave the NPA.

In Denmark, Asmaa Abdol-Hamid participated in the 2007 legislative elections as a candidate with the Red–Green Alliance (*Enhedslisten*), a radical leftist party. Her candidacy unleashed numerous polemics among the left as well as between different feminist movements. She was not elected, but her candidacy was a pivotal moment that questioned Danish society in its form of engagement, or rather, of disengagement, with the Muslim presence.

Asmaa arrived in Denmark at the age of six with her parents, Palestinian refugees, and her five brothers and sisters. They settled in a small village on the Jutland peninsula. Laughing, Asmaa remembers that people on their street would stop to count them. In this small Christian community, religion was a part of the natural environment. The fact that they were practicing Muslims was not a problem for them. Asmaa went to the religious services in the parish with her sisters on certain holidays. Later, when the family moved to Odense, they met other ethnic minorities. Asmaa dreaded living in Odense, in a 'disadvantaged neighborhood,' but after a week, she felt at home. Since 2004, she has worked in the neighborhood as a social worker and was elected in 2005 to the Odense Municipal Council. Her mastery of the Danish language and her oratorical talent allowed her to represent different communities and assure mediation among them. She participated in Muslim associative life as well as in the Red–Green Alliance. When the crisis surrounding the Mohammed caricatures arose, Asmaa was the spokesperson for a collective of eleven Muslim associations that filed a lawsuit against the Danish daily paper *Jyllands-Posten*, the first to publish them.

It is the Mohammed caricature controversy that made Asmaa known to the broad public. A year later, she was already a regular on television when she was asked to present a series of eight shows on this affair. The show, entitled *Adam and Asmaa*, after the names of the presenters – a male atheist and a female believer – presented itself as a sort of dialogue to make two cultures acquainted with one another. The show raised a challenge by pairing and putting on equal footing a man of Danish origin and a Danish woman born to immigrant parents: opening up to cultural pluralism through dialogue and staging a performance that explored the possibilities of a new citizenship. But the public, preoccupied by social problems and impregnated with a politics of fear of Islam, focused on Asmaa's headscarf. Some feminist associations, such as 'Women for Freedom,' openly expressed their hostility, claiming that Asmaa's headscarf was anti-feminist, and that it conveyed the idea that 'an honorable woman cannot go out unless she is covered.' For these feminists, this was equivalent to allowing a veiled woman to openly defend obeying sharia law and Islamic fanaticism on a public television station. It is difficult to escape the cliché that equates the veil, the submission of women and the politicization of Islam. Because she wears a headscarf, Asmaa was not able to act in her own name. In view of her headscarf, neither her personality nor the course of her life in Denmark nor her political engagements counted.

During the 2007 legislative electoral campaign, Asmaa used her 'art of dialogue' to defend her ideas, each time noting: 'I am neither an oppressed woman nor a victim.' She sought to convince Danish society that she adhered to the values of democracy and that being a practicing Muslim didn't prevent her from having 'feminist and socialist' convictions. Her candidacy elicited stronger reactions than she would have imagined. She was accused of insincerity and double-speak. Her refusal to shake hands with male members of parliament was criticized. Journalists never stopped asking her about the veil she has worn since the age of fourteen. She tirelessly repeated that 'no one should be forced to wear the hijab or to take it off.' Her positions on the death penalty, sexual equality and gay rights were also the object of media attention.[20] Despite the clarity of her responses – 'I am a feminist, and against the death penalty, and for gay rights' – the same questions were asked redundantly.

The director of Asmaa's electoral campaign confided to us that she had to take 'citizenship tests' and that she was constantly invited to express her opinion on subjects related to sexuality. The rights of sexual minorities occupy a central role in Denmark's political culture, the first country in the world to legalize civil unions between same-sex couples in 1989. In each public appearance, Asmaa is tasked with justifying how a Muslim can embrace leftist values, which according to them are founded primarily on sexual freedom and the rights of sexual minorities. Each time, she must show her good faith. Freedom of expression is transformed into an obligation, 'forced speech,' as Rikke Andreassen, a feminist academic and supporter of Asmaa, writes.[21]

Despite the accusations of homophobia against her, Asmaa earned the support of a party in the feminist and gay movement, and agreed to participate in a rally in a gay bar in Copenhagen, in a heterogeneous crowd of supporters, including a popular lesbian DJ. Wearing all white with a red headscarf and microphone in hand, Asmaa spoke on social exclusion, the politics of immigration and the rise of the far right. However, far from bringing together two communities, native Danish and migrants, as she had hoped, she lost her credibility, established throughout her life, as an active woman among different audiences. Muslims, until then proud of her success, didn't approve of her rapprochement with the gay community. Following her candidacy, the far-right Danish popular party (Dansk Folkeparti) called for a ban on wearing the veil in parliament, and the Red–Green Alliance, divided on the question of religion, asked her to revoke her candidacy. Asmaa had failed.

Nonetheless, we can reverse this view and say that in fact it was Danish society that failed, a point of view affirmed by Tøger Seidenfaden, editor-in-chief of the center-left newspaper *Politiken*: Asmaa is 'a young woman who completely succeeded in the integration process; she made us take a tolerance test, and we all failed.'[22] Asmaa fulfilled all the criteria of the Danish model of integration, notably success in her studies, presence in the working world, and mastery of the language. She spoke Danish perfectly, even with a Jutland accent. Nonetheless, the adversaries of the headscarf succeeded in putting her in the '*udensk*,' or non-Danish, box: 'foreigner.'

IN COPENHAGEN, AS ELSEWHERE, THE DIFFICULT HYBRIDIZATION OF IDENTITIES

We went to Copenhagen in April 2010. The veil was still eliciting many polemics. We wanted to hear ordinary citizens, understand how they positioned themselves in relation to these debates, and hear them express themselves on the difficulties of intercultural dialogue. Some members of our EPS group had been involved in Asmaa's electoral campaign; several women were part of the feminist movement and members of associations fighting racism. The Muslims in the group had different characeristics and different ethnic origins: migrants from Pakistan and Turkey, medical students, women involved in feminist associations, and converts. The themes of religious freedom, ethnicity and gender appeared forcefully and illustrated the traits of Islam in Denmark.

During our inquiry, the political context in Denmark was marked by the rise of the right-wing neo-populist party (Danish People's Party) and the hardening of immigration policy. A center-right coalition, including liberals and conservatives, had governed the country since 2007. But the rise of xenophobic and anti-Islamic discourse was palpable. The Danish People's Party won two seats in the 2009 European Parliament elections. In our group, the participants were sensitive to the change in atmosphere in Danish society and the growing hostility towards foreigners, particularly Muslims.

Ouzma, a feminist involved in the defense of migrant rights, evoked the beginning of immigration, her childhood: 'I was raised here, and they were wonderful years. When my grandmother, who lived in a small village in Pakistan, came to visit us, she said, "People here are just like Muslims, only without the Koran ..."' The whole group laughed at this anecdote. In the eyes of the grandmother, Danish values were those of all good Muslims. Everyone praised the specific cultural traits of the Danes: uprightness, honesty, kindness. Members of the group aspire to be considered as '*densk*,' but in the eyes of the Danes, they remain foreigners. They don't want to be catalogued as 'Muslims' but find themselves enclosed within the box marked 'Islam.'

Iram, a medical student, explained to us that because she was identified as a 'Muslim,' she had stopped wearing her headscarf two years earlier: she did not want to be the object of discrimination and lose the Danish part of her personality; especially because Danish nurses in the hospital didn't appreciate a medical student, especially a Muslim one, telling them what to do. As soon as she took off her hijab, she immediately noted a change in attitude towards her: praised for her total mastery of the Danish language, she was gently and politely asked about her name and her origins. She realized with some bitterness that, even without her veil, she is associated with her foreign origins. If she was not accepted as a Danish woman when she wore the veil, now that she no longer wears it she remains no less a foreigner. In the eyes of her colleagues, she is labeled a 'Muslim,' or infantilized as a foreigner, remaining someone who comes from somewhere else, implicitly denied an ordinary working relationship with them. Nonetheless, like Imran, many Muslims who immigrated are part of the conquering of new spaces in their lives, professional, artistic and political, aspiring to be recognized as 'ordinary' European citizens, and expressing a desire for discretion in the expression of their faith.

In our Copenhagen EPS group, I was surprised to see that immigrant female Muslim believers were not wearing the headscarf, unlike the female converts. The converts, assured of their Danish citizenship, do not hesitate to affirm their Muslim identity, sometimes with some ostentation. With her black glasses and libertarian discourse, Annette, a Dane who converted and has worn the veil for six years, cultivates her artistic side. She says with humor that she represents 'the smiling face of Islam.' It is she who founded the artistic project Missing Voices in order to promote music among Muslim women. However, she must contend with looks implying her inferiority: 'People look at me as though half of my brain was coming out of my ears,' she said with a touch of irony. Muslim women and women converts tell these kinds of anecdotes that reveal the difficulty of making their two identities, Muslim and Danish, accepted.

The Danish workshop thus confirmed that the question of the veil reveals the hybridization of identities, the articulation between Islam and Europe. The failure of the 'politics of the veil' in Denmark shows that France, where the law bans wearing the veil, is not an exception: it is not the principle of secularism, but sexual norms in public life, as the Danish example has just made clear, that defines the boundaries of exclusion for both Muslim men and women.

THE CONFRONTATION OF THE SEXUAL NORMS OF PUBLIC LIFE

The contemporary norms in the public sphere in Europe impose an agenda on sexuality and pervert the possibilities for the emergence of Muslim actors as citizens. The political domain does not help the Muslim woman any more in affirming herself as an individual. The over-visibility of the 'veil,' its instrumentalization, its media coverage, the effect of shock it produces, all this forms a prism that deforms the political participation of veiled women. Candidates are subject to proofs of citizenship with tests that measure their distance from Islam's values and their affinity with European values of sexual equality.

Sexual questions are more and more subject to the same political demands as other social questions relating to immigration, whether about work, learning the language of a host country, or education. The sociologist Éric Fassin notes that the politicization of questions of gender and sexuality constitutes the extension of the democratic domain towards a 'sexual democratization.' 'Sexual democracy' is a new step where the norms of gender and sexuality gain political importance just like the values of liberty and equality. Sexual norms are not unanimous and profoundly divide European societies. Demonstrations against abortion in Spain and against gay marriage in France are proof of this. In any case, it is on the sexual terrain that the political rhetoric of a conflict of civilizations is playing out. Fassin notes the appearance of an identity defined by democracy, first and foremost in its sexual dimension, an 'us' which is opposed to 'others,' 'prisoners of a culture'[23] where the veil, forced marriages and genital mutilation are imposed on women.[24] As we saw with the Stasi Commission and the German Conference on Islam, far from limiting itself to speech, this rhetoric accompanies new techniques of governance and leads to a new administrative and legal logic in terms of policies of welcoming and integrating immigrants. Foreigners who apply for a residence permit in the Netherlands or naturalization in France or Germany must pass a test that measures their allegiance, a sort of integration 'kit' specific to each country, but which always includes the values of secularism and sexual freedom.

Sexual democracy has its origins in the counterculture and sexual liberation of the 1960s. Since then, secularization has little by little appropriated the domain of sexuality, influencing the relationship between the sexes and displacing the established boundaries between the natural order and social norms. The family, procreation and sexual roles were liberated from the hold of religion and social conservatism. Biological arguments, which until then predetermined the feminine condition, were refuted thanks to mobilization to defend the right to contraception and abortion. Once sexuality and procreation were separated, the possibility of defining another identity for women was conceivable. Like the feminist slogan of the 1970s – 'The personal is political' – debates about women and sexuality crossed the boundary of the private sphere to find themselves in the wake of the political order and culture. The introduction of the notion of gender via feminist literature demonstrates the displacement of sexuality into the domain of public culture. Identity feminism thus participates in the production of the values of equality of the sexes and norms of sexual freedom in public life.

With the cultural and sexual revolution in the West, morals and ways of life have entered a zone of accelerated change where they cease to represent the customs determined by social class and gender. New sociocultural movements have criticized the patriarchal order founded on the hierarchic hegemony of the male sex and the heterosexual norm. The rights of women and sexual minorities today constitute the basis on which public and sexual norms of advanced democracies are defined.

Unlike the morals that arise from the domain of practices and habits, norms refer to a set of rules shared by a social group. Norms have a descriptive aspect that allows us to understand ways of being, thinking and acting in a society. Norms also have an appreciative quality because they define what is good or correct and what is bad or incorrect. Finally, the prescriptive aspect of norms designates what one must or must not do, what is permitted, mandatory or forbidden.[25] In advanced democracies, norms are defined and reproduced by social actors – men and women – via the domain of scientific knowledge. Norms are examined by experts and subjected to the surveillance of public powers. In that norms have a prescriptive character, naming the permitted and the forbidden, they maintain a rapport with authority.

The confrontation with Islam occurs in the register of sexual norms in democracies: Muslim citizens are told to conform to norms in place and are forced to express their personal convictions on arranged marriages, honor crimes, gay rights, etc. Following Foucault's analyses, we can affirm that the sexual revolution encourages individuals to confess, prompting public speech on sexuality.[26] Since then, fault lines and oppositions have appeared between the defenders of norms, from the sexual revolution, and those who search to adhere to Islamic norms. The actors of the religious renewal collide with defenders of the permanent sexual revolution. The two groups find themselves in the same space/time, in European societies, and aim to make their own normative model of the organization of the private and public spaces and the rapports between the sexes prevail. It is a confrontation between two systems of sexuality that focus on the organization of intimate life and the production of public norms. The woman question, and more particularly the question of her body, is at the heart of this power relationship between Islamic prescriptions and secular norms. In this dispute between the sexual revolution and the Islamic renewal in the West, women are at once objects and full-fledged subjects. It is women – feminists or Islamists – who cross the private–public barrier and who participate in the production of sexual and religious norms in public life.

FROM VISIBLE MINORITIES TO ACTIVE MINORITIES

The veil of Muslim women makes visible the sphere of the intimate and sacred, designated by the word *mahrem*. Unlike emancipating feminism, the veil is the symbol of a system of protected and forbidden sexuality. Virginity and religious marriages are valued, and religious codifications of daily behavior, such as the monitoring of social interactions between men and women, are observed. But while adhering to Islamic prescriptions, Muslim women, as feminists, aspire to follow their personal trajectory and conquer new public spaces. This desire to participate in public life leads them out of their homes, transgressing the boundaries between public and private without adhering to the feminist model of emancipation as such.

Unlike 'white' feminists, these Muslim women belong to a visible minority by virtue of their cultural and ethnic traits and of their parents' migrant past. This visibility is also a part of the choice they make to wear the veil: a conscious and voluntary act of their faith. They thus form a visible and active minority. Doesn't the affirmation of their religious identity prove a will to go beyond the social determinism of immigration? Is this then a reversal of the condition of visible minorities, in favor of a new condition of active minorities and the capacity to act or believe? According to Serge Moscovici, active minorities can be sources of innovation and social change, because 'despite meticulous repression, despite the enormous pressures at work to attain uniformity of thought, taste and behavior, not only are individuals and groups capable of resisting them, but they even manage to create new ways of perceiving the world, of dressing, of living, new ideas in politics, philosophy or in the arts, and lead other people to accept them.'[27]

Muslim women undergo double, contradictory pressure: they must conform, on one hand, to the libertarian and majoritarian norms of Europe; on the other, to those of patriarchal Islam. In fact, neither religious orthodoxy nor secular feminists fully welcome their presence in social life. The feminine condition of Muslim women is one of the present-absent. In a general way, women cannot truly be recognized in a world made by men where the masculine model is dominant. That is feminism's conclusion. But Muslim women aim to conquer a world where masculine identification is not solely dominant, as was the case for the identity feminism of the 1970s, but equally identified with a certain feminine identity. Coming from counterculture movements of the 1970s, secular feminism initiated by an active minority has become a majoritarian and master value in European societies. Muslim women are asked for 'consistency': that they identify with this new feminine world and emancipate themselves, or that they remain prisoners of Islam. Pious and faithful while being engaged in active life, Muslim women find themselves in an ambivalent position because they engage in a double distancing from majority norms. This ambivalence requires a reflexive effort towards Islamic prescriptions and adjustments in their behavior in their daily lives in the function of secular norms. They are immediately in the position of an active minority, in other words, a posture at once endured and passive but also claimed and conscious. As Serge Moscovici writes about active minorities, Muslim women, because of their distance from the majority and their dissimilarity from those around them, invent and create new ways of dressing, of perceiving the world and of redefining feminism.

Veiled Muslim women constitute an active minority in the sense that they must doubly invent their place in society. As in the case of feminists in the active minority, they follow life trajectories that are not only untraced, but which are in contradiction with the roles which have previously been assigned to them. These women aspire to stake a place in public life and to reinvent Muslim femininity.[28] Unlike secular feminists, Muslim women consent to acting within the confining framework of religious prescriptions, which forces them to define their relation of dependency and autonomy towards religious authority, in accordance with the interpretation of texts.

In what measure can norms defined by religious authorities be debated by women themselves, as actresses of Islam? In the absence of an Islamic state and an official *oulema*, isn't the European context favorable to the involvement of women in the interpretation and formulation of Islamic norms? The case of a Muslim woman PhD candidate who publicly contradicted Imam Tareq Oubrou proves this. In the article quoted above, Oubrou recommends a certain discretion to Muslim women. He criticizes the headscarf when it is used as an object of seduction and a fashion accessory instead of the expression of Islamic faith. He reproaches young women for wearing the headscarf without performing the five canonical daily prayers. The headscarf is an 'esthetic ostentation' and isn't 'to be taken seriously,' he writes.

Saida Ounissi, a doctoral candidate at the Sorbonne, published an article in the same daily newspaper as the imam from Bordeaux, who, she wrote, 'uses his position as an imam and borrows from theology to call for Muslim women to unveil themselves.'[29] On this occasion, Ounissi pointed out that Koranic verses unambiguously require no woman to veil herself. She herself wears the hijab, but she insists on the fact that it is up to each Muslim woman to comply with this practice, or not. She is not intimidated by the hierarchical relationships that are supposed to exist between Muslim women and an imam. She does not hesitate to publicly call into question the words and position of a religious authority by using her knowledge of Islam and democratic societies. According to her, 'choosing your convictions, your political ideas, your sexual orientation, your representatives' is the very essence of our democratic societies, of which religious freedom is a part. Ounissi carries the singular voice of Muslim women in the position of active minorities. On the theme of the veil, she envisages a detachment and empowerment of Muslim women in Europe. Ounissi, having agreed to participate in our experimental group, met us in Brussels for our research. Ounissi's theological approach brought a new light to the relationship to art and sexuality that dismantles the notion of blasphemy. A minority in the heart of a majoritarian society, a minority in the Islamic movement as well, she is looking for her place in society, which calls for a permanent reflexivity and a critical engagement towards patriarchal authority, holders of religious knowledge and majority feminism.

By affirming that the veil is exclusively oppressing for women, Western feminism, which claims universalism, finds itself in a 'psychology of denial.'[30] However, within feminism, other voices are rising up to criticize this hegemonic thesis. A definition of a plural feminism and different interpretations of emancipation are being debated. Thus in Denmark, some feminist movements, such as 'Feministik Forum' (Feminist Forum) are distancing themselves from the association 'Kvinder for frihed' (Women for Freedom), which discredited Asmaa's candidacy. From their perspective, the practice of veiling must be understood through its different facets: there are many ways of being a feminist and many roads lead to emancipation. The hegemonic aim of the emancipation of women seen as universal and homogeneous is questioned. In what way do white, middle-class, heterosexual, Christian and native Danish woman have a monopoly on feminism?[31] The criticism of majority feminism is a condition of the recognition of the Muslim woman and her public action. A new European and pluralist public culture depends on mutual recognition between two figures of women, and particularly accepting the hyphen between Muslim-European women.

A certain number of performances surrounding the question of the veil indicate two possible paths. In May 2007, during the controversy surrounding Asmaa, the Little Mermaid of Copenhagen, an icon of the city, was found covered with a veil. A foreign religion had taken hold of the national emblem. The Little Mermaid, a converted Muslim, fell under the sway of Islam. This anonymous act was inscribed in a political ideology fed by 'the threat of the Islamization of the country.' Another scenario is capable of opening up a new path towards an alternate politics. This time, the statue the 'Fishmonger's wife' became the object of a public performance. This statue, also to be found in Copenhagen, near Højbro Plads, depicts the wife of a fishmonger, wearing a traditional kerchief. Elisabeth Gerner Nielsen, a leftist MP and a specialist on questions of immigration, had herself photographed next to this statue with a kerchief knotted on her head. This transcultural performance created a sense of correspondence between the veil of immigrant women and the traditional kerchief of Danish fishmongers' wives.

In fact, the veil in the form of a kerchief worn in the past by Danish women, as an accessory to protect them and a marker of respectability, does not belong to such a distant past. A 2010 exhibition of photographs of women from Fanø Island, in Jutland, styled in the old fashion with a *Strude* covering their hair, reminds us of this custom. The Danish photographer Trine Søndergaard, well known in Denmark on the contemporary art scene, wanted to give new life to this clothing custom from the past and interrogate cultural identities beyond distances in time.[32] The reminder of the past facilitated the sense of correspondence between two cultures and their respective religions beyond their differences in time and space. If we consider the Danish kerchief, a traditional accessory and marker of respectability, the Islamic veil ceases to be a sign of alterity. Performance and visual art made it possible to reveal a sense of correspondence by creating a transcultural translation. The visibility of Islam and the veil have lost their troubling aspect and cease to be ostentatious, entering instead into the field of commonality, the perceptible experience of ordinary citizens. An elaboration of the ethical and esthetic norms of intimate life and shared life can be put into place as a horizon of the possible.

7

What about Sharia?

We cannot understand the customs and rules that frame the lives of Muslim believers without discussing their relationship to the Islamic religious corpus, sharia. In the Western media sphere, using this word often leads to confusion and evinces a certain unease among journalists and so-called experts appointed to interpret public manifestations by social actors calling for Islam (or perceived as such), from the most harmless to the most extremist. Sharia, which defines a hierarchy of norms, is a group of prescriptions to which Muslims must submit themselves in the fields of religion, social relations and law. Its sources are the Koranic text, prophetic tradition and Muslim law (*fiqh*). There is not a purely legal vision of Islamic normativity. Some ulemas, as well as lawyers, prefer a legalist interpretation of sharia, while most practicing Muslims limit it to a few rituals. As for Sufi tradition, it favors sincerity in piety and criticizes the literalism of sharia. And, for Islamic reformist thinkers, sharia, as its etymological meaning indicates, refers to a progression – that of the path to follow to become closer to God – and not a code fixed once and for all.

SHARIA AND ISLAMIC NORMATIVITY

In the history of the Muslim world, there is no unique model of Islamic normativity that we can call *the* sharia. It must equally be recalled that in the span of two centuries, the judicial systems of Muslim countries have been transformed to benefit national jurisdictions which are more or less secular and positivist.[1] It is in family affairs, such as marriages, divorce, parentage, and inheritance, that Islamic normativity continues to exert its influence in certain Muslim societies. Turkey is an exception in this area, following the radical introduction of a positivistic vision of law that led to the abolition of sharia. The adoption in 1876 of the 'Ottoman Civil Code,' the *Mecelle*, established a common status of citizenship independent of all religious affiliation;[2] then, in 1926, under the Republic, with the entry into force of the Turkish Civil Code, inspired by the Swiss Civil Code, the equality of rights between men and women was declared – a principle that became an integral part of the Republic.

Since the 1970s, with the rise of political Islam, the notion of sharia – which had been rolled back – was updated in a political rhetoric of contestation. With the return of religion in contemporary societies, the functioning of authority in Islam and its impact on the organization of religious practice once again gained importance.[3] But the political use of the notion of sharia is problematic in the eyes of religious authorities on Islam. The doctrinal absence of clergy in Sunni Islam does not prevent the creation of a hierarchized corps of religious men; as Malika Zeghal notes, 'the equal access to religion that each Muslim experiences is only entirely theoretical, but because it is ideally given by doctrine, it confers an indefinite status on the guardians of dogma.'[4] Who creates the authority to define the norm? Who holds the capacity for interpretation, the *itjihad*? These questions are debated by the four schools of Muslim jurisprudence and by theologians who refer to a complex corpus, while political actors of Islam appropriate authority on the ideological use of sharia for themselves.

Religious authority in Islam has always been multiple, as the Pakistani professor of Islamic theology Muhammad Khalid Masud reminds us. Theologians or ulemas who hold religious knowledge are not necessarily jurists, and there are several categories among them. Thus religious authority can be exercised by 'sufi *shayks*, *muftis*, *qadis* (judges in tribunals), teachers (in schools, *madrasas*), *khatibs* (in Friday sermons in mosques), *muhtasibs* (in markets for public morality), *imams* (who direct the community's prayer in mosques), as well as by people exercising several other professions, named by the State or recognized in the exercise of their role by the community.'[5]

In the modern era of printing and media, Islamic knowledge – the interpretation of the Koran and hadiths – has become accessible to a greater number of people, and each one can refer to Islam's original sources and express his point of view. Thus engineers, doctors or intellectuals with a certain level of knowledge can confront these sources with the way sharia is used – Khalid Masud calls them 'neo ulemas.'[6] The contemporary use of the notion of sharia which pervades the speech of Muslim actors is largely shaped by these neo-ulemas, preachers and intellectuals of Islam.

The issue of sharia obviously does not escape the European Islamic field – it is even a point of 'major fixation' in controversies surrounding Islam.[7] In the eyes of Muslims who want to lead lives in European countries in conformity with Islamic normativity, this question is at once inevitable and equivocal. Inevitable, because Islamic normativity implies social as well as legal norms; equivocal, because in the absence of the Islamic state and institutions, social and legal uses of sharia are fragmented and disparate. The ordinary practices of believers embody social uses of Islamic normativity contingent on the European context. But sharia, as a divine and revealed law, is also the timeless foundation of the principal connection of the Muslim community. This tension between the religious corpus and the practices of Muslims is intrinsic to the study of contemporary Islam.

In the context of immigration, it is exacerbated. Muslims, being free of attachments to the religious institutions of their countries of origin, freely exert their right of interpretation in their religion. Thus they must find a new means of religious learning, deepen their knowledge of Islam and learn to live according to a normative religious repertory in a secular society. They find themselves faced with two forms of contradictory authority. In a new environment, Muslims who live in Europe find themselves forced to think about themselves as a community of believers in the absence of an Islamic state. They cannot ignore secular law in the European societies in which they live, but without the support of religious authorities, they must answer the question: 'What about sharia?' For some Muslim citizens, Europe is a privileged framework in this process, because they are encouraged to live according to their conscience, by abandoning all references to sharia.[8] Others create a 'limited theory of sharia,' a sort of minimalist orthodoxy, by limiting Islamic legislation to cultural practices (*ibadat*) and moral principles (*akhlaq*).[9] Freed of all political systems – Islamic state and caliphate – a new historical condition is thus emerging for the forming of sharia by the immense majority of Europe's 'ordinary Muslims.'

In their mental universe, sharia thus does not take up a large place as a legal system and even less as a penal code. But those who we interviewed feel that they are constantly questioned by its political and media representations. In their eyes, Islam dictates a way of life that is above all dissuasive, which can in no way be reduced to criminal sanctions or corporeal punishments like stoning. The literal application of sentences linked to heavy-handed interpretations of a supposed 'Islamic penal code' seems unthinkable and unacceptable to them: sharia does not concern them, it is possibly the concern of their coreligionists in the distant countries of Europe. In a self-confident way, and even with some pride, they affirm their feeling of belonging to the European cultural area, even more so as they distance themselves from sharia.

WHEN MUSLIMS OF EUROPE REJECT SHARIA

Salima, twenty-eight, was born in Valencienne, in the north of France. A modern single woman with a business degree, she is the oldest of six in a family of Algerian origin. When I met her in December 2009, she was working in finance in Geneva. She likes to ski and hike, sports which, she told me, made it easier for her to respect Muslim clothing norms – because her faith is something she has taken on herself in her personal and professional life. Before moving to Switzerland, Salima worked for six months in humanitarian assistance in Afghanistan and then in Pakistan.

Alerted to a professional opportunity by a headhunter, she moved to Geneva because the city offered her the possibility to take Islamic theology classes. She makes no secret of her admiration for the Ramadan family's contributions to Islamic education, notably the Islamic Center of Geneva directed by Hani Ramadan. Salima is determined to pursue her career while cultivating her faith and living in accordance with the law of Islam. But concerning sharia, she explains, 'As a woman, it's difficult to submit myself to sharia laws [...] I was born here [in Europe], so the idea of public punishments in certain Muslim countries, like stoning and lashings, shocks me.'[10] She confidently affirms her feminist conscience and belonging to Europe.

One often hears Muslim minorities in Europe idealizing the countries, where Islam is a shared religion. But those among them who followed their dream of living in an Islamic state elsewhere, of moving to an Islamic land, nonetheless return to Europe quite disappointed. David, who converted to Islam at a very young age, was married according to Islamic law in Malaysia. Today he is active in Muslim associative life in Geneva. He precisely describes his trajectory from Malaysia to Switzerland, the country where he was born: 'I tried to live in a Muslim country. I went to Malaysia, but life there didn't suit me. Living in a Muslim society that applies sharia law was not acceptable to me. Now, I know I am Swiss. In any case, according to sharia, I have to respect the laws of the country I live in as long as it allows me to be a Muslim. In this way, I am not in at odds with my values and principles.'[11]

For Muslims who want to practice their faith without calling for the application of sharia, Europe is becoming a privileged space. As David observes: 'To practice my religion, I don't need police or

Islamic judges.' Taken together, the Muslims of Europe seem to acquiesce to the idea of living their faith without renouncing the 'Western mindset.' For Issam, whom we interviewed in Toulouse, this Western mindset is clearly constitutive of his personality. Born in France of French-Moroccan nationality, he is representative of an entire generation. He mentions discrimination in France and the postcolonial syndrome in Morocco. His trip to Australia helped him underscore the fact that he belongs to different places. Today he teaches in a private Muslim school. When he is asked about the application of sharia, he explains, 'Since I was born and grew up in France, the Western mindset is dominant; it's the Western dimension of my personality that dwells in me ... Having been immersed in a culture, the French culture in particular, which defends the rights of man, that makes it so you're against corporeal punishment, for the legal equality of all people, and for abolishing the death penalty. We are all sensitive to this type of thing, a sort of humanism that is a bit modern, contemporary.'[12]

DECONSTRUCTING TWO UNIVERSALS: TARIQ RAMADAN'S ATTEMPT AT *AGGIORNAMENTO*

As for Tariq Ramadan, he proposes keys for understanding the new conditions of Islamic faith in Europe. He identifies the minimal conditions allowing Muslims to live in a secular society without hindering their belonging to the community of believers. How do we redefine Islamic faith today in the heart of European societies? Ramadan aims to respond to this major question. By basing his answer in part on Islam's sacred texts and in part on an analysis of contemporary society, he aims to contribute to the constitution of a new Muslim conscience of European citizenship.

European integration first requires Muslims to abandon their perception of a binary world: *Dâr al-islam* (the house of Islam) against *Dâr al-harb* (the house of war). Ramadan considers Europe above all as a land of peace (*Dâr al-sulh*). Next, he develops the notion of *Dâr al-shahâda* (house of witnessing Islamic faith), to designate all territories where Muslims can freely practice their religion: everywhere where this right is guaranteed, the materialization of the Muslim conscience is witnessed.[13]

Secondly, he aims to bring Islamic thought to the temporality of the present, and he subjects it to the test of contemporary questioning. Basing his inquiry on the fundamental sources of Islam, the Koran and the *Sunna*, Ramadan notes the distinction between what in Islam is immutable (*thâbit*) and what is subject to change.[14] According to him, the order of faith cannot avoid the critical exercise of reason to remain faithful to the teachings of Islam. A double movement, from texts to contextual realities, determines the terms and the stakes of the compromise and conditions all actualization of the interpretation of religious norms.[15] He thus writes that 'Those who know texts (*'ulamâ'an-nusûs*) and those who know contexts (*'ulamâ'al-wâqi'*) must now work together, on equal footing, to set in motion this radical reform we call for.'[16] Ramadan enumerates the key areas – medicine, arts, culture, male–female relations, ecology, economy, secularization, politics, philosophy – in which this investigation to update Islamic norms must be led. Nonetheless, he considers it necessary to maintain a dialogical relationship with theologians of Islam, the authority of religious figures, in order to redefine Islamic norms in the European context.

Thirdly, Ramadan tasks himself with thinking about the Islamic religion and sharia in relation to the universal. His task is even more difficult as the West has the hegemonic intention to impose its conception of the universal. Nonetheless, he says, all spiritual or religious traditions have considered the universal. Spirituality and monotheistic religions associate the universal with truth, in the a priori and the transcendent. Recognizing what is unique and practicing rites imply that each person considers ethical requirements to be universally true.[17] One must refer to a Being, an Idea or a Path that *states* the essence of the human experience. Nonetheless, for Ramadan, this choice of an 'a priori universal' does not necessarily imply that religions and spirituality have no legitimacy to construct a universal based on the exercise of reason.[18] Referring to the sources of these monotheistic religions as well as to Hinduism and Buddhism, Ramadan explains that the two approaches are not mutually exclusive. One must adopt a humble outlook to recognize the necessary multiplicity of paths and bring the essence of one's own in dialogue with others.[19] For Ramadan, reaching the universal through the exercise of reason is the 'condition for being capable of understanding the reason of others' universal.'[20] Instead of making do with two distinct universals, comparing their respective values in view of establishing a hierarchy, he defends the idea that 'the only universal is a shared one.' The shared universal imposes the double fundamental recognition of the common (the universal) and diversity (sharing).[21] He thus questions the possible sources of pluralism in the very definition of the universal: 'Never claim ownership of the center by denying the legitimacy of points of view' but instead determine 'intersecting spaces' where we locate equality, rather than integrating difference. This is Ramadan's ideal model for a shared universalism.[22]

The grounding of Islam in Europe makes it necessary to rethink the encounter with the Other. Living with the Other, with his different skin, clothing, beliefs, customs, habits, psychology and intellectual logic, leads us back to ourselves, to our interior horizons, to our intimacy, writes Ramadan.[23] In his view, being a Muslim implies faithfulness to a spiritual dimension, a connection to transcendence and at the same time strong social engagement. He thus defines the contours of a 'citizen's religiousness'[24] by encouraging Muslims to demand their right to be full citizens. His position is therefore not about defining the living conditions of Muslims in Europe as a religious minority, nor about asking them to blend into the cultural majority of the countries in which they live. He implicitly recognizes their capacity not only to transform their relationship to Islamic normativity, but also to question the Western universal.

How do people preserve a close relationship with Islamic prescriptions while fully entering into European reality? Reaching consciousness of the multiplicity of allegiances is a source of tension for the Muslims of Europe, as well as for Tariq Ramadan himself as a Muslim and European intellectual. His position expresses a plurality of affiliations in tension with one another. The difficulty of addressing different audiences, of being in between two worlds, Muslim and Western, is familiar to him. His efforts aim at the opening up of a space for updating Islamic norms in Europe without breaking the link with theologians in the Muslim world. Ramadan wants to be heard by the West without losing the attention of the Islamic world, and this delicate position feeds suspicion on both sides. His care to not question the scriptural sources without the consensus of theologians caused a scandal in France when, instead of firmly condemning the stoning of women practiced in some Muslim countries, he called for a moratorium on this medieval practice.

It is in the heart of European societies that the question of creating a link between people from different parts of the world with distinct cultural identities and religious traditions has become a major concern. The public visibility of Islam, which presents itself as an infraction of the boundaries drawn between 'foreigners' and 'us,' is the source of discord for shared norms and questions European societies about the meaning of commonality. Nonetheless, the new public fabric creates an unprecedented proximity in composite cultures and allows for the initiation of a process of interaction and mutual transformation. The possibility of making connections requires the act of intruding into the domain of others' convictions, and transgressing established boundaries. This transformation plays out as a cultural interpenetration.

THE ARCHBISHOP OF CANTERBURY IN 2008: TAKING 'MULTIPLE AFFILIATIONS' INTO ACCOUNT

A comparison of Tariq Ramadan's thoughts and the Archbishop of Canterbury's positions clears this ground. The first is Muslim, the second Christian, but they both aim to deconstruct two universals and explore forms of interaction between secular and religious norms. Because they take the risk of transgressing the boundaries established between Islam and Europe, neither one has been spared criticism.

In the venerable Anglican Temple Church in London, in 2008, a conference speech by Rowan Williams, Archbishop of Canterbury, on the necessity of finding a 'constructive arrangement' with some aspects of Islamic law caused an outcry.[25] His proposal implied entering into a dialogue with Islam, relating to the advice of thinkers of Islam, notably Tariq Ramadan. The Archbishop of Canterbury's plea in favor of accommodation with Islam and, moreover, his use of the notion of sharia created a polemic which led him to lose political support and exposed him to virulent attacks by the media. Stigmatizing the archbishop's words, they amplified the negative clichés of sharia and torpedoed the possible public debate about the question of religious pluralism: a new show of Islamophobia, this time targeting a non-Muslim, in order to erect in public signs saying 'Entry barred to Islam.' However, it seems important to reproduce the archbishop's words, because they signal the existence of new dynamics of interaction and the horizon of the possible in European public life.

Rowan Williams begins with the assertion that a pluralistic society must take into account the presence of citizens with 'multiple affiliations.' If these different attachments are marginalized or hidden because they are part of the private sphere, the ghettoization of social life will become inevitable. According to him, these multiple attachments must be recognized as legitimate and comprise the object of debate on shared priorities and common interests. In line with Habermas, the archbishop gives a central place to the public sphere as a place where everyone's affiliations can appear and be recognized in a democratic debate on the meaning of commonality.[26]

Williams pleads for the recognition of social identities which, according to him, constitute a dual identity: that of citizen and believer. His critical reflection focuses on the 'abstract universalism' that relegates anything that concerns religions, habits and customs to the private sphere. 'Secular' laws tend to dissolve these specific features in the name of universalism; instead, he says, they should play a 'role in the support and monitoring of these multiple affiliations.' The public non-recognition of social and religious identities can lead to the creation of mutually exclusive isolated communities in which individuals find themselves subject to repressive constraints and injustices. The Archbishop of Canterbury thus joins critics of a multiculturalism that has led to communities separated from one another. But instead of privileging cultural homogeneity and the hegemony of national values, as is frequently the case in critiques of multiculturalism, he does not hesitate to engage in a dialogue with Islam. According to him, the public sphere must allow for the appearance of different religious and cultural affiliations and their reciprocal compromise because questions of freedom cannot be resolved only by public rectification.

It is in public space, as a place of interaction and rectification, that Rowan Williams defends the need to think about the rights of religious groups in a secular state. Referring to Islam and Orthodox Judaism, he explores in particular the compromise in norms surrounding sharia. After demonstrating the limits of abstract universalism, he aims, by relying on the work of Islamic thinkers, to dispel some common misconceptions about sharia. Beginning with Tariq Ramadan's work, Williams interprets sharia as the expression of universal principles of Islam instead of comparing it to a system of rigid codification. He takes from reformist thinkers of Islam the idea of updating religious law by reason founded not on traditional Muslim schools of law, but on the religion's universal principles.

The archbishop also discusses the question of women's rights in Islam and the ban on religious conversion, two key points for updating sharia, according to him, because of the considerable gap in these areas with European norms. In a society where freedom of religion is guaranteed, one group cannot, he tells us, ask that religious conversion be banned and punished. In the European context, the ban on a Muslim converting to another religion is a contradiction with freedom of conscience – and moreover affects relationships between Islam and other religions. Williams thus brings up a subject likely to concern Muslim citizens in Europe more in the future. Another thorny subject is the family code and the rights of women. Williams adheres to the notion that the recognition of an additional jurisprudence, in terms of the Islamic family code, can have as a consequence the reinforcing of retrograde elements within communities, notably as concerns the role and freedom of women. He rightly draws attention to the importance of distinguishing between customs and cultural practices and religious prescriptions, as in the case of honor crimes. He suggests that lawyers would do well to inform themselves on the differences between these cultural prejudices and religious prescriptions.

The idea of an 'overlapping consensus' of different moral doctrines, developed by the philosopher John Rawls[27] is continued in the archbishop's reflections, which call for the public recognition of religious and cultural affiliations in order to allow for an overlapping of social relations and a public rectification of freedoms. According to Williams, in order to engage in deep reflection on relations between Islam and British law, one must 'deconstruct' simplistic oppositions and mythologies which surround the nature of sharia as well as the heritage of the Enlightenment. If we want to avoid legal universalism leading to a sort of sterile positivism, theoretical and theological aspects must be taken into consideration.

Tariq Ramadan and Rowan Williams thus both note the multiple affiliations of citizenship. Their underlying idea is that of a 'citizen's religiousness' which defines the dual identity of believer and citizen. From their respective points of view, both think about the question of Islam beyond immigration, without reducing it to the rights of minorities. They bear witness to the necessity of thinking about Islam's grounding in the West and approaching European pluralism in a new way, by calling for a critical interrogation of monocultural universalism. Our interrogation continues theirs in that, in this book, we are trying to understand the development of Islamic normativity in relation to European codes and imagine the conditions of a process of interpenetration of European citizens.

CONTROVERSIES ON 'ISLAMIC COUNCILS' IN GREAT BRITAIN, 2008–09

By calling for 'accommodation' with Islamic law in his 2008 speech in Temple Church, the Archbishop of Canterbury was not well received. On the contrary, an Anglican who wished to engage in a constructive dialogue with Islam was the object of criticism by his peers: instead of a politics of accommodation, his detractors countered him with a call for British values and 'one law for all.' In this controversy, even in a country considered 'multicultural,' we once again observe the rise of identity nationalism.

The British model is known as a producer of relative legal pluralism in that it tolerates some of the legal traditions of migrant populations and their religious and communal norms. British jurisprudence is often described in relation to this culture of compromise, as Jean-Philippe Bras, a professor of public law at the University of Rouen, reminds us: the model of 'common law,' which privileges arbitration and mediation, is the antithesis of the French legal model, which is affirmative and integrationist, with a secular and centralizing tradition.[28] Nonetheless, controversies surrounding Islam, mostly analogous on both sides of the Channel, blur these differences and favor a dynamic of convergence between two legal models in their treatment and resolution of conflicts. While recognizing that the intervention of the Archbishop of Canterbury would be unimaginable in France, Bras observes that the British debate on sharia follows a similar path to 'French-style controversy.'

Despite the political and ideological character of public debate on sharia in Great Britain, Islamic law has found a field of application in the Sharia Councils and Muslim Arbitration Tribunals. The vast majority of these Islamic councils operate within mosques, like the first, inaugurated in Birmingham in the early 1980s, in the Jami Mosque. These religious authorities work in the service of the Muslim community and rule on legal questions such as, for example, the authentication of acts of marriage and divorce or commercial transactions. These councils also rule on cases involving alimony, child custody and inheritance. As Jean-Philippe Bras points out, from a pragmatic standpoint they offer simple procedures that are quick and inexpensive, unlike civil courts – to the extent that even non-Muslims often prefer to go to them to settle their disputes. These Islamic councils also have proximity to the community thanks to their judges' knowledge of Islamic law schools and the plaintiffs' languages of origin (often Pakistani Urdu). They are, as Bras shows, veritable support institutions for the integration process of Muslim communities.

As for Islamic Arbitration Tribunals, which since 2007 have been subject to the British Arbitration Act, they are defined as 'organs of internal regulation' of Muslim communities.[29] They are also spaces where an effort of interpretation (*ijtihad*) is emerging, with the effect of reactualizing Islamic normativity.[30] These tribunals help Islamic law evolve towards the norms of Western law: they seek to officialize Islamic councils – until now informal – and also help clear the way for a form of codification of religious rules. Since 2007, the network of Islamic Arbitration Tribunals has been directed by Faiz-ul-Aqtab Siddiqi, born in 1967 in Pakistan, and groups together five of England's large cities (London, Birmingham, Bradford, Manchester and Nuneaton). A lawyer and specialist in both British and Islamic law, Faiz Siddiqi has a degree from the University of Liverpool and from Al-Azhar in Cairo. Since 1994, he has directed the Hijaz College Islamic University, located on the outskirts of the city of Nuneaton in the Midlands, the seat of the Islamic Arbitration Tribunal founded in 1994, a few months before the death of his father, Abdul Wahab Siddiqi, a sheikh in the ancient Sufi brotherhood Naqshbandi Hijazi, whose body lies in a mausoleum at the building's entrance; he is considered to be the first Islamic saint to be buried in European soil.

In May 2009, we met the young Faiz Siddiqi at Hijaz College in Nuneaton. Islam is quite a presence in this small city, where nearly 30 percent of the population is comprised of immigrants. The factories that once drew cheap laborers closed in the 1980s after Margaret Thatcher's neoliberal reforms. The crisis is evident in the many boarded storefronts and empty streets. It is for this reason that Sheikh Siddiqi put in place a project of 'spiritual renaissance' among the youth. In the high school, students wear long white tunics and the traditional embroidered skullcaps. Over their tunics, they wear green vests with the school's insignia, a heteroclite mix of English and Pakistani madrassa uniforms.

Faiz Siddiqi explained to us that he created the network of Islamic Arbitration Tribunals in 2007 to fight forced marriages in the Muslim community. For him, the object of this network is not to interfere in divorces and marriages, since Islamic councils are sufficiently competent in these areas. Rather, it is about creating a legal framework that is more homogeneous between different Islamic councils so that all who use them are treated in the same way. The idea is also to take charge of internal affairs in the community, such as forced marriages or quarrels over the leadership of mosques. Siddiqi in no way hopes that sharia will replace the British Constitution, only that it complements and enriches the legal system in the United Kingdom. But can British law accommodate it? Faiz Siddiqi believes so: 'My knowledge of Islamic law helps me make proposals that will allow British law to evolve, and my knowledge of British law helps me adapt Islamic law to the British context. I think that the two together can create a new synergy. Laws have a spirit, and the spirit of the law remains the same.'[31]

The anchoring of Islam in the West occurs through the rapprochement of legal systems and results from the multiplication of points of contact between Islamic norms and positive law. In the case of British colonialism, the codification of Islamic law occurred through legal accommodation concerning the family code in South Asia.[32] In the contemporary and post-colonial period, it is immigrants who reactualize the question concerning the family code in Great Britain. The rapprochement and arrangement between two legislative codes are a source of litigation and conflict when sharia leads to explicit violations of positive law – for example, in forced marriages, polygamous marriages, unilateral repudiation or honor killings.[33] It is in these 'gray zones' that public affairs and controversies we have studied suddenly emerge in the most vivid way.

In the heart of the Muslim community, there is no consensus on the necessity of a codification of religious law or on the recourse to Islamic councils. The imam Muhammad Shahid Raza, the director of Muslim College, London (an institute for training imams and leaders of the Muslim community), is a doctor of Muslim law, trained in India. He is also one of the founders of the Federation of Muslim Organizations in Leicester, one of the first bodies to facilitate interreligious dialogue among the Muslim community. He understands the problem of Islamic councils from the perspective of equality between Muslims and other British citizens before the law. He does not favor the idea of two parallel legal systems and considers that the recognition of Islamic councils can cause even more exclusion for Muslims.

Imam Raza instead prefers recognition of the English system of Muslim religious marriage (*nikah*), by putting in place councils of experts in Islamic law. Thus mosques could have the right to register religious marriages as well as civil ones, as is the case for British churches.[34]

Our interview with Judge Khurshid Drabu, a legal advisor at the Muslim Council of Britain, proves the multiplicity of voices in the Muslim community. According to him, Islam is an essentially public faith which as a consequence cannot become a solely private affair. It is this public aspect of Islam that disturbs the British legal system. Drabu sees in Islamic councils structures of jurisprudence that allow British Muslims to live in conformity with the Koran. Nonetheless, for him, Islamic councils are not yet sufficiently mature to become true arbitration tribunals. He believes that Islamic councils discriminate against women, not intentionally, but because of a lack of sensitivity to women's rights guaranteed by Islam. This is why Judge Drabu wants to create a training program for muftis in Islamic councils, so that they can become judges who are truly competent in matters concerning the rights of women.[35]

These controversies reveal the will of Muslims in Great Britain to define an Islamic normativity and to put it to the test of European codes. In Islam, there is neither a recognized source of authority nor any central system of control capable of serving as a guide. The individualization of belief, the rival doctrinal conceptions, the fatwas pronounced by imams in far-off countries prove the diversity of paths taken and the plasticity of normative registers in direct contact with sharia.[36] But in the legal field, a process of accommodation is under way. Beginning with empirical elements, lawyers in effect reflect on the possibilities of articulating norms and different legal systems. On the other hand, on the national level, the public debate continues to operate according to polarization and presuppositions of incompatibility between Islamic and liberal norms. Opposing the image of the West, founded on a universalist ethic of the rights of man, and one of the Muslim world, finding refuge in a communitarian position, this debate on values thus does not reflect the composite reality of ordinary Muslims.

IN LONDON, BRITISH ISLAM AND REDISCOVERED CITIZENSHIP

We brought together our EPS group in London on 3 October 2009, to discuss the controversy sparked by sharia with British Muslims. The Muslim participants, mostly from South Asia, particularly Pakistan, reflect the history of immigration in Great Britain. But their ethnic origins scarcely seemed important to them – they almost never mentioned them in the course of our discussion. It is the definition of their citizenship as British Muslims that appears to them to be the central issue. As one of the participants explained, in Great Britain, Islam developed largely out of the daily experiences of immigration, independent of what was going on in Pakistan or Bangladesh or India. A significant number of converts to Islam, who have no national allegiance besides British, are uniquely positioned representatives of this hyphenated identity. They are British-Muslims.

Each one of the participants has his or her way of living the faith, creating diversity, which makes it difficult to talk about

'Muslims' as a sociologically homogeneous category. In the group, some Muslims called themselves secular, and women in veils called themselves feminists. Among them were a knowledgeable imam and follower of Salafism, with divergent positions on the question of sharia. Khola, a woman in her forties, directs the women's area of the Masjid Tawhid Mosque in London and made a name for herself with the positions she took on the debates provoked by the intervention by the Archbishop of Canterbury. She studied Islam and feminism at the School of Oriental and African Studies (SOAS) in London after receiving a degree in Islamic law from the same university. For her, sharia is a necessity for Muslims. Living in Great Britain, she is familiar with religions other than Islam and does not hesitate to legitimize her faith with a mirror comparison to Judaism: 'For me, sharia is a way of being Muslim and following religious prescriptions in the same way a Jew does by respecting the Shabbat.' She explains the 'power of belief' as its continuity: 'The fact that people have followed the same rituals for centuries is the beauty of sharia.' Born in a religious family – her father and brother are both imams – Khola was introduced to religion in her youth. She calls herself a Salafist and voluntarily presents herself as a conservative. Nonetheless, she is interested in the question of feminism and is inspired by the writings of the Moroccan feminist Fatima Mernissi and her Egyptian counterpart Leila Ahmed.[37] She criticizes her opponents for not taking into consideration the 'Islamic renaissance' developing in the Western world under the influence of modern Islamic thinkers who demonstrate the compatibility of Muslim law with the European notion of the rights of man and women's rights.

In this way, Khola is representative of an elite Muslim feminism emergent in Europe since the 2000s, as the results of our vast inquiry prove. Succeeding in university, continuing to doctoral studies on Islam and intervening in public debates are the distinctive traits of these young women. They access the secular and liberal cultural capital of European countries, but they also benefit from professional opportunities offered by Islamic networks. They call for Muslim normativity, but they also question themselves about their beliefs, religious practices, dogmas and the validity of Islamic prescriptions in the English context. Far from being static, their sometimes contradictory responses prove the reflexivity of Muslim women toward their faith, seen through the prism of their lived experience in Europe.

In light of the trajectories of the members of our EPS group, we were able to understand the controversy over British Islamic councils in a new way. Sometimes considered as religious authorities in the heart of the Muslim community, treating the problems of immigrant populations confronted with the difficulties of integration in the margins of the host society, they find themselves reappropriated by this new feminine, urban elite and the new generation of British Muslims. These Islamic councils offer the opportunity for a consensual overlapping of relationships that Muslims have with Islam and British law, in view of accommodation between these respective norms. Instead of applying a coercive legal doctrine, they play an intermediary role between Muslims and broader society by accompanying Muslims in their daily lives and their ethical development. Unlike national justice, which is perceived as distant, procedural and conflictual, these Islamic councils of sharia provide a familiar and intimate framework, and respond to ethical concerns and the request for psychological counsel by those who use them. An imam affirmed for us that Islamic councils propose a 'reconciliation clinic' for familial disagreements where they 'care for the souls' of believers. In fact, they owe their popularity to this alternative and informal mode of resolving conflicts.[38]

Some members of our group know these authorities well from having participated in the work of Islamic councils. Cassandra, an English woman who converted to Islam, was part of a commission tasked with drafting a type of religious marriage contract at the initiative of the Muslim Institute. She thinks that the inclusion of women in negotiations is essential for integrating women's rights. As for Heba, a young veiled believer with a doctorate from the University of Sussex, she sees sharia as a way of life, because she doesn't trust Islamic councils in mosques to protect women's rights provided in the Koran. Other Muslims take the same position against sharia, because any recourse to Islamic law would represent for them a step backward by giving power to religious fundamentalism. This was the position of Taj, one of the theologians in the group, well known for the public positions he has staked in favor of secular Islam.

THE 'DERAILMENT' OF BRITISH ISLAM

In 2009, all of these interventions confirmed that Great Britain's Muslims were often, and had long been, active in associative life. Many among them work in Islamic foundations and mosques, are part of Muslim networks and, through these associations, serve as an interface between the Muslim community and public powers.

They fully demonstrate that there are many interpretations of Islamic norms and practices of accommodation in conformity with the liberal values of British society, and that they are present in legal institutions as well as in associative life and daily life.

But this society has also been at the center of global and local dynamics of radicalization which have hindered this endogenous process of accommodation. A series of events has thus 'derailed' British Islam from its path towards integration via multiculturalism. The fatwa against Salman Rushdie in February 1989, the sending of British troops to Afghanistan in 2001 and Iraq in 2003, the Al-Qaeda attacks in London in 2005, and the government's enactment of the Prevent program in 2007 to fight terrorism: all these events have disturbed a progressive and peaceful process, caught between terrorist acts, wars, radicalization and security politics. Far from favoring a peaceful and inclusive multiculturalism, they have reactualized, as we have seen, the affirmation of the British national identity. The feeling that a threshold of tolerance had been transgressed, that liberalism had reached its limits, that segregation and communitarianism had led to radicalization, was largely shared. Insular Great Britain, a country with a liberal and multicultural tradition, saw itself converging with the identity dynamic at work in other countries in continental Europe.

The British government's enactment of the Prevent program, which aims to eradicate the sources of violent extremism, can be seen as the beginning of security politics and the end of multiculturalism. Put in place after the 7 July 2005 attacks, this program was meant to survey and 'de-radicalize' the Muslim youth of the country. In reality, it became a new technique of governmentality of citizens from the Muslim faith. Some denounced this policy as a significant industry with public financing given to Muslim organizations and experts to help the government in its fight against terrorism. The program was seen as responsible for a schism inside Muslim populations. Muslim organizations that received funding thanks to the Prevent program were regarded with suspicion. They nonetheless opened the door to new opportunities for some Muslim actors, notably women, who use these spaces to make themselves heard in public debates and who play an active role in the anti-radicalization campaign.

For the participants in our EPS group in London, this series of events – from the fatwa against Salman Rushdie up to the end of multiculturalism – represented an abrupt break in the ordinary lives of British Muslims. Since then, Islam has been in the forefront of the media's attention on the national as well as the global level, against the wishes of Muslims. Participants said they were struck in the literal sense of the term – 'we are hit' – by the Rushdie affair and the 2005 attacks in London. Ever since, they have been 'under the spotlight,' constantly asked about their faith and suspected of being involved in terrorist networks. They complain of and fear being 'burned' by this excess of attention.

The immigrant's one-time status on the margins of society is gone. Migrants and their descendants now attract the attention of public opinion. We invited participants to clarify their identity, allegiance and loyalty. The change in status of Muslim immigrants, who, once invisible, have become overly visible, is a phenomenon that we have observed in all European countries. But this reversal was more violent and global in the British case. The fatwa against Salman Rushdie and the 2005 London attacks constitute crucial moments in the collective memory of Great Britain's Muslims: participants pointed to these events as the moment when global Islam's influence affected their trajectories and pulled the plug on insular and multicultural British Islam.

These Muslims find themselves faced with a difficult task: reconciling their religious identity and their British citizenship. This is what members of the EPS group in London undertook by joining in a polyphonic dialogue. The few who have fixed ideas – such as the imam who puts his ethnic identity first, or those who believe only in Western secularism – don't control the orientation of the debate among the group. Most Muslims face head on the question of their 'double belonging,' and the convergence between two spheres of their identity: their attachment to British citizenship and the Muslim faith. They share the same line of thought as Tariq Ramadan and Rowan Williams, whose research follows a double logic, thinking about European Islam and religious pluralism in Europe.

Navid, the editor-in-chief of a Muslim newspaper, retrospectively analyzes what it means to be a Muslim in England. Islamic identity today, he explains, is not based on an ideal as it was in the 1980s, but on contextual experience. The traumatic events which have occurred in Europe are points of departure for rethinking collective memory and identity. The personal interpretation of these events by participants in the EPS group helps them question their identity and citizenship. Navid goes back twenty years to the *Satanic Verses* affair. That was a key moment, he says, for becoming conscious of what it meant to be a British citizen and a Muslim. For him, the person who had the most pertinent response was the now deceased Sheikh Mohammed Abdoulkhair Zaki Badawi, the former director of Muslim College, whose moderation and religious tolerance were publicly recognized. A theologian of Egyptian origin, Zaki Badawi founded Muslim College in 1986. He gave a central place to interreligious dialogue and did not hesitate to criticize imams who did not teach in English in their mosques. A pioneer in the definition of British Islam, he was nonetheless a traditional ulema who inspired respect. Navid affirms that Zaki Badawi held a visionary position during the Rushdie affair and that he was ahead of his time: Badawi publicly declared that 'if Salman Rushdie came to find refuge with me from the fatwa, I would protect him because he is my fellow citizen.' He thus created a proximate relationship with the writer Salman Rushdie and not with the imam Khomeini. He prioritized his British citizenship over Muslim fraternity. Navid regrets that no Muslim organization has since understood the visionary implication for Muslims of what Zaki Badawi said: 'Only later, after many years, did British Muslims understand that he was right ... They should have reversed themselves on the *Satanic Verses* affair.' Navid thinks that this episode was the beginning of the question of citizenship in the discourse of Muslims in Great Britain. This 'key event' taught them the importance that their British citizenship had for them.

This self-questioning, and the necessity to return to the past, to revisit the Rushdie affair and to recognize the errors, in particular the violent and emotional reaction by Muslims, is a shared concern. Judge Khurshid Drabu, mentioned earlier in reference to Islamic councils, who has a degree in English law and is from Kashmir, is one of the founders of the Action Committee for Islamic Affairs created after the Rushdie affair. He admits that Muslims, including himself, had emotional reactions at the time, and that they were misled, instead of looking for institutional and peaceful forms of intervention as British citizens; British citizenship, he underlines, implies accepting the principle that in a liberal society, thoughts, publications, books, caricatures and art cannot be censored. Milad, originally from Afghanistan, works in Muslim networks and participates in the Prevent program. He repeats Judge Drabu's argument in the EPS group by insisting on the fact that Muslims must learn to not be immediately reactive by burning flags. They should find other means of action: 'Before the Rushdie affair, Muslims living in Europe didn't have representative bodies. Today we are used to intervening as Brits and Muslims. It is because we were born here that we feel British. That's my case. In Afghanistan, I would feel like a foreigner. Great Britain is my home and my children's home.'

That multiculturalism ran out of steam is not only a judgment of political figures and European intellectuals. It is an assessment, a lived reality for Muslims. Multiculturalism did not allow them to live sheltered from 'shariatic' and global dynamics: the fatwa by Iran's Supreme Leader, the war in Iraq, terrorist actions supported by Al-Qaeda ... The repositioning of Muslims in relation to these events nonetheless has opened up the possibility for a critical reflection as well as an anchoring in British citizenship. Beyond discussions on the rights of minorities, religious liberty, cultural racism and discrimination, Muslims find themselves forced to 'deconstruct' their relationship to sharia and to reconstruct their British Muslim citizenship. This consciousness of citizenship was acquired by the 'derailment' of their established Islamic identities.

8

Halal Lifestyles

Islam is a religion that provides the faithful with a manual of civility in their relations with others. It is a modus vivendi that maintains them in their daily faith and helps them respect the meticulous division between conduct that is licit and illicit. Muslims demonstrate their belonging to the community of believers, the *oumma*, by obeying God, but also by their appropriate cultural practices, food guidelines, way of addressing others, and dress codes. Faith as a form of believing and individual spiritualism is thus not sufficient. Muslims must perform a variety of material or physical acts to make their faith manifest in the community. These acts must extend to all areas of life: besides cultural prescriptions (*chahada*, prayer, fasting, pilgrimage, charity), social etiquette and 'good manners' (wearing the veil, growing a beard, avoiding co-education) are important in daily life.

FROM SHARIA TO THE AUTHORIZATION OF DAILY HALAL

This law resides in the believer's body, and is incorporated in practices and ritual forms. The anthropologist Mohammed

Hocine Benkheira talks about the 'love of the law' in that believers submit themselves of their own free will to prescriptions and Islamic norms.[1] Religious rituals are indistinguishable from the theological strategy of salvation, and from the requirement that the faithful master their bodies, physical appetites and passions.[2] Food guidelines are only one manifestation of this body policy and self-mastery which leads to individual salvation, to 'humanization.' One must make the body a place where 'animalism and humanity' are confronted, into a 'place that is fit to reside.'[3]

In terms of food guidelines – the ban on consuming pork and the obligation of ritual slaughter – the verses of the Koran are very specific. In his book *Le Licite et l'illicite en islam* (*The Licit and the Illicit in Islam*), the theologian Yusuf Al-Qaradawi quotes sura 6, verse 145: 'Say, I do not find within that which was revealed to me [anything] forbidden to one who would eat it unless it be a dead animal or blood spilled out or the flesh of swine – for indeed, it is impure – or it be [that slaughtered in] disobedience, dedicated to other than Allah.'[4] By pronouncing God's name, the believer proclaims that he commits this act towards a living being only with God's permission. Each ban on a food is linked to a hygienic concern or the good treatment of the animal. As for the ban on pork, the reason given is the 'impure' way this animal feeds.[5]

Benkheira situates the theological significance of the distinction between licit and illicit in the framework of an anthropological analysis. According to him, the animal is a mediating category for thinking about the organization of the world. Animal classifications allow us to create the category of humanity based on major oppositions between savage/domestic, carnivore/herbivore, and demonic/divine. The principal criterion for distinguishing between licit and illicit species is their respective way of feeding: animals that feed on meat are prohibited, as are those that feed on garbage. In order to understand this rule, he writes, we must recognize the sometimes explicit assumption according to which food transmits its properties to the eater.[6] Avoiding certain animal species implies avoiding their qualities: a man who ate their meat would end up resembling them. The ban on the meat of carnivores is explained in a general way: you must not eat the meat of meat-eaters, so as to not inherit their violence, their aggression and their savagery.[7]

How, then, can we understand the meaning of the taboo against pork? Can the prohibition on carnivores help explain why pork is banned? In taxonomic classification, pigs are shown as an animal with strong canine teeth, and thus as carnivores. Moreover, in the Muslim bestiary, pork is also a symbol for appetite, love of the world and terrestrial life.[8] Gluttony, cupidity, and an absence of jealousy are other qualities associated with pigs. For some Muslim legal scholars, the extended consummation of pork would weaken 'a man's jealousy for his family's honor.'

Under what conditions, then, is it possible to eat meat without falling under the sway of animalism? The detailed classification of species allows for the creation of a list of animals which are licit (halal) to eat under Islamic law, which prescribes their ritual slaughter in a very detailed protocol. The animal must be well treated before and during slaughter. No needless suffering may be inflicted on him, no sharp blade, and he may not be sacrificed in front of another animal.[9] Invoking Allah's name is also important – legal scholars insist on this point – because in Islam, animals are

God's creatures, and men can only kill them by obtaining divine permission. Canonical texts codify the ritual death of an animal according to rites of sacrifice.[10] The ritualization of slaughter aims to avoid the objectification of the animal and the identification of man with a predator. The central point is to 'civilize' man by assuring that he will not lose his humanity.[11]

THE 'ECLECTIC USE OF HALAL'

Bans on specific foods in these religious precepts are scarcely applied in contemporary societies. In Europe's industrial slaughter-houses, preserving these rules has become a subject of debate and negotiation between businesses, veterinarians, leaders of Muslim associations and theologians.[12] Because of consumers' mistrust of the halal label, more and more Muslims defend the need to go from meat-eating to a 'vegetarian diet,' which they justify based on the Koran and the ethics of Islam.[13] Muslims seek to relocate Islamic ethics through the prism of their European experience. Their call for halal converges with the vegetarian movement, the organic market, naturopathy, etc.

Muslims ask for legal advice (fatwas) in different areas, ranging from physical hygiene to family relations and financial transactions.[14] If their main motivation in religious interpretation is avoiding evil and sin (haram[15]), those who live in Europe also seek an 'Islamic license.' They base their decisions on the advice of Muslim legal scholars, for whom licitness is the primary rule, and bans are an exception. If the notion of haram indicates that which is forbidden, imposes a law and evokes punishment and fear, the notion of halal is suppler, and defines on the contrary licit acts.

Etymologically, the word halal comes from the word *hall*, which signifies the act of resolving, of freeing in one way or another.[16]

Young Muslims in Europe aim to distinguish themselves from their 'parents' Islam' by substituting the halal principle for the forbidden haram. The transmission of religion through the family is in effect suited to their attempts, because an Islam of the forbidden handicaps them in the solicitations of secular life. They overcome this dichotomy by adopting a religiosity oriented by the permissible and by creating for themselves places for the apprenticeship of Islam. For example, they create 'halal circles,' places where conversation is guided by someone knowledgeable on texts by Muslim thinkers, such as Saïd Nursi, in order to learn and practice an Islam different from the one imposed on them at home.[17] This form of apprenticeship of religious knowledge through discursive practices, called *sohbet*, occupies an important place in the Sufi tradition of Islam. Young people are reviving this tradition in the European context in order to create an Islamic modus vivendi to apply in their daily lives. By finding a foundation in religious texts, they form their ideas according to what is allowed in Islam more than what is forbidden, opening up the possibility of adapting themselves in an inventive way to modern forms of leisure and entertainment, by organizing alternative parties, graduation ceremonies and birthdays without alcohol.[18] In this way, writes the Swiss political scientist Patrick Haenni, halal 'tends to imply not only conformity with what is forbidden, but also a certain ethics of religiosity, […] from an individual concern for health to the desire for fair trade.'[19] The emergence of this Muslim culture of consumption, writes Haenni, is open to cultural extraversion, with 'hedonistic, individualistic and market friendly traits.'

Rachid Id Yassine, a researcher involved in our EPS group in Toulouse, described the 'eclectic use of halal' in all parts of social and cultural life: eating habits, hygiene, feelings, sexuality, art and leisure, finance and social engagement.[20] This extension of halal expresses European Muslims' attraction to lifestyles that are not strictly Islamic. The activities they call halal do not at all concern the strict observance of the Muslim religion, signaling the weakening of the principle of mastery of appetites required by the faith. Believers thus become users and consumers of halal markets. They multiply their ethical requirements and associate halal with organic, ecological and fair trade. Because of this, Islamic halal is converging with the most popular contemporary cultural trends, intersecting with New Age and 'bobo' (bourgeois bohemian) generations in European countries.[21] The quest for halal love, 'well-being' and 'personal development' is also becoming a part of Muslims' lives. New careers in 'Islamic coaching,' with experts certified in different forms of physical and psychological therapies, are tracing the boundaries of an alternative market of 'Islamic well-being.'[22]

Islamic norms are thus subject to modern imperatives of ethics and expertise, which are allowed to define halal. Instead of traditional religious authorities of Islam, those knowledgeable about *fiqh* who debate norms, today experts put the halal seal on meat, candies, drinks, cosmetics, leisure activities, mortuary rights …[23] This call for 'all halal' signals Muslims' entry into the ordinary communal life of European societies. The halal certification demonstrates the move from religious claims to social gains. With this certification, Islamic normativity escapes religious authorities and becomes a business. Halal lifestyles also circumvent secular powers and their bans in the public sphere. We thus see an expansion of public life in the development of new Islamic markets and the emergence of its users and consumers.

THE SURPRISING FRENCH POLEMICS IN THE 2010S

At the end of the 2000s, a series of polemics emerged in France following the scandal over a fake halal certification in the agrifood sector, sparking a series of interrogations about the authenticity and legitimacy of halal in a secular republic. Consumers learned in a televised documentary that products labeled halal did not adhere to the norms of ritual slaughter.[24] The scandal encouraged the monitoring of meat by Muslim experts: entrepreneurs specialized in the halal label to ensure the traceability of products from the slaughter to the condition of the meat up to distribution, as well as their financing. But the debate on halal, far from remaining limited to the community of Muslim consumers, rapidly spread across society. According to the political scientist Gilles Kepel, the halal affair thus revealed what 'was developing in Islam's relation to France.'[25]

The controversy began when the fast food chain Quick decided to extend halal choices in their French stores in 2010. In these restaurants, ritual slaughter and the ban on pork would be respected: hamburgers were to be made of halal beef, and pork would be replaced by turkey. This offer, inspired by economic incentives aimed at conquering new segments of the market, was interpreted by opponents of halal as a sign of the 'forced Islamization' of France. Marine Le Pen, the feminine face of populism, set the tone, as she had in the controversy surrounding prayers in the street. She defined the political terms of the confrontation with Islam: denouncing the decision to offer halal food as a 'communitarian dispute,' a 'diktat' imposed on French citizens, she affirmed her adherence to republican principles and distinguished herself from older generations of the far right. In her offensive against halal, she thus reversed the image of exclusion, the minority/majority relationship, by speaking about French people as a group threatened with exclusion and discrimination, 'despised in their own country.' In 2012, during the presidential elections, she declared that a number of French people would unwittingly eat halal meat because meat distributed in Île-de-France would be 'exclusively halal,' which was of course inaccurate.[26]

Other political personalities on the right as well as the left entered this polemic to condemn the offer of halal as noncompliant with republican principles. The UMP government fanned the flames. School cafeterias, the labeling of methods of slaughter on products that were sold, and the principle of secularism on the 'republican plate' were all put forth.[27] The prime minister, François Fillon, even took a position in the affair, calling ritual slaughter a 'remnant of ancestral traditions that no longer have much meaning.'[28] His statement, which targeted Muslims and halal, offended the sensibilities of Jews, whose representatives, such as the Chief Rabbi, Gilles Bernheim, expressed their fear that these polemics would spread to the Jewish community and put in peril religious rituals like kosher, ritual slaughter and circumcision.

The fight against Islamic halal even pushed certain radical circles to promote the consumption of pork as a national symbol, imposing it on the 'republican table' as a condition of Muslims' integration. The 'return of the pig' in polemics also revived the question of Muslims' citizenship in the present and that of Jews in the past, both suspected of not respecting the French way of life and kept at arm's length from the communal table with regard to their own beliefs. In his book *La République et le Cochon* (*The Republic and the Pig*), Pierre Birnbaum showed the importance of food for understanding the exclusive visions of the nation.[29] The return of the pig in effect reawakens memories of shared sociability from century to century, when consuming pork was the norm. This animal occupies an important place on the farm, in the country, at banquets, just as it does in books, where novelists describe tables where its meat is enjoyed. In France, eating is not an exclusively individual act, limited to the private sphere; the shared table symbolizes a public activity where citizens collectively affirm their fraternity.[30] The republican table is a privileged place for learning the tastes of and the conditions for belonging to public space. While the pig is a symbol of innocence, sensitivity and intelligence in children's stories, for Jews and Muslims it is the animal emblematic of impurity. Birnbaum shows how nationalist thought made the question of food a standard against Muslim migrants, but Jews similarly find themselves implicated. Celebrating the pig and banning kosher food in the name of a common food culture signals a return to ethnic nationalism, feeds xenophobia and sends us back, he claims, to the distant past – one of the signal measures of the Vichy government, as he reminds us, was the ban of ritual slaughter and the prohibition of kosher meat.

The controversy over halal also calls into question the exemption that Muslim and Jewish ritual slaughters receive from the rules governing animal slaughter in France, which requires animals to be stunned before they are killed. Because of this, the field of confrontation extended from the freedom of religious practice to the protection of animals: a campaign to turn French citizens against Muslim ritual slaughter was launched in 2010 (without much success) by defenders of animal rights who considered halal slaughter as suffering inflicted on animals.[31]

As in the other controversies studied, the controversy over halal in France thus inflamed 'media imaginaries' which contributed to social panic and the polarization of society.[32] Yet another public controversy was turned into a missed opportunity for debate … The pig, a symbol that affirms the French convivial tradition, was even raised as an emblem of the resistance of the Republic against halal … Muslim ritual slaughter, reduced to the – symbolically charged – act of throat-slitting was stigmatized as a manifestation of barbarism in which animal suffering was ignored. The questioning of the agrifood industry was muted, although a number of rigorously documented studies[33] denounced its practice of cynically monetizing animal suffering – since it obviously had nothing to do with Islam. The unforeseen European convergence of halal with organic norms and the similarities between Muslim and Jewish ritual slaughter were similarly ignored. The very French polarization of the 'Republic versus Islam' again stifled the potential for a new public, intercultural and religious link among citizens – through the medium, in this case, of the animal. It is here in these questions that are pushed to the side of daily life that the creative possibilities of our contemporary societies reside.

HALAL AND THE 'REPUBLICAN TABLE' IN TOULOUSE

We went to Toulouse, the first city where we conducted our research, on 14 June 2009. When we brought our first EPS group together at the Grand Hôtel d'Orléans, I didn't yet know whether this research scheme would allow for the creation of a space for listening, exchanging thoughts and configuring the possibility of an alternative public space that would not be dominated by prejudice and muzzled by distrust.

When the ten participants began to arrive, I observed that they avoided socializing between genders. The women sat around one side of the table. The men sat at the other side. Thus the Islamic spatial segregation of women and men was respected. Only one woman, the oldest of the group and the only one who didn't wear a veil, sat next to the men. The four other women were younger and veiled and came from Algerian or Moroccan backgrounds, but were all French nationals. Zeyneb, a high-school student, is an artist and a singer active in Muslim associations. One of the women has a degree in math, and the other two are students in physics and science at Paul Sabatier University. They are members of associations like Étudiants musulmans de France (Muslim Students of France)[34] or Médecins du monde (Doctors of the World).[35] The male members of the group are equally active in the associative field in France. Among them are antiracist and pro-secular activists, a French convert to Islam, a Muslim slam and rap musician, and the director of a private Muslim school. Two of them have beards, a sign of their Islamic faith. Most of them, like the women in the group, are of Maghrebi origin and are French nationals.

For this new generation of young Muslims, their French nationality is established, at least in terms of their identity. Houria, a mathematician at a university who wears the veil, says that secularism is important to her and that her life is in France. Seeing a photo of a woman protestor who covers herself with the French flag, she comments: 'I think she means that being Muslim doesn't mean being less French.' France is her country: 'If I believed in reincarnation, I would say that I already lived in France. That's the feeling I got the first day I walked through Toulouse.' This feeling of familiarity and affection for France is equally shared among the other Muslim citizens. It is in France that they 'feel at home.' Their sense of a connection between the place where they live and their most intimate feelings is reminiscent of the German notion of *heimat*. However, in *heimat*, this identity is created by the relation between man and his environment only if the individual has been exposed to a specific language and culture since birth. Yet we find this assimilationist identity among Muslim immigrants in Europe.

In resonance with public debates in France, we notice that the group appeals to the notion of secularism. Two participants, one the Jewish daughter of a deportee and the other the Muslim son of an immigrant, make themselves the spokespeople of secularism in the group. Chantal is a retired physical education instructor. She is a member of Riposte laïque (Secular Response), an association hostile to signs of Islam in Europe,[36] and of the group Ni putes ni soumises (Neither Whores nor Submissives) against the oppression of Muslim girls.[37] She represents a feminist version of secularism that has consolidated around controversies over the Islamic headscarf in France. Abdallah, an Arab teacher in a public high school, instead defends the progressive version of secularism as it has been adopted by modernist elites in Muslim countries. He calls himself a 'secular militant of Muslim culture.' These two defenders of secularism are not from Christian backgrounds and do not represent 'native French citizenship.' It would be difficult to charge them as being 'Catholic-secularists,' those who defend the principle of secularism while remaining attached to Christian values. Nonetheless, their references to secularism are expressed in a didactic, even authoritarian, manner and question the other members of the group who are younger and more devout. These two, one Jewish and the other Muslim, remind the young people of the importance of secularism in France's history and the necessity of learning about it. They are eager to lecture the others, affirming that religion is an obstacle to progress for society in general and for women in particular. This didactic form of secularism does not take into account what others have to say, but dictates principles rather than listening.

Nonetheless, among the Muslim members of the group, adhesion to the principle of secularism is a part of their universe, as is the refutation of communitarianism. Anouar explicitly says so: 'Me, I've always said that secularism doesn't belong to people who don't believe … Secularism belongs to everyone, both to religious people and non-believers. So it is a principle of civil society, it's like a referee between two teams, it has to make sure everyone plays by the rules.' One of the veiled girls regrets that 'secularism is turned against Islam, against our religion.' An incantatory discourse on secularism that aims to exclude more than include loses its influence among Muslims who search for a life in conformity with their faith.

Over the course of these discussions, they become aware that the more they appropriate Islamic normativity in their lives and invent practices of accommodation, the more their tie to their faith is transformed. As the Islamic religion has materialized in new forms and normative practices, it readjusts to European secular norms. In a paradoxical way, it is the believers' quest for a life in conformity with Islamic normativity in a secular society that transforms modalities of belief. For European Muslims, the question of coherence with or deviance from faith is a personal concern, as a subject of both internal debate and collective reflection.

THE BAN ON 'HAM' MOCKED BY MUSLIM HUMOR

We played a short video on the ban on 'ham' to enliven our discussion in the Toulouse EPS group. The film was published on a website created in 2008 following a series of public controversies surrounding Islam.[38] Its founders explained that they wanted to fight prejudice against Islam with humor. They started with the idea that disputed topics surrounding Islam, notably the headscarf in schools, divorces over non-virginity, the Danish caricatures, and the ban on mosques in housing projects, revealed divisions and tensions within French society. It was in this climate of distrust and mutual incomprehension, where one side turned to communitarianism and the other to Islamophobia, that they aimed to use comedy to create a link between worlds which, in their view, were growing apart. They needed to learn to live together, reestablish dialogue and 'relax in order to make the "clash of civilizations" a farce and not a drama.' This was the ambition shared by the comedians and artists participating in this site. They share their formula for cohabitation: 'That is what living together is: being able to laugh at your neighbor and at yourself.' They believe in the power of laughter to bring cultures, groups and divided publics together.

The film *Jambon* was made in this spirit of engagement with Muslim humor. The first scene brings the spectator into the kitchen of a middle-class home. A father calmly feeds his three-year-old daughter. But the mood is ruined when he finds a package of uneaten ham in the garbage. Apparently, this is not the first time this has happened in the house. He asks his daughter to go get her brother, an adolescent. The son enters and the annoyed father, holding the package of ham, asks him: 'Do you know what this is?' The boy looks apathetic, and sighs. The father gets mad: 'Let's be clear here, Mathieu!' he says. 'You give me a dirty look when I get a beer out of the fridge and you change the channel when a girl is too liberated on TV, that's one thing! When you're a pain in the ass to your mom 'cause her skirt is too short, you start to annoy me! But when you throw the ham we bought in the garbage, I say NO!' The boy remains silent. The father starts to yell: 'Look at me when I'm talking to you! Do you know who you are?' The father calls him by his traditionally French name: 'I'll tell you who you are. You're Matthieu Bué! You're François Bué's son! It might piss you off, but booze and naked chicks and pork, we like that in this family! Understand? You understand that you can't throw food in the garbage?' The boy, who is still quiet, looks at his feet. 'Say something, goddammit!' the father yells again.

Finally, pushing the package of ham under the table with a disgusted look, the boy yells 'It's haram!' The father furiously replies: 'Let me tell you something: you're not going to make the rules around here just 'cause you've been brainwashed by the "Salam aleyk" of the Mohammads in the neighborhood! Stop it with this crap! What's next, huh? What are you going to do? You're going to get on your hands and knees and yell "*Allah Akbar*!" I'm warning you, if I see you do that, I'm going to kick you in the ass so hard you'll end up in Mecca! I make the rules around here! Do you understand?' The boy mumbles: 'Yes, Dad!' and leaves the kitchen. Then we see the father with his head in his hands, asking what he is going to do about his son. When the little girl comes back into the kitchen, he apologizes for yelling at her brother and offers to take her to the merry-go-round to take their minds off it. The girl sweetly responds to her father: '*Insh'Allah*!' The video ends with a close-up of the father's distraught face.

Watching this film, the members of the Toulouse EPS group laughed. They found the anecdote to be exaggerated, but saw that it partly reflected the reality of the Muslim fixation with food rules and the ban on pork: 'Even if it's a caricature, the film is inspired by reality, by real facts.' This judgement by Sabiha, a young student in physics at Paul Sabatier University, was shared by the group.

In effect, the film recognized the new sociology of Islam, the emergence of Islamic norms, from the permitted halal to the forbidden haram in secular societies, the phenomenon of young converts to Islam, and the worries this raises in French families. A package of ham in the garbage illustrates the confrontation between two norms and two cultural habits. The sense of remorse one often hears in the expression 'we're no longer at home' undergoes a paroxysm. With the ham affair, the film shows that the effects of immigration don't end outside the home, but that they infiltrate the interior, in kitchens, in food habits. Islam from the streets moves from the exterior to the interior, into the heart of family life. The boy is socialized in the neighborhood with his Muslim friends. Not only is he familiar with Muslim manners and sayings, but he even adopts for himself the Islamic habitus of the youth in his neighborhood. For the father, this becomes a defiance of his parental authority in his own home. He feels distraught because he cannot even recognize his son as his offspring anymore because he has stopped belonging to the French family by moving towards a foreign religion. The father tries to remind him of his name, to make him remember his 'native' French identity. The opposition between two cultures is simplified in the stereotypes that capture the current conflict surrounding Islam. 'Ham, alcohol, beer, wine and chicks' appear as traits of French tradition, a life of pleasure, while a religious lexicon – haram, Mohammad, *salam aleyk*, *Allah Akbar*, Mecca, *Insh'Allah* – is used to distinguish an Islamic way of life.

The film reflects the confrontation between two lifestyles, but beyond that the incomprehension between Islam and the West. For Nasreddine, a PhD student in law and a participant in Islamic networks, the father symbolizes the Western world that is no longer in step with what is going on around it or in its home. In his opinion, the father, like the Western world, experiences incomprehension of and anxiety towards Islam. But he wants to be able to exert his authority. The fact that Islam is represented by his own son only aggravates the situation, because the one who calls himself a Muslim is his own offspring, present in the family home.

In fact, converts to Islam make the endogenous nature of European Islam evident. In this phase of post-immigration,

Muslims intimately participate in the cultural fabric of European societies. Nonetheless, this intertwining of Muslims in Europe, their proximity and their relationship with European citizens, doesn't lead to hospitality. The inability of the father, an inheritor of the West, and the son, turned towards Islam, to engage in dialogue proves it, as Nasreddine highlights: 'We see it, there's no dialogue between the father and the son, like between the West and Islam, only an expression of authority: "I'm the father, I am in charge, I make the law and you follow my authority." This is what Europeans are really saying: "There are laws, this is our country, there are our values, and it's up to you to live in conformity with our laws."' For him, this is a bit like what is currently going on in Europe.

THE IMPORTANCE OF 'WORKING ON PATIENCE' AND THE POPULARITY OF 'HALAL HAM'

That said, he also observes that the father is not the only one responsible for the lack of dialogue: the son doesn't facilitate the relationship with him, just as the Islam of Muslim converts, and sometimes the Islam of European Muslims, is ostentatious and provocative. They are often more attached to the exterior signs of Islam than to the concern for religious tradition. Muslim participants in the group recall the existence of the Islamic principle of not throwing away food and consider the son's gesture non-Islamic. By putting the accent not on the ban on pork but on the ban on throwing away food, they displace the discussion and they consider converging with the father, finding common ground for agreement. Anouar calls himself an 'Algerian in memory and French in nationality, European in culture and Muslim in religion and secular too.' He intervenes to say that Islam bans throwing away food. But 'when young people enter into a religion, they attach a lot of importance to what is ostentatious, to exterior signs.' What makes dialogue impossible is that if on one side there is 'the intolerant person, the father,' on the other there is 'someone who doesn't know the religion, the son.' His interpretation of the film is not far from the contemporary reality of the relationship between the majoritarian society and Muslims: on one side, 'the father uses discourse he sees on TV; on the other, the impatient youth doesn't know the religion enough, he makes mistakes and is in contradiction with some of Islam's values.' For him, it's the son's job to 'work on patience' because 'he brings something new and it is up to him to be patient with his father, with the majority.' We can extend the young man's case to Muslims in general. Confrontation with the majoritarian society is not accepted and is not even considered Islamic. The themes of 'patience' and 'restraint' we heard in our Bologna EPS group reappeared as a means of behavior and action that Muslims of Europe hoped for.

Nasreddine provided a critical analysis of Muslims, including himself. He says that he recognizes himself in the relationship with the father, because he himself went through the same thing: recalling his adolescence and his conflictual relationship with his father in the 1990s, he explains that he was 'in a group that was called "Islamic Awakening" back then' while his father was 'a pretty secular person.' He judged his Algerian father as insufficiently Muslim, even 'a bit lost' (*rabbi yahdi*). But deep down, he admits, laughing, it was he who was a bit lost back then. He thinks that the young convert is in a similar state of mind and that he judges his father for not taking the right path. He clarifies the convergence between the phenomena of converts and the Islamic Awakening: in both cases, there is a new manner of returning to religion, of interpreting and rediscovering it. The two phenomena converge in the form of a radical adhesion to Islam, which claims to break the chain of historical continuities and religious traditions. Islam without its cultural particularities is the shared dream of neo-Muslims and fundamentalists, a dream that has become a reality in the conditions of European immigration. The political scientist Olivier Roy speaks of 'holy ignorance' to describe the myth of a pure religiosity formed outside culture in modern fundamentalisms.[39]

This separation of religion from its culture of origin has unexpected and undesired consequences, creating practices that are not in conformity with purist ideologies of Islam. For many of those who see themselves in it, this religion is the basis through which European culture is transformed and adopted. The Islamic habitation of cultures in European countries thus sets in motion a process of interpenetration between the secular and the religious domains, making space for unexpected hybrid forms. A mutual transformation of European culture and the Muslim religion are quietly at work. This occurs in the micropractices of Muslims, in their ordinary, daily lives, in their food habits. The quest for normative conformity with halal has become an affair of consumption and a lifestyle.

Without renouncing Islamic normativity, they wish to adhere to traditions of the French *terroir*. The surprising popularity of 'halal ham' demonstrates this. A participant observed this tendency without a value judgment: 'Now, when they go into halal butchers, Muslim people who are very observant or not observant ask for ham; of course, it's not from a pig, but looks like ham …' Another adds, 'Yeah, yeah, they say: "We eat ham too, but halal ham!"' They conclude, laughing together, that this 'integration is a bit off-track' … The Islamic prescription banning pork takes a track in favor of traditions belonging to the French *terroir*.

In the post-immigration phase, the pig has become a central public figure around which Islamic interdictions and European food traditions are confronted and overlap: asking for halal meat has less to do with the religious customs of immigrants and their descendants than with a Muslim normativity reinvented in interaction with European lifestyles. This new religious normativity is their certificate for adopting lifestyles, but also a way of affirming their difference and their social distinction: the new way of being Muslim includes an Islamic styling of trends in modern life. European Muslims have thus adopted a logic of conquering spaces in secular life, bringing an Islamic label to styles of consumption and leisure activities, as well as artistic and musical creations – even if merchandising and the ethnicization of Islam don't resolve all tensions between rigorism and hedonism.[40]

It is notably in hip hop, the music of a marginal urban youth, that the implication of Muslims in the heart of a global cultural movement emerges, by promoting 'fusion' – or confusion – between genres with an Islamic influence, which since the 1980s has been present in the musical artistic scene in Europe.[41] Muslim musicians inscribe their religious references in their songs by denouncing injustice in the world, by the use of Islamic sounds inspired by Sufism, as well as in their performances of piety onstage. The artist-believer seeks not to forgo Islamic interdictions: as the Belgian anthropologist (of Moroccan origin) Farid El Asri writes, he make himself a 'witnesses of faith' by translating Islamic references in a new scenography, mobilizing prophetic traditions in gestures and allusions to verses of the Koran, using objects like prayer beads, dress codes and symbolic places.[42] It is an expressive, even demonstrative, religiosity which casts Muslim musicians as interpreters both of hip hop and new European Islamic norms.

Practicing music is not at all prohibited in the Koran, but later and particularly moral exegesis calls for the faithful to survey the content of songs, to avoid inciting debauchery and ecstasy. The conservative Qatari theologian Yusuf Al Qaradawi says that Islamic legal scholars agree that songs are not banned in themselves, but that they become illicit when they are associated with other forbidden things. Because, for him, music and singing often go along with 'luxury, circles of drinking and forbidden all-night parties.' There is also a way of singing that can have a 'certain attraction and style that excites the instincts,' revealing temptations and passions. Singing must not excite 'base instincts,' subjecting man to temptation and making the 'bestial side' of him dominant.[43]

Muslim musicians are confronted with potential religious illicitness in the musical field, lived by some as a dilemma between their adherence to their faith and their attraction to music. The case of the French female rapper Diam's illustrates this: born in 1980 to a French mother and a Greek Cypriot father, she announced the end of her brilliant career in 2012, four years after converting to Islam. This caused a scandal when clichéd images of her exiting a mosque wearing an Islamic veil in 2009 were published in the press. Her departure from the music scene sent the signal that Islam was incompatible with the genre of modern music, and with women performing in public. It was an astonishing paradox to see bans which had become outdated resurface in European societies because of a young artist convert.

We don't know whether Zeyneb, the veiled high-schooler in our EPS group in Toulouse, was inspired by Diam's, but she did aspire to be a singer. She clearly expressed her desire for an artistic career while also expressing her religious reservations. The dominant interpretation of Koranic prescriptions on modesty and the principle of *awra* in fact do not encourage women to sing before a mixed audience in the presence of men.[44] The most rigorous and sectarian exegesis even affirms that once one has accepted the principles of Islam, one must be 'consistent' with the faith and subject the spheres of modern life to the transcendence of religion. Words like 'desire' or 'frustration' would not find their place in the believer's universe.

MUSIC, FOOD AND SEXUALITY, CRUCIBLES FOR NEW FORMS OF ISLAMIC NORMATIVITY

It is undoubtedly in Birmingham, a multiethnic city marked by the culture of rebellion of its youth, where we can observe the investment that young Muslim generations have in the musical field in Europe, with all the dilemmas it implies. Birmingham is characterized by a strong migrant presence, majority Pakistani and Indian, but also Yemeni and Somali, with new arrivals from eastern Europe. Many Islamic networks are in place in the city,[45] which has a reputation as a breeding-ground for the 'English Taliban' and has been considered since the 7 July 2005 attacks in London as a hotbed of 'home-grown' terrorism. In 2009, Islamist groups and the British far right faced off in urban riots over the engagement of British troops in Afghanistan and Iraq. This explains the local importance of security politics and antiradicalization programs for youth, such as Prevent.

During our inquiry in Brimingham, women spoke to us about the urban riots, the radicalization of youth, the anger of their own sons, their 'bad Muslim boys.' They insisted that it was necessary to understand their desire to revolt and express themselves. Music, according to them, is a source of expression of injustice and allows these youths to channel their emotions. Themes like the occupation of Gaza and the killings of their brothers and sisters are certainly serious and politically radical. Nonetheless, religion also brings them an element of serenity, the possibility of moving from street fighting to street praying.

Islamic hip hop is a way for youths to gain a sense of pride and popularity, as was once the case with the Black Power movement. In their words – *I am dirty, but I point towards a good direction* – they affirm that in Islam, they orient themselves on the right path even though they are marginal and sinners. They turn to this hip hop culture because it values their engagement with Islamic normativity. And music, they say, creates friendships among Muslims from different ethnic backgrounds, between African, Caribbean, Jamaican and other friends. Hip hop signifies the hybridity of differences. Young Muslims, both men and women, are carriers of a new culture with the imprint of Islam and are actors in intermingling and creativity. This is evident in the fusion of musical genres, pluriethnicity, the polyphony of languages, the blend of clothing and the adjustment of social labels.

They constantly define their faith through the prism of their European experience. It is in the areas of art, food and sexuality that norms around body policies face off in Birmingham, as they do elsewhere in Europe. Two extreme figures, the woman in a burka and a homosexual believer, crystalize the tension between personalization and faith, Islamic normativity and the European culture of sexuality, in the most paradoxical way. Wearing the burka, including by European women converts to Islam, is an intensification of the Islamic norm. By such a policy of the total covering of the body, the woman in a burka, as a demonstration of her faith, believes that she incarnates Islamic law, sharia. This demonstrative religiosity aims to escape the influence of the values of sexual freedom. The other is the figure of the homosexual Muslim believer who wants to participate in the defense of minority sexual rights without being forced to renounce his faith. The creation of an 'inclusive' mosque in Paris on 30 November 2012 thus became a new link between sexual identities and beliefs; its founder explained his intention to open an alternative religious space that would include Muslim men and women in the situation of 'identity dissonance' – in other words, sexual minorities.[46]

A differentiated grammar of religious sexuality distinguishes between these two figures. One affirms purity in the extreme, the other deconstructs categories of the impure. One breaks with the values of sexual freedom and the availability of women, the other adheres to a culture of sexual minorities. The new Islamic normativity invents itself in these two forms, the burka and the inclusive mosque. By their radical nature, these practices signal a transgression of sharia. These new and strange figures who are difficult to define and problematic to label cause a scandal in European societies, but they are also unusual in Muslim tradition.

Encouraged by active minorities exploring cultural and religious norms, they are truly a part of the new order of European Islam.

The question of coherence or incoherence between ancestral sacredness, personal experience and global modernity underlies these practices. Tensions between the revealed text and the context of life, between transcendence and imminence, between piety and desire, abstinence and appetites, are intrinsic to the practices of ordinary European Muslims, including in their most radical forms. The question of the authority of religious knowledge is raised in relation to these lifestyles. The emergence of young Muslim theologians with their European lives and scientific education in religious facts marks a renaissance in these new questions raised by the anchoring of European Islam.[47] Their job of interpenetration not only depends on their capacity to overcome the complexes of Muslims in Europe as regards the religious authority of majority Muslim countries, but especially to attest to the singularity of this European Islam. As the young Muslim musician, with his long, ostentatious beard, pleaded in our Toulouse EPS group: 'We have to avoid frustrations and find grounds for adaptation with the ancestral and the sacred. Religion must show that it accepts youths, like they accept it.'

The process of transforming the link between Muslims and modes of believing is under way in the contemporary era in Europe. The theological sense of normativity is taking on new sociological significations. As in its birth, Islam is confronted by other religions, other norms and other habits from which it must distinguish itself. It was notably in its relation to Jews and pagan Arabs that the first Islam established its singularity. Today, once again, the horizontal relationship to religion is becoming decisive in the subjective and theological concerns of Muslims. They aim to distinguish themselves from their neighbors of different religions, but also from traditional interpretations of Arab-Muslim Islam. It is in this way that the ban on pork, an omnipresent question since the dawn of Abrahamic religions, has forcefully reemerged in the European context, where the three monotheisms fight for their place.

9

The Jewish Cursor

Public controversies not only take place in the abstract sphere of ideas, through conceptual debates between well-identified parties: in conflicts over territory and identity, they also involve corporeal practices, eating practices, and even animals. In France, the pig thus appears, as we have seen, as a 'national emblem,' but it has been similarly chosen as a public figure across Europe: in order to mark the territory of shared identity, this animal plays a leading role in a repertoire of actions against Muslims' halal; in order to stigmatize them by pointing out Islamic food regulations, pork has been emphasized by radical nationalist groups in the 2000s as the trait of majoritarian culture.

This is proven by example in France, with the organization of public demonstrations for '*apéro-saucisson-pinard*' ['sausage and wine cocktail'], synonyms of the values of the national *terroir* – ultraprovocative and very minoritarian, their echo has remained limited. In 2010, on the anniversary of the 18 June 1940 call by General de Gaulle for resistance to the Nazi occupation, several organizations from the far right, including the Identity Block, thus wanted to organize a 'sausage and wine cocktail hour' in the

Goutte d'Or neighborhood in Paris, home to a majority Muslim population. In so doing, they hoped to call for a sort of 'resistance' against the 'occupation' of the 18th arrondissement evident in street prayers and 'in the adversaries of the wines of our *terroir* and our meat products.' Similarly, in Italy, activists with the Northern League frequently and ostentatiously ate sausage in front of Muslim religious places; and in 2008, militants in the neo-fascist Forza Nuova group organized a public 'pork roast' cocktail hour during their anti-Islamic and anti-mosque demonstrations.[1]

The pig is inserted into campaigns against the construction of mosques and is used to profane the site of their construction. 'Pig walks' were organized in Bologna and Padua. In 2000, militants with the Northern League in Italy threw pig urine over the construction site of a future mosque in Lodi in order to demonstrate their opposition to the 'rampant Islamization of the Paduan countryside.' Again in Italy, during Ramadan in 2007, the former prime minister Roberto Calderoli (a member of the Northern League) provided a pig to a local committee for a 'walk' on the construction site of a mosque in Bologna. In April 2004 in Rimini, Islamophobic extremist Christians coated the main entrance of the mosque with pork fat, writing the slogan 'Christ the King.'[2] In December 2009 in Castres, a city in the south-west of France, pig's feet and ears were found in front of a mosque.[3] And these Islamophobic and very symbolic aggressions multiplied across Europe throughout the 2010s.

The pig is thus used to intimidate Muslims and profane their religious spaces, even though they do not consider the animal itself a symbol of profanation. They told us this several times during our inquiry. For example, Yassine, a young man of Moroccan origin living in Bologna, who finds it amusing when he sees the grotesque actions of nationalist fanatics who aim to prevent Muslims from constructing their mosque by profaning the sites with pig's heads: 'Everyone thinks that we Muslims cannot touch pigs. Although I can touch a pig and walk it with me like a dog with no problem. I can't eat it, of course, because God forbids me to eat its meat. But he doesn't tell me not to touch it.'[4]

WHEN CONTROVERSIES OVER ISLAM COLLIDE WITH THE JEWISH QUESTION

Controversies surrounding Islam lead the Jewish religion and its religious regulations into debates and put it in tandem with Islam. The 'return of the pig' – to use Pierre Birnbaum's expression – stirs up the memory and the status of Jews in Europe. He writes that 'in the past, as today, Jews find themselves abandoning their "ancestral customs" in the name of a biological view or universalist secularism whose cultural perspective remains anchored in Christianity.'[5] Without seeking to, Jews find themselves implicated in controversies surrounding Islam, such as ritual slaughter, circumcision, religious tribunals, the ban on images or debates about the 'Judeo-Christian roots' of Europe. Contemporary debates on Islam retroactively shape the place of Judaism and Jewish identity, making them again publicly visible although their status as a religious minority no longer poses a problem.

Judaism and Islam have in common their attachment to the law as their frame of organizing life and both return to canonical textual sources, the Halakhah and sharia, respectively, as the foundation of their religious practices.[6] With their similar prescriptions and prohibitions, these two monotheisms were in fact associated in controversies in Europe, although the parallel rise of anti-Semitism and Islamophobia created distance and mutual hostility between them.[7] In post-Shoah Europe, a process of reconciliation with Jews was under way, and notably led to the growing affirmation of the 'Judeo-Christian roots' – and no longer the 'Greco-Roman' ones – of European civilization, while disavowing its Arab and Muslim heritage. The proximity and separation between Jews and Muslims thus requires a double view in order to read the Muslim presence in the mirror of the history of the Jewish religion in Europe and rethink the Jewish condition in relation to Islam and the stakes of the present. The mixing of temporalities – the past of Judaism and the present of Islam – in European history in effect makes the mutual recognition and apprenticeship of co-citizenship more difficult.

The observance of religious rituals, such as circumcision and kosher/halal eating, not only provokes hatred and resentment in segments of opinion towards religious minorities in Europe, but also leads certain governments to use techniques that retrace the boundaries between religions and regulate their proximity with secular modernity. It is in this process of accommodating and excluding religious practices that the Jewish question becomes a cursor between Europe and Muslims.

The distance that separates Jews and Muslims is not fixed: it varies according to historical eras and dominant mentalities. Different historical interpretations of the constitutive myths of the relations between Jews and Muslims exist. The cursor moves according to the way that affinities and rivalries between the two religions are perceived and constructed. Historians are divided between schools of harmony and conflict.[8] The first school believes in the possibility of an interreligious utopia. They refer to moments of their coexistence in history in medieval Spain and the Ottoman Empire – where Jews were granted the status of protection (*dhimmi*).[9] In her book *Becoming Ottomans*, Julia Phillips Cohen notes that in the second half of the nineteenth century, the Jews of the Ottoman Empire recognized themselves in the 'imperial citizenship' and became a 'model *millet*.'[10] The identification of Jews with the Ottoman Empire was reinforced by the appropriation of its symbols, such as the crescent moon, the star of the Empire or the stylized signature of the sultan (*tugra*) that is found on Jewish ritual objects like the prayer shawl (*talit*) or the silver spice tower. This imperial citizenship, which appeared as a promise of the Tanzimant reforms (1839–76) and the legal equality of non-Muslim subjects, nonetheless did not prevent the later deportation of the Armenian people or the recurrent anti-Semitic acts of the young Republic.

Unlike the school of harmony, the school of conflict insists on the continuity of the mutual hatred between Jews and Muslims over the long term. Unlike those who believe that anti-Semitism could disappear with the realization of peace between Israel and Palestine, these historians believe that anti-Semitism's deep roots can be found in the origins of Islam.[11] Today, most Muslims reject this idea, and support an idealized narrative of the Middle Eastern past by evoking the values of tolerance and hospitality. For them, Islamist extremism's acts of hostility and violence are exclusively explained by the state of Israel's colonial politics in Palestine. The eventual links between political Islamism and anti-Semitism – which are sometimes very real, even if they are not indicative of an imaginary 'essence of Islam' – are admitted only with difficulty.

Symmetrically, in representations by some Jewish groups, old Western anti-Semitism has since been displaced towards new Islamist incarnations. If the history of European Jews remains marked by the weight of memories of the Shoah, the massive presence of Muslims and Islamist extremism today constitute for them new sources of concern. They fear again becoming the target of Muslim anti-Semitism and losing what they have acquired in a wave of Islamophobia. It seems to them that the past returns in present conflicts: the 'Jewish question' has a new meaning in that it has become a benchmark, a cursor in the contemporary interface between Europe and Islam. Judaism and Islam are both opposed to the norms of secular modernity.

THE LONG HISTORY OF THE HALAKHAH AND SHARIA IN CHRISTIAN EUROPE

The complex and tragic German case illustrates the importance of putting contemporary histories of these two religions of the Book, Islam and Judaism, in relation to one another. Today, one cannot help but be astounded by the repetition, in relation to Islam, of themes of controversies surrounding Judaism in Germany in the nineteenth century. Jewish rituals were then commonly considered 'Oriental': disputes that occurred about the presence of Jews as a religious minority two centuries ago, notably about the construction of synagogues, wearing the kippa in courts, the exemption of Jewish children from physical education classes during Shabbat or religious education in public schools, present troubling similarities with current controversies surrounding Islam, as has notably been shown by Shai Lavi, a Jewish sociologist of Israeli law.[12] During the second half of the nineteenth century and the beginning of the twentieth, Jewish rituals were at the center of confrontations between German nationalism and Jewish particularism. Two Jewish prescriptions, kosher butchery and the circumcision (*brit milah*) of boys, thus became central in public debates. Although these two rituals are different, in the eyes of some German elites they marked a troubling difference in Jews to the morals of the majority. Described in discourse with scientific pretensions, Jewish traditions were then qualified as uncivilized and outdated superstitions.[13]

Circumcision is a biblical prescription marking the rite of passage on the eighth day after the birth of a boy. According to the Old Testament, it is the sign of an alliance between God, Abraham, and his descendants engraved in the flesh. Over the course of history, it gained an additional significance, becoming the sign of belonging to the community of believers. Circumcision and the obligation to eat kosher were perceived as distinctive practices of the Jews of Europe. In the first case, the difference remains in the familial sphere. But in the second, with the existence of kosher butchers, it is obviously more visible. And in both cases, it is a question of flesh and the use of a knife and the spilling of blood, topics of concern in German society. The American historian Robin Judd, in her book on *Contested Rituals* in Germany,[14] details the disputes around these two rituals during the Weimar Republic (1918–33). She shows how they began as early as 1850, then radicalized during the unification period in the 1880s and 1890s before being prohibited by Nazi power in 1933. Despite rhetorical changes over time, Jews are still reproached for remaining outside the majority, of being cruel towards animals, of spilling blood and of not respecting the criteria of hygiene and health.

Current debates on the religious practices of Muslims in Europe have seen a resurgence of these old conflicts in the collective conscience. We saw this in the debate over halal, a distant echo of the debate over kosher. Circumcision, a prescription common to Jews and Muslims, equally returned to notice when the Cologne regional court in June 2012 condemned the practice of this rite, considered a crime.[15] This decision primarily targeted Muslims, but it also has implications for the Jewish population of Germany.

Muslims also practice circumcision in reference to Abraham. Even if this tradition is not prescribed in the Koran, it is nonetheless part of prophetic tradition and is recommended by the *Sunna*. Circumcision, a pre-Islamic custom continued in Islam, has attained the significance of a rite of passage. Accompanied by a ceremony including festivities and the sacrifice of a lamb, in the popular milieu it symbolizes the entry of the child into the religious community.[16] This religious norm is also a cultural custom that signals belonging to the community of Muslims. As in the case of Judaism, it is the distinctive trait of Muslim men in a religious framework, but also a marker of parent–child and man–woman relations. This rite is transmitted from one generation to the next and it is not customary for Muslim women to marry a man who is not circumcised. Converts to Islam are encouraged to follow the initiative rite of circumcision in order to be a part of the religious corps. Even non-practicing Muslims adopt this religious and customary tradition from one generation to the next without questioning it much.[17] The fact that they are migrants to Europe and have a new way of life does not prevent them from continuing this 'ancestral' practice.

THE LESSONS OF CONTROVERSIES ABOUT CIRCUMCISION

In November 2010, the circumcision of a four-year-old boy living in Cologne with his parents of Turkish origin would in no way have been unusual, if there had not been a medical complication which led to the child's admission to an emergency room for bleeding a few days after the procedure. The city's prosecutor then charged the doctor who performed it. The legal inquiry led to a national controversy, and also led to a debate in the Council of Europe. The decision of the Cologne regional court to ban the act of circumcision, considered a violation of the physical integrity of children, caused a scandal among different audiences, moving outside a debate among circles of experts. A legal polemic had already been initiated by a legal professional, Holm Putzke, who published several articles in favor of the penalization of circumcision. The judgment of the Cologne regional court, inspired by his reflections, marked a new step in the legal regulation of the religious practices of Muslim citizens. The judges decided to rule against circumcision despite the absence of medical negligence and the consent of the parents. The 'well-being' of the child was advanced as the major argument: his body was changed in an irreversible way, which signals a violation of his physical integrity. It was a violation of his autonomy and his freedom to choose his religion later in life.

An ancestral and familial practice recognized in European history more as a marker of Judaism than of Islam thus became a public affair. Two constitutional principles thus came into conflict in the case of circumcision: freedom of religious practice and the respect of the corporeal integrity of the child.[18] On one side, the representatives of the three monotheist religions formed a united front to condemn the judicial interference in the domain of faith; on the other, representatives of scientific knowledge, doctors, pediatricians, and lawyers advanced the interests of the child in the arena of the confrontational debate.[19] The characterization of circumcision as an act of mutilation, barbarism, indeed of religious fundamentalism, expresses its anti-religious sentiment in particular towards Muslim and Jewish communities; this is what the Iranian-German intellectual Navid Kermani describes as the triumph of 'vulgar rationalism.'[20]

The spokespeople for Turkish immigration did not hesitate to warn the decision-makers that this legal decision was a strong signal to Muslims 'that they are not part of German society and that they are not welcome.' As for the president of the European Conference of Rabbis, he considered the decision as 'the gravest attack against Jewish life in Europe since the Shoah.'[21] With the involvement of the spokesperson for Judaism, the debate in Germany, charged with history, turned away from the Muslim case of Cologne towards the Jewish question and forced politicians, beginning with the Chancellor, Angela Merkel, to find an accommodation without calling into question the achievements of religious freedom for Jews. To calm collective passions, a new law was adopted, authorizing circumcision with reinforced medical inspection: the presence of a doctor became mandatory for all circumcisions unless they occurred in the first six months after the birth of the child. In the case of Jewish circumcision prescribed for the eighth day, this allows a religious practitioner (*mohel*) to complete the procedure. But what about Muslim practitioners (*sunnetci* in Turkish)? This exception made for the Jewish practice represented in the eyes of some a certain infringement of equity explicable by the historical debt of the Germans. In any case, legal power showed a certain restraint in its desire to interfere in the affairs of the Jewish community.

Anti-circumcision policies spread to other European nations, notably Switzerland and Austria: two hospitals, one in Zurich and one in Saint-Gal, decided to temporarily suspend circumcision except in case of medical necessity; and in an Austrian province, circumcisions for non-medical reasons were prohibited in all public hospitals. In the case of France, it may seem paradoxical, as the French political scientist Dominique Schnapper has noted, that this country, often criticized as 'integrationist,' adopted a pragmatic, tolerant position on the practice of circumcision even as it was causing a vast public controversy in Germany on democratic principles. How do we respect the boundary between private and public and reconcile the foundational value of respect for the person and the freedom to remain faithful to religious traditions? All European democracies face these fundamental questions.[22] Those asked about the Muslims' practices are not inscribed in frameworks of established thought, notably multiculturalism and the rights of religious minorities, but elicit new societal debates and mobilize a bioethical sensitivity. Once more, it is notable that European countries, despite their historico-political particularities, converge in their attempt to frame Islamic difference in light of a contemporary ethical sensitivity. A process for the redefinition of the Islamic religion emerges, taking into account secular values and discourse about rights, particularly those of women and children. The separation of the religious prescription of customs from the medicalization of rituals is again at stake in order to distinguish the sphere of the religious from the secular.

The controversy over circumcision cannot be debated solely by focusing on the religion of migrants. The inclusion of Jews has brought the memories of pre-Shoah history into debates.[23] As in the case of ritual slaughter, circumcision caused a scandal as an archaic and barbarous practice, and Muslims as well as Jews saw their religion deemed 'pre-modern,' seen as incompatible with modern European values.

These two distinct controversies showed the importance of religious practices shared by Jews and Muslims and which are foreign to European Christians. Nonetheless, the meaning of these controversies is not reducible to an expression of anti-Semitism and Islamophobia. According to Shai Levi, the rise of xenophobic motivations must be understood in relation to the deployment of ethical arguments.[24] The emergence of a new humanist ethic goes back to the end of the eighteenth and beginning of the nineteenth century in Christian Europe. According to him, it is in this context that these preoccupations with the allegedly inhuman nature of ritual sacrifice and circumcision must be situated. These two practices are criticized as a source of suffering inflicted on living things, defenseless creatures. The new ethical sensibility is supported by the development of medical sciences as much as it is by a state that is assumed to be 'liberal,' which governs 'private' morality as much as it does 'public' behavior. The protection of the child and the animal justifies the growing intervention of the state into the private sphere, the once protected space of the intimate.

In Judaism as in Islam, religious customs constitute rules for living daily life, while the modern approach of Christian secularism considers animal slaughter and circumcision a ritual, and thus as transcendent of worldly life. According to Lavi, ritualization operates through attempts to reform Jewish traditions by aligning them with Protestant practices. One of the arguments against kosher slaughter proposes that this practice is not a part of the Jewish religion, but represents a simple ritual. Opponents base this on the fact that the detailed description of the act, particularly the use of a knife and the prohibition against stunning the animal, cannot be found in the biblical text. In the case of circumcision, ritualization took place in a different way. In the middle of the nineteenth century, a debate was raised when some Jewish parents living in Germany refused to practice circumcision on their newborns. But when they tried to register their children as eligible members of the Jewish community, even though circumcision was not a precondition for becoming Jewish, Orthodox rabbis did not allow them to: they affirmed that circumcision was an obligation, aligning it with the baptism of Christians as a rite of passage, a precondition for acceptance into the community of believers.[25]

As the American anthropologist Talal Asad shows in his book on the genealogies of religion, with secularization, a modern acceptance of ritual replaces the traditional notion of practices proscribed by a manual of rules which details appropriate conduct in conformity with the law.[26] He notes that the term 'ritual' is foreign to the Jewish tradition, and that Jews refer instead to *mitzvah* (obligation or commandment) or *Halakhah*, in reference to a particular prescription or to the entirety of the religious code.[27] Similarly, Muslims speak of sharia, Islamic law, as a source of guidance in their lives and daily practices. The ritualization of religion signals its retreat into a well-defined sphere, the sphere of the private, and its adaptation to the understanding of religion as a personal and spiritual activity. This implies the separation of belief in practices, the retreat of religion in the cultural domain from the organization of daily life. Like Judaism in Europe,[28] is Islam in the process of becoming a private and ritualized religion?

THE 'JUDEO-CHRISTIAN ROOTS' OF EUROPE

While aligning itself with modern and Protestant conceptions of religion, Judaism also had to undo its identification with the 'East.' The Jewish religion, far from being associated with Christianity, was long considered as revelatory of Eastern religions and foreign to Western Christian culture.[29] The idea that ritual slaughter was not part of the biblical world, but came from pagan traditions in Ancient Egypt, was based on this view: Jews fleeing Egypt around 1500 BC supposedly incorporated this practice into their religion. It was only in the nineteenth century that Judaism acquired the definition of a religion.[30] Jews themselves participated in defining what has been called *German Jewry*, a fact clearly recognized by liberal Jews, who identified themselves as German citizens of mixed confession. This was also true of Orthodox Jews, who sought autonomous recognition as a community of faith.

The assimilation of Jews is the product of a dialectic of the West versus the East: it is through recourse to an orientalist model that the dichotomies Jew–Arab, Ashkenazi–Sephardic, secular–

religious were reproduced and maintained over the course of history.[31] The Jewish question thus acted as a cursor, because the emergence of the Judeo-Christian link becomes possible as long as the Jew is separate from the East, from the Arab. With the orientalist paradigm, the cursor moves by creating the separation of Jews from the East, including Sephardic Jews, who are originally from there. Power operates by imposing homogeneity on practices, but also by instituting difference. The American philosopher and historian of religion Gil Anidjar shows how the European idea was constituted as power through the separation between 'the Jew and the Arab.' According to him, throughout its history, Europe produced mechanisms of alterity and hostility in which the Jew became the interior and theological enemy while the Muslim was designated as the exterior and political enemy.[32] The benchmark for measuring the Europeanness of Jews was thus determined by their proximity to Christianity and their separation from Islam. Then, in the post-Shoah period, the link reestablished between Jewish and Christian identities led in a concomitant way to the distancing of Muslims and the heritage of Islam in European history.

In France, the affirmation of a Christian European identity removed from its ties with the Arab-Muslim world notably emerged with the publication of a book in 2008.[33] In it, the medieval historian Sylvain Gouguenheim refutes and corrects the argument about 'Europe's debt to the Arab-Muslim world' as bringing Greek thought to the West. According to him, it was at the Mont Saint-Michel in the first half of the twelfth century – fifty years before the translation of Aristotle's works into Arabic – that James of Venice supposedly first translated Aristotle into

Latin.[34] Gouguenheim reexamines the formation of the cultural identity of Europe by underlining the role of monks and copyists in the transmission of Greek knowledge; he affirms that the matrix of European civilization resides essentially in its Greek roots and that it is in no way indebted to the Arab-Muslim world.

This simplification of entities of identity, Christianity and Islam, the East and Europe, by echoing the thesis about the 'conflict of civilizations' gained him entry into public debate. This literary event, which would not have garnered much attention in light of the almost unanimous judgment by the scientific community about its meager value, nonetheless provoked a lively polemic. Some praised Gouguenheim's thesis in the media, while others signed a petition rejecting it.[35] The philosopher Alain de Libera, the author of *Penser au Moyen Âge* [*Thinking in the Middle Ages*],[36] considers it a form of 'scholarly Islamophobia' whose goal is to separate 'The Greek from the Arab, and thus the Arab from us.'[37] The notion of 'an essential Christianity of Europe' aims to exclude the Islamic world from modernity. This thesis contributes to the 'Hellenization of Christian Europe' and rejoins the general debate about European identity and its Christian heritage.[38]

This debate emerged as a central preoccupation in the years 2003–05, with the Turkish candidacy for the European Union, which, along with the continuation of public controversies on Islam, played a catalyzing role in the quest for European identity and its civilizational boundaries.[39] During these debates, the definition of a European Muslim became problematic, to the detriment of the recognition of the Muslim presence in Europe over the long term.[40] The necessity of including a reference to Judeo-Christian roots in the European Constitution was defended by some as a cultural basis for defining this identity. Even if this proposal was not included,[41] the question of European identity continued to gain ground among intellectuals, citizens and politicians in public debates and mobilize collective passions. Traditionally 'European' subjects such ase the environment, agriculture and the Constitution were perceived as questions far removed from citizens' preoccupations, the domain of expertise and bureaucracy. In short, the more citizens were impassioned about defending their identity, the more they turned away from the future of Europe and the project appeared to them as imposed from above as the work of political elites. The return of identity quickly presented fertile ground for neo-populist movements on the right who deployed their Eurosceptic and xenophobic politics.

One might also wonder whether the affirmation of a notion of a Europe based on identity leads directly to a politics of exclusion. The genealogy of the Judeo-Christian reference provides a field of analysis for understanding how the return to identity can become a political instrument of exclusion: the term 'Judeo-Christian,' as the Canadian philosopher Anya Topolski explains, has had different meanings in different eras, some contradictory.[42] Two very different stories about the content of this signifier have thus appeared in Europe, the first in the 1830s and the second in the post-Shoah period. The founder of the Protestant school of Tübingen (Germany), Ferdinand Christian Baur, forged this notion based on a theological vision that had existed since the fourth century, according to which Christianity would succeed Judaism. But he adapted it to make Protestantism the successor of 'Judeo-Christianism.' The idea of a 'pure' Europe could only be found in the Christianity of 'gentiles,' that is non-Israelites. For Baur, Christianity needed to be freed from the past, from its Judeo-Christian 'chains' and from Catholicism 'contaminated' by its interactions with Judaism, paganism and Islam. Anya Topolski thus shows how the use of the term 'Judeo-Christian' in the nineteenth century as well as in contemporary Europe is linked to the construction of an identity supported by the desire for unity that necessitates an exclusion. The widespread idea that a strong Europe needs a strong identity prevents us from thinking of an alternate Europe, one of the *communitas.*[43] In opposition to the idea of a collective identity, the etymology of the Latin term designates people linked by an 'obligation' and not by what is 'unique' to them. The common is not characterized here by the 'unique' but by the 'common,' that which is not finished or completed.

For Topolski, whose analysis is particularly pertinent, it is a question of knowing whether Europe can shape itself as a *communitas*, whether it can be conceived of as a community or shared responsibility. This question is related to the one asked in our inquiry. We are looking for possibilities of a horizontal pact between individual beliefs and different, even antagonistic convictions. We are asking how links can be created in a multicultural, plurilingual Europe composed of different religions and ethnicities. How do we share responsibilities? In the inquiry we conducted among ordinary people about their possibilities for making a community, we did not avoid the subjects of conflicts. On the contrary, we often began with discord, with sources of problems or the basis of scandal. If controversies have a disruptive effect on shared meaning, they can also put people and foreign publics – even hostile ones – in contact with one another. Through controversies, we looked for possibilities of 'making common,' the potential for public creativity in European public space.

THE IMPOSSIBLE CO-CITIZENSHIP OF EUROPEAN JEWS AND MUSLIMS?

The possibility of a dialogue in this public space necessarily occurs through the mutual recognition of Jews and Muslims in their shared responsibility and their European co-citizenship. In this path, the Israeli-Palestinian conflict comes between them and becomes an obstacle so that Jews and Muslims interconnect in European realities: many among them in fact tend to transpose their relationship as co-citizens onto a conflict external to Europe. Jerusalem or Al Quds, a sacred place in the Jewish and Muslim religions, touches on the intimate convictions of both and the political stake it represents takes primacy over the countries to which they belong. It is not that Jews and Muslims don't know each other. But their knowledge of the other does not have a transformative effect if the other's story does not touch them at heart and does not provoke moral sympathy, as the Palestinian philosopher Sari Nusseibeh puts it: without working on inspecting the self or reflexivity, one can remain walled inside one's own body.[44]

Controversies surrounding Islam, as we have seen, lead Jews to emphasize their own history in the discussion of present stakes. Debates around halal and circumcision also invite Muslims to engage in relation to the past of Jews. But which one? The Shoah presents problems for them. As migrants, they do not feel implicated in or responsible for the horrors of the European past. And they often express their reticence about the fact that the memory of the Shoah takes up all the space and that other memories, such as those of slavery, colonialism or the Algerian War, are thus obscured.[45] In an unexpected way, controversies surrounding Islam also echo the Jewish past and force us to create parallels between two moments in history, two religions and two respective ways of reacting to the secular modernity of Europe.

Yet the intersection of these histories opens up the possibility for another relationship to the memory of the Shoah. In light of controversies in the present around Islam, the religious dimension of the killing of the Jews of Europe resurfaces: in effect, we see how debates about the daily practices of Jews and Muslims are not trivial, and constitute the heart of their relationship to politics. Controversies lead Muslims to connect themselves to the history of the Jewish religion in Europe, think about Islamophobia in tandem with anti-Semitism, and rethink their relationship to the memory of the Shoah. But the story of the Shoah's potentially transformative effect on representations of Muslims can only occur if memory resonates closely with their life experiences, which requires citizens to become implicated not as the passive objects of commemoration, but as active agents of memory.[46] Rethinking the memory of the Shoah with the history of migration necessitates a 'multidirectional approach of memory.'[47]

Among Turkish migrants in Germany, we observed the emergence of new ways of connecting to the Jewish past. Zafer Senocak, a Turkish writer and poet, noticed that Turkish immigrants did not feel concerned with German history: in his novel *Dangerous Kinship* (1988), considered a leading text of the 'Turkish turn in contemporary German literature,'[48] he addressed the history of 'dangerous' affinities between Turks, Jews and

Germans over three generations in the post-1990 period in Berlin. The different memories in question, including those of the Shoah and the Armenian genocide, are put in relation in the novel: how not to obscure them, how to make them return to the present, these are the questions that constitute the book's central theme. It is not the story of the respective culpability of Turks and Germans or the heavy charge on successive generations that is foremost in the author's mind. Instead, he aims to see how the culture of memory in Germany constitutes and transforms itself in relation to other memories. By situating his story in the period after the fall of the Berlin Wall, he interrogates himself on post-Shoah Germany reconfigured by unification and migration. Feeling actively implicated and sharing historical responsibility, he writes not as an ethnically different subject, but as a responsible citizen who adopts German history as his own, albeit in a critical manner. Thus he follows the heritage of German intellectuals who have worked critically on memory. He asks his Turkish compatriots living in Germany the central question: 'doesn't immigrating to Germany also imply entering into the arena of the country's recent history?'[49] He attempts to narrate immigration and different memories of Germany that intermix and 'touch' each other. This represents a double intimacy, because each one is touched by the other in a corporeal relationship as well as in its effects: by grasping the memory of the Shoah, Turkish migrants 'emigrate' into the German past and into their own past. Zafer Senocak thus recognizes the centrality of the Shoah in European history as the condition of Turkish-German citizenship.

He explains that a European conscience cannot exist without learning about the inhumanity of Auschwitz. We do not know exactly why the dying Jews were called 'Muslims' in the camp's language. The enigmatic use of the German word *Muselmänner* (Muslims) designated men at the end of their strength, exhausted by labor, who had consumed their reserves of muscle and fat, the walking dead. By retracing the theological-political history of Europe, Gil Anidjar showed how the use of this term can be situated in the gray zone of dangerous porosity between Jews and Muslims in their distinctive regimes as enemies from the interior and exterior: a Jew becoming 'Muslim' before dying is the resigned and 'fatalistic'[50] Jew. This qualification would then refer to their fatalism and docile acceptation of their destiny attributed to Islam and the Orient. In any case, Auschwitz is situated at the heart of European history in the prolonging of theological-political relationships between modernity and the three monotheisms. New arrivals in Europe, Muslim and non-Muslim migrants, as well as citizens of candidate states for integration into the European Union, such as Turks, cannot ignore this reality.

In February 2011, I was part of a French delegation invited to visit Auschwitz as part of the Aladdin project.[51] There were many of us. At one point, in the Birkenau camps, I found myself in front of clothes, suitcases and objects left by some of the millions of innocents who were assassinated. I thought of passages from a book by the Hungarian writer Imre Kertész (who won the Nobel Prize for Literature in 2002), born in 1929 in Budapest to a Jewish family and deported at fifteen in 1944 to the Auschwitz-Birkenau camp. In *Fatelessness*,[52] he subtly describes the living conditions of Jews in Budapest during the Second World War: wearing the yellow star, looks by non-Jews, forced labor, 8pm curfews, raids that surprised Jews in their daily lives, the lies of Nazis who asked for volunteers to work in Germany, transports in cattle cars with no water, the 'selection' (a synonym for immediate death) upon arrival at Auschwitz, the transformation of men into deportees, the lack of privacy in dormitories, sickness, the interminable wait in quarantine, hunger, unending transfers from camp to camp, the loss of all solidarity. In this book, he recounts, with some detachment, his quasi-agony and his transformation into a 'Muslim,' near death.

Jews arrived by train in Auschwitz after a long and terrible journey, many of them believing what the Nazis had told them: they would work, and be reunited with their families, identity cards, documents and suitcases, everything that was in front of our eyes. This description of Jews as docile and naïve, incapable of suspecting these were lies – and even less the inhuman programming of their organized extermination by the Nazis – seemed to me a singularity of the Jewish genocide. I told a man standing next to me, a Muslim theologian and renowned intellectual in Turkey, about these passages from the book. After attentively listening to me, he evoked his own memories of the genocide of 1915. The Armenians also believed what the Turks told them when they were asked to leave their homes: they thought they would return at the end of the war with Russia. A taboo fell, a major piece of the official Turkish version, casting doubt on the absence of intentionality by those in power during the Armenian genocide.

At Auschwitz, we were witnesses to crimes of inhumanity committed against Jews; connected to our own history, we were thus united against any inhuman act. Since the 2000s in Turkey, taboos about the Armenian genocide have indeed fallen as more and more citizens publicly express their feelings of responsibility towards the Armenian victims of the 1915 genocide. After the assassination of the Armenian Turkish intellectual Hrant Dink on 19 January 2007 by a young Turkish nationalist extremist, thousands of indignant citizens spontaneously came together, chanting: 'We are all Hrant, we are all Armenians.' This form of public expression of indignation created an emotional and political shock which shattered the official taboo. On 15 December 2008, an 'apology letter' signed by thousands of Turkish citizens was thus addressed to Armenians, opening a breach in the politics of revisionism.[53] With the growing number of signatures, this 'act of citizenship' linked to individual conscience became an act of collective memory: this autonomous work of memory in the heart of a population constituted a new form of political action, surpassing established frames and transforming the relationships between citizens.[54]

Citizen initiatives and performances attest to the sort of multiplicity of politics of memory that are spreading in contemporary Europe. In the period marked by the fall of the Berlin Wall, the memory of the Shoah has been reconstructed in the present in a lively and creative way, in encounters with 'others,' including migrants, Jews and non-Jews, in a multicultural Europe.[55] This has opened a new space for the Jews of Europe to rethink their citizenship in light of the possibility of a link to the present with others. In the post-war period, Jews agreed on one point: there no longer existed a collective Jewish life in Europe. This type of life could exist only in Israel or, to some extent, in the United States. As the American historian Diana Pinto reminds us, Judaism was then perceived in Europe as a past notion and was not thought of in relation to its future.[56] For her, the question is whether or not

Jews can affirm an active presence in contemporary Europe by rising to the challenge of pluriculturalism and multiculturalism. In any case, Jews and Muslims are entering through very different paths into a new phase of their shared history in Europe: they find themselves questioned in their co-citizenship, a challenge for a democratic future of Europe and its new multicultural orientation.

CONCLUSION

European Muslims Taking to the Stage

This book, based on a long-term inquiry, has shown that since the 1980s, Muslim religiosity, once seemingly limited to the spheres of immigrants, has affirmed itself throughout social life in Europe. Muslims claim the right to live their religion and to follow Islamic prescriptions while accessing the spaces of communal life, work, education, and recreation in European societies. The manifestation of Islam in European public life signals a new step in the integration of Muslims and their settlement, while still sparking real polemics. Obviously, the public visibility of Islam and its major symbols – mosques, veils and halal – still represents a problem in the eyes of citizens attached to the secular and Western values of Europe. Islam becomes a public affair, debated by all, a subject that mobilizes actors and collective passions.[1] Controversies surrounding Islam lead to the emergence of new ruptures and alliances around norms, values and identities, and they change the democratic agendas of European countries. Islam has become an unavoidable source in the creation of policy, both for those who fight against it and for those who claim it.

In an unexpected way, and without seeking to, Islam has thus become a decisive factor around which the normative orientation of European societies has become a source of debate. The future of the European Union, imagined and wished for in the wake of Western civilization and its Christian heritage, consequently takes these unexpected paths opened up by dynamics coming from the East. These require it to revisit the forgotten pages of a shared past that is still present: this is what I want to show in this conclusion by placing the results of our inquiry into the larger perspective of a confrontation between the challenges of the present and the persistent force of unresolved conflicts of the past.

TOWARDS A POST-WESTERN EUROPE?

Europe's first step towards a 'post-Western' orientation began with the fall of the Berlin Wall. In November 1989, the moment of hands held out between East and West and the reuniting of Berliners was eternalized by the photographer Raymond Depardon. Berlin, he said, was the hope for peace, the city that represents 'the future of Europe turned towards the past.'[2] But the reunification of Berlin alone did not assure peace in Europe. With the destruction of the wall, the seeming cohesion of the former Yugoslavia shattered. Haris Pasovic, the director of the East-West theater company in Sarajevo, vividly remembers this moment: 'We were sitting on the wall. When it fell, all of Yugoslavia crumbled with it. We were the first victims of its fall.'[3] The most European of the Eastern countries, after forty years of 'socialism with a human face,' the inheritor of Tito, fell into a chauvinist nationalism with the neo-fascism of Milosevic. There, in the heart of Mitteleuropa, the Muslim presence in Europe was tested in the 1992–95 war in which Serbian power led to a policy of destruction and the ethnic cleansing of Muslim and Croat groups in Bosnia.[4]

The events in Bosnia brought the Muslim presence in the heart of Europe into the light of day. During the civil war, the destruction of the Mostar Bridge (9 November 1993) was a precursor and the sign of a new Europe that is still emerging today. This bridge was constructed in 1566, when the sovereignty of the Ottoman Empire extended to Budapest. It was planned by an engineer named Hayreddin – a disciple of Sinan, the master architect of Suleiman the Magnificent – and built over the Neretva river in order to link the mosques and markets on either bank. Over the course of centuries, it became an icon of the city, a European patrimony. Its destruction put not just Bosnia in peril, but also the European project. In order to make sure that 'Europe does not die in Sarajevo,' an alarm was sounded in 1994 by the French intellectuals Bernard-Henri Lévy and Alain Ferrari in their documentary film *Bosnia!* Jean-Luc Godard vowed the same in his 2004 film *Our Music*, so that the bridge once again became a link and incarnated the hope of Europe. The French architect Gilles Péqueux, responsible for its reconstruction, explained with force the importance of the historical stakes of this architectural gesture: 'Mostar is in a sense where the East and the West held out their hands to one another.'[5]

Yet the Mostar Bridge did not become the symbol of reconciliation in Europe. The reunification of the continent remained marked by the destruction of a hideous wall. The wall remains the object of commemorations and animates collective memory, while the bridge has been filed away into the archives and relegated to the city's history. As Paul Ricœur has written, there is no 'just memory' but 'the worrying spectacle of too much memory here, too much forgetfulness there.'[6] But history is also a product of phenomena hidden in forgotten folds, written in absence. If the fall of the Berlin Wall turned the page on communism, the destruction of the bridge opened another, making the troubling presence of Muslims in the heart of Europe emerge. Through these destructions, the imprint of the long term surfaced, and the traces of two historical poles of influence in the Balkans, the Ottoman Empire, and the Soviet Union, find themselves at the center of current rivalries in Europe. On one side, the Christianity of the East, freed in the fall of communism, and on the other Islam in the West are fighting for their place in Europe. The return of Eastern Christianity, the Orthodox Church in the center of Europe and the presence of Muslims in European immigrant countries destabilize current definitions of Western and Christian Europe. Yet a new step in the rapprochement of the Catholic Church and the Eastern Church is under way; in November 2014, Pope Francis traveled to Istanbul, the city where the Patriarch of Constantinople Bartholomew 1st signaled a breakthrough in this direction.

Classically, European modernity is essentially attached to its Greco-Roman heritage, while those of two other civilizations, Slavic-Byzantine and Ottoman-Muslim, remain unknown, even ignored, as the British sociologist Gerard Delanty has revealed.[7] According to him, European modernity is not the fruit of one sole civilization, but the conjugation of these three. Dynamics of

Europeanization have in effect followed a process of borrowing and interaction between these three civilizations. Certainly, avenues of modernity have not been the same in each one. If, for Western Europe, the route that has been adopted has led to cultural rationalization (Protestant reform, Enlightenment, secularization), the Russian and Turkish cases have in their extremes pushed the project of political rationalization by secular and Jacobin states. And today, societies in countries which were formed by Russian and Ottoman heritage share the same difficulties, finding themselves in a Western Europe centered on itself.

THE DIFFICULT RECONCILIATION OF THE INTERSECTING HERITAGES OF EASTERN CHRISTIANITY AND WESTERN ISLAM

Hagia Sophia in Istanbul and the Mezquita Cathedral in Córdoba are two jewels of the global cultural patrimony inherited from the Christian and Muslim civilizations. These religious places, one of Eastern Christianity and the other of Western Islam, incarnate the juxtaposition of layers of history, Byzantine and Muslim, Arab and Hispanic, as well as the sedimentation of eras – the Middle Ages, the Reconquista in Spain, the fall of Constantinople, successive conversions from one religion to another, the imprint of the powers of empires and nations, and the deletion of traces of memories. These two sites are still the object of a symbolic battle between religions and civilizations today. Calls to change the names of these sites thus constitute indicators of the ambiguous relationship of the past and the controversial orientation of the future.

Mythic moments of coexistence between different religions and civilizations – Muslim, Jewish and Christian – in the history of the fifteenth to the nineteenth centuries today elicit a new interest in a Europe in search of historical sources of pluralism.[8] But if it remains a reference model in the matter, the remembrance of the cohabitation of three monotheist religions in Andalusia is the subject of battles of memory and current conflicts of identity.[9] For example, Hamza Salah, the rector of the Khalid Ibn Walid Mosque in Paris, explained in 2009: 'I always refer to this diversity in Andalusia – you know, Christians, Jews, Muslims who live in symbiosis and harmony. That is what I would like to see in the future in France and Europe: I want to see the Andalusia of tomorrow, the Córdoba of tomorrow, the Grenada of tomorrow.'[10] These places represent the stakes of civilizational memory not only in Europe. In New York, the construction of a mosque named the House of Córdoba near the Twin Towers, destroyed in the September 11 attacks, elicited strong reactions from American citizens who said they were worried about preserving the memory of victims; but the Muslim promoters of this project defended it as creating a platform for interreligious dialogue, like that which prevailed when Andalusian Spain was under Muslim rule.

With the Alhambra of Grenada, the Great Mosque of Córdoba, beginning in the eighth century, is certainly the most prestigious witness to this Muslim presence in Spain. In contemporary language, for the inhabitants of Córdoba and for its visitors, the Mezquita is one of the major monuments of Hispano-Muslim Andalusian architecture. Built by Umayyad caliphs, it was expanded several times by their successors. In the interior, a forest of marble columns and double arcades in brick and white stone create the impression of infinity, translating a singular esthetic of transcendence. When Córdoba was retaken by Christians in 1236, the Mezquita was converted into a church. In the sixteenth century, a cathedral in a sumptuous baroque style was built in the center of the monument. Today the Mezquita Cathedral is the primary church in the diocese of Córdoba and the practice of Muslim worship there is formally prohibited – the minaret was not destroyed, but hidden inside the cathedral's tower.[11]

On 8 December 2006, a Spanish psychologist and convert to Islam, Mansur Abdussalam Escudero,[12] dramatically renewed an ancient request: authorization for Muslims to pray inside the Mezquita Cathedral. That day, he put his prayer rug in front of the edifice and performed his prayers as television cameras followed him. Escudero said that his objective was not to bring back the past, or recover or appropriate this place for himself, but to make it a unique ecumenical place in the world. In order to do so, he sent a letter to the Spanish prime minister, José Luis Zapatero, suggesting the reopening of St Sophia in Istanbul to all believers. But this was in vain. The Bishop of Córdoba, Juan José Aenjo, rejected his call by stating that a Catholic church cannot be shared, as Muslims do not have the same conception of God as Christians (Father, Son, and Holy Spirit). In order to put an end to these calls, the bishop proposed in 2010 changing the name of the monument: he asked the city to renounce the term Mezquita and keep only the 'Cathedral of Córdoba.' According to the bishop, the term 'mosque' would create confusion among visitors, and since it had been centuries since the building had been used as such, it would be inappropriate to call it a mosque today. However, neither the residents nor City Hall supported this proposal. This 'war of words'[13] is inscribed in the list of emblematic quarrels and illustrates the disputes over the heritage of the Muslim past in Spain today. In our EPS research group organized in Córdoba on 21 February 2010, participants shared their worries in the face of these attempts at distorting the past, removing the Muslim heritage from the Spanish patrimony and the rise of nationalist movements that were inspired, in justifying their current Islamophobic policies, by the 'hunt for *moros*'[14] during the Reconquista period.

St Sophia, the ancient Christian church built in Constantinople in the sixth century and which became a mosque in the fifteenth century is also the subject of forceful polemics in contemporary Turkey, where policies of reinforcing the Muslim identity are gaining ground. With the creation of the secular Turkish Republic, St Sophia was transformed into a national museum. Asking for its reconversion to a place of worship touches different layers of history and civilizations in the collective conscience. St Sophia, which means Holy Wisdom – *Hagia Sophia* in Greek – is a place of worship and memory for Byzantine Christians and for Ottoman Muslims. Occupying a unique place in the patrimony of civilizations, it survived historical upheavals, conquests, conversions, the fall of empires, and the birth of nationalisms by successively adjusting to these contexts.[15] After having served as the center of Eastern Christianity for more than a millennium, with the conquest of Constantinople in 1453, Hagia Sophia became the imperial mosque of Istanbul. The conquerors transformed this Byzantine space by integrating it fully into imperial and Islamic collective memory. In this new Islamic context, Hagia Sophia was consecrated, at the initiative of Sultans engaged in its restoration and transformation, into a place of worship and a religious symbol of Islam. Distinctive signs of Christianity, such as steeples and altars, were removed, mosaics were covered, and Islamic architectural elements like the *mihrab*, *minbar* and minarets were added; and Ottoman sultans promoted the creation of texts, the production of myths and fables allowing for the narrative of the conversion of Hagia Sophia into an imperial mosque.[16] It exerts particular influence on classic Turkish and Ottoman architecture. Mosques by the architect Mimar Koca Sinan (1489–1588), characterized by their domes and slender minarets, have thus been seen as a mediation between the Byzantine and Islamic architectural traditions. With the dawn of the Turkish Republic, Hagia Sophia was adapted to the politics of secularization and was transformed into a national museum in 1934. It is thus neutralized in the new context of the secular Republic, which wants to detach itself from its imperial and religious roots. The idea of reconverting it into a mosque is still promoted by some, and profoundly worries others. Turks continue to call it by its original Greek name while adapting it to the Turkish language, as *Ayasofya*.

Like the Mezquita of Córdoba, Hagia Sophia continues to be a battlefield for memories and religions today, and crystallizes the disputes between secular and religious people, Christians and Muslims, West and East. The multiple filiations of these places of worship and their genealogy, rooted in several civilizations, make the echo of these debates spread beyond the boundaries of Spain and Turkey to a European and transnational public sphere.

THE UNPRECEDENTED ANCHORING OF ISLAM IN EUROPE

The German philosopher Jürgen Habermas laments the fact that European citizens are not sufficiently concerned with the affairs of the European Union, and that the absence of a public European sphere leads to a democratic deficiency.[17] He is completely right to say that citizens are not mobilized around the construction of Europe: during our inquiry, we noted that the EU does not provide a frame of reference for citizens to formulate their problems or seek to move beyond antagonisms. The invitation to discuss topics concerning Europe even decreased interest in the debate.

But a transversal space of debate is opening up around the question of Islam. In other words, the European public sphere is being constructed where we least expect it, around affairs concerning Islam. Islam's place in Europe, its places of worship, and the heritage and current presence of Muslims constitute subjects of debate, hot topics that carry heavy baggage in terms of reciprocal affects and resentments that mobilize collective passions. The public sphere is the site of this interface of encounters and confrontations as well as a place for exchange and mutual accommodation. It is through the quasi-volcanic eruption of Islam that Europe is led into a hot zone of transformations and permutations.

Modern societies have been defined by Claude Lévi-Strauss as 'hot societies.' He distinguishes them from 'cold societies,' whose dominant concern is 'the desire to preserve their essence.'[18] They seem to him to have 'a particular wisdom that leads them to hopelessly resist all modification to their structure that would allow history to intrude into them.' The three major characteristics of cold societies as described by Lévi-Strauss are the preservation of their standards of living, their fertility rate, and the consent of the majority. We find these characteristics in Muslim immigration in European societies: the immigration question is often understood as a disruptive element in terms of the fertility rate, a threat to standards of living, and a means of shattering majority consent. It seems that European societies borrow the traits of cold societies in that their major concern is to resist all modification, particularly when it is caused by the presence of Muslims. While so-called stagnant societies enter a hot zone in history through acceleration and changes, notably emerging nations and Arab revolutions, European societies tend to cool. Nonetheless, Islam is making them enter into a hot zone in history with new social realities that make the preservation of the old world difficult.

Islamic actors are reproached for acting out of step with secular values, of making 'space/time' from 'elsewhere' appear in European public life, and making use of references that are 'external' to national boundaries; their stories and life trajectories are seen as coming from the countries their parents came from via satellite channels in their living rooms and native languages spoken in their homes. Their eruption into the public sphere is thus perceived as an act of the imminent transgression of national boundaries and a perpetual source of concern because of their multiple identities and their loyalty to the host country. They are here, but they're also there; they are often sent back to their parents' origins through labels such as 'from a migrant background' and therefore they are not completely included in the nation or recognized as citizens. Their very presence signifies the encroachment of national borders with other countries and the irruption of the 'Middle East' into

Europe. Their supposed insertion in transnational networks of commerce, entertainment, communication, humanitarianism and also terrorism is a source of suspicion perceived as the symptom of the failure of Muslim integration in Europe.

This is all the more true as the public presence of Islam brings its symbols and signs which point to the long term of the religion, even its immutable character, into daily life in the present. The lives of Muslims are part of the religious social imaginary and they recognize each other by adhering to Islamic prescriptions and also constructing, in a genealogical way, chains or mimetic continuity with the prophetic tradition. The *Sunna* tradition allows for the introduction of another temporality into the present, going back to the time of Mohammed. Comprised of the Prophet's sayings and deeds, it acts as a complement to divine revelation and the Koran's message by providing a common matrix and repertoire of actions that connect Muslims under the conditions of immigration and acculturation with the dawn of Islam. While we have the tendency to oppose religion and the political domain, the expression of faith, as we saw apropos prayer, is a daily form of public action and appearance on the public stage. Muslims also bring the phenomenological dimension of politics into daily life.

The proliferation of the use of a very selective lexicon attests to the emergence of Islam in public life in Europe. Notions like sharia, halal, fatwa, hijab, burka and jihad enter media and political debates. These religious notions that belong to a specific cultural area and another era, considered pre-modern and archaic, have become used in daily speech while adopting a European flavor. But the adoption of an Islamic lexicon in the European context creates deviations from the original theological meaning of these notions: their use in another context changes their meaning, as we saw in the case of the transformation of sharia law in halal lifestyles.

More broadly, the lived experience of Islam in Europe implies a process of interrogation and reflection on the part of Muslims who see their faith and their practices questioned through the prism of perceptions that are sometimes depreciative of others. They contend with offensive images of their prophet, depicted as a 'terrorist' or a 'pedophile.' Verses from the Koran are taken out of their theological context and quoted in films or ad campaigns that aim to stigmatize supposedly violent and retrograde aspects of the Muslim religion. Some want to burn the Koran, and others, like the ultranationalist Dutch MP Geert Wilders, demand that it be banned in the same way as *Mein Kampf*.[19] Nonetheless, we must remember that European disputes about the sacred symbols of Islam do not originate in the present, but go back at least to the twelfth century: the figure of the Prophet is worrisome and his different representations are most often at the center of theological rivalries and controversies.[20]

Despite differences between countries and immigration profiles, the same recurrence of controversies and convergence in how the Muslim presence is treated, named, and framed is evident everywhere. In fact, the European public field is reconstructed around Islamic controversies. Borrowing an Islamic lexicon, using representations of the Prophet and quotations from the Koran in repertoires of action, bringing in personalities for or against Islam, and creating unusual and sometimes fatal alliances are common traits of publics where controversies emerge. The coupling of 'original' citizens and migrants, 'courageous' natives and 'emancipated' Muslims, is one example. We saw militants bracing themselves in defense of their country's culture aligning themselves with Muslim figures who criticize Islamic norms, in particular concerning equality of the sexes.[21] We thus see appear in the same space/time cosmopolitan assemblages of disparate elements, actors and themes that blend the sacred and the profane. Controversies create proximity, assemblages between audiences that would otherwise not know about each other.

WHEN ISLAM CONTRIBUTES TO THE EVOLUTION OF THE EUROPEAN PUBLIC SPHERE

As we saw in Chapter 2, the public sphere is not an empty and neutral space, but is comprised of hierarchizations between spaces and social classes through distinctions like center/periphery, city/projects, literate/illiterate, and excluded/included. As long as Muslims remain restricted to housing projects, practicing their religion in their places of work, and constructing their mosques in industrial parts of cities, the signs and symbols of Islam are not troubling. It is the demand for their equal presence in spaces reserved for 'original' citizens that garners public attention. This visibility, although it attests to the integration of immigrants, elicits unease and triggers polemics.

Participation in the public sphere requires a measure of conformity with established frames of action and a relative acceptance of the values of the majority. But in the eyes of some, the entry of Muslims with their faith and their distinctive behaviors into public spaces produces a disruptive effect, the sign of an anachronism, and creates a rupture in the frame of public life.

As Erving Goffman wrote, ruptures in frames are introduced by those at the bottom who come from somewhere else, like Muslim migrants.[22] Public space is a place where citizens come together and create a consensus, the possibility of dissensus, and a place for uncertainty.[23] The visibility of Muslims raises the question of what is consensual in public space. Controversies erupt when common sense, the accumulation of shared opinion, and evidence are fragmented and appear as incompatible judgments.[24]

Islam thus often emerges as an unacceptable alterity in the cultural context of Europe in that it disturbs the cognitive frameworks of common life and its space/time. All human and social actions unfold as chronotopes, literally space/time where daily realities take shape. According to the Russian historian Mikhail Bakhtin, space/times in the public sphere are social and historical products that different groups of individuals create in different ways in various eras.[25] In the current era in which societies are penetrated by migratory and global dynamics, an approach to the public sphere fixed in space/time, like the monocultural model of the national community, becomes constraining for democracies. The public sphere needs polyphony and dialogism – even the carnavalesque[26] – to account for the variety of concurrent 'nows' and seize the complexity of contemporary experience.

Yet as we have seen throughout this book, Muslim actors have become visible in Europe in the measure that they become singular, distinguish themselves, and make themselves noticed. Wearing the hijab, building mosques and minarets, and eating halal represent many distinctive signs of this quest for singularity in the Muslim experience. This visibility evokes unaccustomed forms in Europe, from clothing to architecture, a new semantics (hijab, burka, minarets, halal), and behavior in conformity with religious norms of purity and modesty. According to the philosopher Hannah Arendt, the courage to appear, which consists of leaving the private sphere to manifest one's singularity, is the very proof of citizenship.[27] In this perspective, one acquires the status of citizen through action and appearance. Muslims thus prove their citizenship and display their singularity in public spaces.

The public sphere and public space are notions that overlap. The public sphere evokes in particular freedom of expression, communication and discussion – and sometimes the tendency to confuse media debates with it, which are only one element. As for public space, it is the idea of a public 'stage,' "in other words a stage where actors and actions as well as events and social problems become publicly visible.'[28] In its treatment of the presence of Islam, the media exacerbates its visual traits and the polemical aspect of debates. Islamic visibilities are represented in their excessive forms, considered in a spiral of aberration and alterity. Sensations, scandals and outrageous positions replace rational protocols of public debate. In our inquiry, we wanted to inversely reconstitute the democratic potential of public space as both a stage for the appearance of actors, ordinary Muslims, and a space of debate and exchange. In the organization of our research in the EPS, Muslim participants had the opportunity to turn away from media hegemony that made them feel captive. They were able to apprehend their daily reality in the presence of other citizens, including Catholics who help immigrants in the field, young people in antiracist movements, Jews involved in interreligious matters, converts to spiritualism, as well as alternative globalists, ecologists and cultural mediators … EPS gave participants the chance to meet each other, become aware of each other's presence, and move beyond simplistic antagonisms and binaries.

PERFORMANCES AND ARTISTIC CREATION INDICATE TO EUROPE A HORIZON OF POSSIBILITY WITH ITS MUSLIMS

Art revealed itself as a facilitator for an intersubjective debate, even around works considered by some as blasphemous. The most difficult subjects, such as sexuality and religion, came up, as we saw in the EPS in Brussels during a debate with the artist Mehdi-Georges Lahlou. Artists aim to take account of the tensions between European lifestyles and Islamic halal norms. The topic of food, where pork products occupy a central role, illustrates this point. Artists of Muslim culture adopt pork as the distinctive symbol of life in Europe and juxtapose it with signs of identity in Islam. The public figure of the pig is not only used by movements on the populist right, who use it to stigmatize Muslims, but also by some artists who inversely use it as a symbol of integration. Artists aim to familiarize themselves with pork and domesticate it while creating a shock effect. In the work by the Turkish Berliner artist Nezaket Ekici *My pig* (2004), we see a woman dressed in a black burka, in fact the artist herself, who is petting a little pink pig and walking it on a leash like a dog. Sarah Maple, another young artist born in England to a Muslim mother and a Christian father, also uses her own body to create unsettling scenes and situations. In a controversial work, *Haram*, the artist wears an Islamic headscarf and cradles a piglet. This work, shown in the Salon Gallery in London in 2008, caused an outcry in some segments of the

English Muslim community, which considered it a blasphemous criticism of the Koran and the ban on eating pork.

Sarah Maple said that she wanted to play with the discrepancy between this Koranic rule and the superficial repugnance that Muslims feel towards the animal itself. She defends herself: 'My work does not criticize Islam as a religion. I start with my experience: I grew up in a mixed family as a Muslim, I was in a Catholic school, and so on. For me, things could always be summed up this way: "I would like to be a believer, but I want to be able to do what my friends do."' Her comments reiterate the dilemma facing young Muslims who want to live ordinary lives in Europe. In the frame of our research, when we asked them to respond to these artworks, Muslims reiterated several times that the Koran simply bans eating pork and does not call on them to hate the animal, which is a creature of Allah. A young Muslim woman's interpretation of Sarah Maple's painting *Haram* illustrates the 'unusual anchoring of Muslims' in Europe. When she saw the image, she said to us, 'This image is really beautiful! The woman seems totally maternal and a little authoritarian. She's protecting her pig, a symbol of people who eat pork … In my mind, the pig is pejorative, it's settled. That said, an artist has to shock people. This image makes me think. Maybe she adopted it … And she has her nails polished … Normally, you can't wear nail polish, otherwise ablutions don't work. It's rare to see a veiled girl with nail polish … These are the details that make me think … For me, this means that the woman adopted the West! That's a cultural dialogue.'[29] The evolution of her thoughts shows the development of reflexivity, the process through which Muslims try to understand their own transformation in their lives in Europe.

The pig in the arms of a Muslim woman becomes the metaphor for the adoption of Europe by Muslims. It is primarily women who familiarize themselves with European lifestyles both in their maternal and intellectual positions.

As we saw, ordinary Muslims often display their citizenship in performative acts by creating a link between themselves and Europe. To countertheir overexposure in the media, they return to their faith and to virtues like patience, discretion, and silence. With a rich repertoire of humorous actions and visuals, Muslim citizens, like non-Muslims, aim to work around bans in public space. Against the ban on the construction of minarets in Switzerland after the referendum, a contest for the most beautiful minaret in Europe was organized in 2010 by several NGOs, including the Multicultural Youth Council (COJEP), the Organisation of the Islamic Cooperation (OIC), specialists (architects, photographers) and religious representatives (Jewish and Protestant). The Madni Jamia Masjid minaret in Bradford was chosen from two hundred which participated in the competition.[30]

In September 2010 in France, the day before the law creating a ban on the full veil, the burka, in public places was adopted, two young French women in their twenties enacted a performance entitled 'NiqaBitch': covered in burkas that went to their hips but with bare legs, they walked down the streets of Paris mocking the ban on the full veil. They pushed codes to their extremes, producing a hybrid figure both Muslim and European, but faceless and unidentifiable.[31] The juxtaposition of opposite codes, the veil and nudity, the act of covering up and uncovering simultaneously, created a transgressive and humorous effect. Public space became a carnavalesque place for the reversal of regulations.

The creation of new esthetic forms can also signify the desire to go beyond antagonisms, the incommensurability between norms, and identity divisions between Europeans and Muslims. We saw this in the case of the Cologne mosque. In the same way, the Penzberg mosque, winner of the most beautiful building in Bavaria, whose architect is from a Muslim Bosnian background, illustrates the role of esthetic forms in the cohabitation of communities. The mosque's minaret, made of steel, remains silent, but the words of the call to prayer are inscribed on it in calligraphy; and instead of the muezzin's call to prayer, the minaret lights up at the time for prayers.[32] The form of minarets thus became a source of architectural inspiration for the adaptation of Islam into the European landscape. Public space became a place of exploration of new norms and esthetic forms, and Islamic visibility ceases being an essential and caricatured sign of alterity. This visibility is carried by people and human faces. Discovering the possibility of showing their presence, Muslims can thus become engaged in the affairs of the city.

Proof of this citizen engagement is offered by the Not In My Name campaign, founded by British Muslims on 10 September 2014, to denounce the atrocities committed in Iraq and Syria – including beheadings of European citizens – by the self-proclaimed 'Islamic State,' also known as Daesh. This movement allowed for the public appearance of voices and faces of ordinary Muslims who say, as Muslims, that these horrors cannot be committed in their name.[33] The Not In My Name movement is a form of action through the performance of citizenship in public that follows the idea that 'the personal is political.' Every participant lends his or her face and appears in his or her singularity on the public stage.

They show the multiplicity of the faces of Islam and the European polyphony of Muslims. Like other British Muslims who twenty-five years ago rediscovered their citizenship by denouncing the fatwa against Salman Rushdie, the Muslim initiative Not In My Name is the expression of their co-citizenship with 'original' Europeans. European Muslims defend their Islam against that which wants to destroy all possibility of a link with others, which aims to destroy Christians in the East and Jews in the West, as well as Muslims who have veered from the proper path, beginning with women.

Jihadis and Islamophobes fight the productive process of cultural blending and defend an impossible purity in identity, religion and nations. This is why they sabotage common life, prevent debate, and destroy spaces of encounter through verbal violence or physical elimination. The antidote against the cycle of extremism lies in the possibilities of making public, of passing from placing differences side by side to intermixing them. This is where Europe's exception resides, in its creative freedom, in its propensity to invent itself with others, in the act of interweaving the social fabric. Like a magic carpet, Europe shows a horizon of possibility with its Muslims.

NOTES

INTRODUCTION

1 'Gilbert and George: Scapegoat' exhibition, Thaddeus Ropac Gallery, Paris, November 2014 (see the exhibition catalogue, with text by Michael Bracewell).

2 *Time Out*, 8 September 2014.

3 'Gaz hilarant: la drogue qui fait faveur en Angleterre,' *Les Inrocks*, 2 October 2014. The Jamme Masjid Mosque in Brick Lane was originally, in the eighteenth century, a Protestant church. From 1898, it was a synagogue, before transforming in 1976 into a mosque for London's Bengali community. Since 2009, this site of Muslim worship has been distinguishable by its minaret, with a soaring metallic needle.

4 For the use of the notion of urbicide, see Canto-Sperber, Monique, *Le Bien, La Guerre et la Terreur*. Paris: Plon, 2005, p. 30.

5 See Göle, Nilüfer, 'The terrorist instant,' in *Islam in Europe: The Lure of Fundamentalism and the Allure of Cosmopolitanism*, trans. from the French by Steven Rendall, Princeton, NJ: Markus Wiener, 2010.

6 Expression used by the French far right before being adopted by some media intellectuals like Alain Finkielkraut.

7 Boltanski, Luc, Énigmes et complots. Une enquête à propos d'enquêtes. Paris: Gallimard, 2012, p. 22.

8 Ibid.

9 Göle, Nilüfer, *EuroPublicIslam: Islam in the Making of a European Public Sphere*, 2009–13 , EHESS (Ecole des Hautes Etudes en Sciences Sociales) in Paris. This project was financed by the European Council of Research under the Seventh Framework Programme of the European Commission (7ePC/2007-2013, grant agreement ERC-2008-AdG- 230244). See the project's website: europublicislam.hypotheses.org.

10 This itinerary led us from Toulouse to Sarajevo by way of Istanbul, Milan, Bologna, Cologne, Berlin, London, Lyons, Birmingham, Brussels, Geneva, Paris, Cordoba, Amsterdam, Copenhagen, Madrid, Oslo, Rotterdam, Treviso and Vienna.

11 De Michelli, Francesca, Alejandra Magnasco and Vrian Chauvel, *EuroPublicIslam. Itinéraires d'une recherche européenne*, coproduced in partnership with the audiovisual department at EHESS, 2013. The subtitles in French and English were created by Pierre Guenoun. The French version of the film is available on Canal U (Webtv for higher education), url.ca/j9qf9; the version with English subtitles is available on the EuroPublicIslam website: url.ca/j9qg5.

12 For the loss of artisanal work in modern societies, see Sennett, Richard, *The Craftsman*. New Haven, CT: Yale University Press, 2008.

13 Art historians have shown that in ancient rugs from the East or Byzantine art, we can follow the evolution of transformation at the level of details, in the representation and stylization of the most common motifs (Riegl, Alois, *Questions du style. Fondements d'une histoire de l'ornementation*. Paris: Hazan, 2002).

14 See Frontisi-Ducroux, Françoise, *Ouvrages de dames. Ariane, Héléne, Pénélope* … Paris: Seuil, 2009.

15 For a more detailed account, see the collective works: Göle, Nilüfer (ed.), *Islam and Public Controversy in Europe*. London: Ashgate, 2014; Göle, Nilüfer (ed.), *En quête de l'islam européen*. Perpignan: Halfa, 2015.

16 Göle, Nilüfer, *Musulmanes et Modernes. Voile et civilisation en Turquie*. Paris: La Découverte, 1993; trans. as *The Forbidden Modern: Civilization and Veiling*. Ann Arbor: University of Michigan Press, 1997.

1. EUROPE: NO ENTRY FOR ISLAM?

1 Pamuk, Orhan, *Other Colors. Essays and a Story,* New York: Vintage International, 2008.

2 Baubérot, Jean, *Histoire de la laïcité en France [History of Secularism in France]*. Paris: PUF, 2005; *Laïcité 1905–2005: entre passion et raison* [*Secularism 1905–2005, between passion and reason*]. Paris: Seuil, 2004.

3 The Stasi Commission was established on 3 July 2003 by Jacques Chirac, then president of France, at the height of the debate on veils in schools. Comprised of twenty members, the commission was assigned

to draft a report on the application of the principle of secularism. It delivered its conclusions on 11 December 2003. Following this report, the National Assembly and Senate adopted the law banning religious symbols in public schools on 15 March 2005. The text of the law is available on the website www.legifrance.gouv.fr.

4 Gauchet, Marcel, *La religion dans la démocratie: Parcours de la laïcité [Religion in Democracies: The Path of Secularism]*. Paris: Gallimard, 1998. Taylor, Charles, *A Secular Age*. Cambridge, MA: Harvard University Press, 2007. These two reference works show the genealogy of secularism through the history of Christianity. It is worth noting that the secularism transmitted to other cultures was adopted by non-Western countries like India and Turkey by means of colonialism or modernization.

5 When I was publishing my book on the phenomenon of the veil, French editors, unprompted, asked me to leave out the first section, which focused on the history of secularism in Turkey, because they saw no link between this and the question of the headscarf. For them, this was a Turkish anomaly. Since then, it has become unthinkable to discuss the question of the veil without its relationship to secularism. My book was eventually accepted in its full form by the publishing house La Découverte. Göle, Nilüfer, *Musulmanes et Modernes [Muslims and Moderns]*. Paris: Éditions La Découverte, 1993.

6 Noiriel, Gérard, À quoi sert l'identité 'nationale'? *[What is 'National' Identity For?]* Marseille: Agone, 2007.

7 This ministry, created by the decree of 18 May 2007, was abolished on 13 November 2010. French intellectuals circulated a national petition to denounce the creation of this ministry as a violation of the French notion of citizenship and demand its abolition. 'Nous exigeons la suppression du ministère de l'Identité nationale et de l'Immigration,' *Libération*, 4 December 2009.

8 Sarrazin, Thilo, *Deutschland schafft sich ab. Wie wir unser Land aufs Spiel setzen* [*Germany Does Away with Itself: How We Are Gambling Away Our Country*]. Munich: Deutsche Verlag-Anstalt, 2010.

9 Ibid.

10 *Heimat* refers not only to the native land, or home town, but also to the childhood home. *Heimat* thus contains the notion of 'home.' The emotional attachment to one's place of birth and sites of socialization plays an important role in it.

11 Sarrazin, *Deutschland schafft sich ab*, p. 308
12 'Do you not like Turks, Mr. Sarrazin?', interview published in the daily newspaper *Die Welt*, 29 August 2010. www.welt.de/politik/deutschland/article9255898/Moegen-Sie-keine-Tuerken-Herr-Sarrazin.html.
13 Conte, Édouard, 'Peut-on devenir Allemand?' ['Can you become German?'], Études rurales, 163/164. *Terre, Territoire, Appartenances*, July–December 2002, pp. 67–90.
14 Scheffer, Paul, 'The multicultural drama,' *NRC Handelsblad*, 29 January 2000.
15 'Angela Merkel admet l'échec du multiculturalisme allemand' ['Angela Merkel admits the failure of German multiculturalism'], *Le Figaro*, 17 October 2010.
16 Habermas, Jürgen, 'L'Europe malade de la xénophobie' ['Europe is sick with xenophobia'], *Le Monde*, 4 January 2011.
17 Ibid.
18 Ibid.
19 Rancière, Jacques, 'Racisme, une passion d'en haut' ['Racism, a passion from above'], *Médiapart*, 11 September 2010. www.mediapart.fr/node/92825.
20 Modood, Tariq, *Multiculturalism: A Civic Idea*. Cambridge: Polity Press, 2007.
21 Geisser, Vincent, *La nouvelle islamophobie [The New Islamophobia]*. Paris: La Découverte, 2003. Contemporary Islamophobia follows the traditions of the Middle Age Christian anti-Mahometanism and colonial-era Arabophobia.
22 Ibid., pp. 10--11.
23 Allievi, Stefano, *Conflicts over Mosques in Europe: Policy Issues and Trends*. London: NEF/Alliance Publishing Trust, 2009.
24 Geisser, *La nouvelle islamophobie*, p. 51.
25 Ibid., pp. 95–112.
26 Ibid., p. 76.
27 Gresh, Alain, 'A propos de l'islamophobie: Plaidoyer en faveur d'un concept controversé' ['On Islamophobia: A plea in favor of a controversial concept'], Les mots sont important Net, 4 March 2004. lmsi.net/A-propos-de-l-islamophobie.
28 See Fourest, Caroline and Fiammetta Venner, 'Islamophobie?', *ProChoix*, 26/27, 2003, and Pascal Bruckner, 'L'invention de l'"islamophobie",' *Libération*, 23 November 2010.

29 Houellebecq, Michel, *Platform*, trans. Frank Wynne. London: Random House, 2002, p. 349.
30 Ibid.
31 Muslim associations filed a complaint against the author for 'inciting religious hatred,' but not calling for the book to be banned. They took issue not with the fictional world, but the author's repetition of the narrator's and characters' 'socially unacceptable' opinions. Michel Houellebecq was tried for making racist insults and acquitted.
32 'Le roman et l'inacceptable. Sociologie d'une polémique: autour de *Plateforme* de Michel Houellebecq,' in Meizoz, Jérôme, *L'œil sociologue et la littérature*, Geneva: Slaktine Érudition, 2004, pp. 181–209.
33 The first part of this pamphlet was published on 29 December 2001 in the newspaper *Corriere della Sera*. Published by Rizzoli in 2001, and in French in 2002 by Pilon and translated into several other languages, it became an international bestseller. It was quoted by newspapers and political parties, which found in it 'expert' support for political, religious or social positions opposed to the integration of Muslims and Islam. The text was added to the curriculum of numerous Italian high schools.
34 Fallaci, Oriana, *Inshallah*, Milan, Rizzoli, 1990.
35 Cousin, Bruno and Tommaso Vitale, 'Italian intellectuals and the promotion of Islamophobia after 9/11,' in George Morgan and Scott Poynting (eds), *Global Islamophobia. Muslims and Moral Panic in the West*, Farnham: Ashgate, pp. 47–65.
36 Fallaci, Oriana, *The Rage and the Pride*. New York: Rizzoli, 2002.
37 Fallaci, Oriana, 'Il nemico che trattiamo da amico,' *Corriere della Sera*, 15 September 2006, quoted in Bartolomeo Conti's doctoral thesis, 'L'emergence de l'islam dans l'espace public italien: les leaders musulmans entre intégration et intégrisme' ['The emergence of Islam in Italian public space: Muslim leaders between integration and fundamentalism'], EHESS, Paris, 31 October 2011.
38 Interview with Michel Houellebecq in the magazine *Lire*, September 2001.
39 Cousin, Bruno, 'Quand le racisme se fait best-seller. Pourquoi les Italiens lisent-ils Oriana Fallaci?' ['When racism becomes a bestseller: why do Italians read Oriana Fallaci?'], *La vie des idées*, 3, 2005, pp. 71–7.
40 Bosetti, Giancarlo, 'Madame et son ennemi' ['Madame and her enemy'], *Reset DOC*, 5 February 2008. www.resetdoc.org/story/0000000727. Giancarlo Bosetti is the founder of *Reset DOC*.

41 Giroud, Françoise, 'Voyage au bout de la haine' ['Journey to the end of hatred'], *Le Nouvel Observateur*, 30 May 2002, quoted in Geisser, *La nouvelle islamophobie*, pp. 47–8.

42 See Ockrent, Christine, *Françoise Giroud, une ambition française*, Paris: Fayard, 2003, and Laure Adler, *Françoise*, Paris: Grasset, 2011. These two books retrace the novelistic destiny of France Gourdji, the daughter of a family of Jewish Turkish origin, who through sheer determination became Françoise Giroud, incarnating 'French ambition' and whose path situates her squarely in the dawn of modernity, and the entrance of women into professional and public life.

43 Giancarlo Bosetti notes with a touch of irony: 'I am grateful to Madame for describing to me in an extreme, heated and inflammatory manner a small vice, kept at a low temperature by reflexive editorials, explained in a gentle way, a regime of real or simulated moderation.' www.resetdoc.org/story/00000000721.

44 Treviso interview, with the mayor, 17 June 2009.

2. ORDINARY MUSLIMS

1 Haag, Pascale and Cyril Lemieux, 'Critiquer: une nécessité' ['Criticizing: a necessity'], in Pascale Haag and Cyril Lemieux (eds), *Faire des sciences sociales: critiquer*, vol. 1. Paris: Editions de l'EHESS, 2012, pp. 13–27.

2 Cf. Aykac, Cagla, 'Personnage publics de l'islam en Europe: scandales, controverses, et performances ['The public personas of Islam in Europe: scandals, controversies and performances'], Unpublished doctoral thesis, ed. Nilüfer Göle, École des Hautes Études en Sciences Sociales, Paris, 2 March 2010.

3 Hirsi Ali, Ayaan, *Infidel*. New York: Free Press, 2007.

4 Cf. Levy, Bernard Henri, 'Connaissez-vous Ayaan Hirsi Ali?' ['Do you know Ayaan Hirsi Ali?'], *Le bloc-notes de Bernard-Henri Lévy*, 7 February 2008, www.bernard-henri-levy.com/connaissez-vous-ayaan-hirsi-ali-594.html. Cf. also 'L'UMP demande un passeport français pour Ayaan Hirsi Ali' ('The UMP asks for a French passport for Ayaan Hirsi Ali'), *Le Nouvel Observateur*, 11 February 2008.

5 CILE, Center on Islamic Legislation and Ethics.

6 Fourest, Caroline, *Frère Tariq. Discours, stratégie et méthode de Tariq Ramadan* [*Brother Tariq: Tariq Ramadan's discourse, strategy and method*]. Paris: Grasset & Fasquelle, 2004.

7 Ramadan, Tariq, *The Quest for Meaning: Developing a Philosophy of Pluralism*. London: Penguin Books Ltd, 2012.
8 Ramadan, Tariq, *Western Muslims and the Future of Islam*. New York: Oxford University Press, 2004, pp. 44, 68.
9 Roussillon, Alain, *La pensée islamique contemporaine: acteurs et enjeux* [*Contemporary Islamic Thought: Actors and Stakes*]. Paris: Téraèdre, 2005, p. 165; cf. Tariq Ramadan, *Radical Reform: Islamic Ethics and Liberation*. New York: Oxford University Press, 2009.
10 Interview with Issam, Toulouse, 25 April 2009.
11 Interview with Sherine, Copenhagen, 9 February 2010.
12 Interview with Zeyneb, Treviso, 19 June 2009.
13 Interview with Muhammed, Rotterdam, 21 January 2010.
14 *Itinéraires d'une recherche européenne* [*Itinerary of European Research* was written and directed by Alejandra Magnasco, Francesca De Michelli and Brian Chauvel with support from the audiovisual department of EHESS.
15 Interview with Salima, Geneva, 11 December 2009.
16 Arendt, Hannah, *The Life of the Mind*. New York: Harcourt Brace Jovanovich, 1971.
17 Tassin, Étienne, 'Les gloires ordinaires, actualité du concept arendtien d'espace public,' *Sens public*, 15/16, July 2013, pp. 23–38.
18 Goffman, Erving, *The Presentation of Self in Everyday Life*. New York: Doubleday/Anchor Press, 1959.
19 *'Ibâdât* refers to 'religious affairs and pillars of Islam whose goal is to maintain and reinforce faith and the concept of *Tawhîd*.' Cf. Ramadan, *Western Muslims*, p. 68.
20 *Mu'âmalât* refers to general rights and social affairs. This term signifies the sphere of the negotiable that is widely open to interpretation and creativity in Islam and thus that which is subject to change, 'the area of social affairs (al-muamalat).' Ibid., p. 85.
21 Bracke, Sarah, 'Subjects of debate: Dutch Muslim women responding to interpellations about women's emancipation,' Paper presented at the conference 'Islamic Feminists, Islamist Women, and the Women in Between,' Paris, 18/19 January 2013.
22 Rosanvallon, Pierre, *Le Peuple introuvable: Histoire de la représentation démocratique en France* [*The Lost People: History of Democratic Representation in France*]. Paris: Gallimard, 1998, pp. 341–3.

23 Boal, Augusto, *Theater of the Oppressed*, trans. Emily Fryer. London: Pluto Press, 2000.

24 Haag, Pascale and Cyril Lemieux, 'Critiquer: une nécessité' ['Criticizing: a necessity'], in Haag and Lemieux, *Faire des sciences sociales: critiquer*, vol. 1, pp. 13–27.

3. CONTROVERSIES SURROUNDING MUSLIM PRAYER

1 Hadith, sayings by the Prophet Mohammed, and authentificated by the chain of transmission from the Sahih of the Imam Al-Bukhari, which means 'the authentic [words] of the Imam Al-Bukhari.' This collection is a reliable (re)source for Muslims.

2 Mahmood, Saba, *Politics of Piety: The Islamic Revival and the Feminist Subject*. Princeton: Princeton University Press, 2005, p. 126; for an analysis of prayer as a performative ritual, see the fourth chapter, pp. 118–52.

3 Jouili, Jeannette S., 'Devenir pieuse: Femmes musulmanes en France et en Allemagne entre réforme de soi et quête de reconnaissance' ['Becoming pious: Muslim women in France and Germany between self-reform and the quest for recognition'], Doctoral thesis defended in 2007 at EHESS, under the co-direction of Nilüfer Göle and Werner Schiffauer.

4 Ramadan, *Western Muslims*, p. 119.

5 *Mosquées de Paris*. Documentary directed by Jean Michel Riera and Franck Hirsch, L5A3 PROD, with the support of the City of Paris and the Institut des Cultures d'Islam, France, 2009, 52 mins.

6 'Marine Le Pen compare les "prières de rue" des musulmans à une "occupation"' ['Marine Le Pen compares Muslims' "street prayers" to an "occupation"'], *Le Monde*, 11 December 2010. abonnes.lemonde.fr/politique/article/2010/12/11/marine-le-pen-compare-les-prieres-de-rue-des-musulmans-a-une-occupation_1452359_823448.html.

7 'Guéant: Les prières de rue doivent cesser' [Guéant: Street prayers must end'], *Le Figaro*, 14 September 2011. www.lefigaro.fr/actualite-france/2011/09/14/01016-20110914ARTFIG00722-gueant-les-prieres-dans-la-rue-doivent-cesser.php.

8 MASDJID (mosque): *The New Encyclopedia of Islam*, 3rd edn. Plymouth: Rowman and Littlefield, 2008, pp. 361–2.

9 Giacomo Biffi elaborated this vision in a pastoral theme entitled 'The City of San Petronio in the Third Millennium' (*La città di san Petronio nel terzo millennio*, Bologna, 2000), quoted in Bartolomeo Conti's doctoral thesis, 'L'emergence de l'islam dans l'espace public italien,' pp. 211–12.

10 Machiavelli, Marta, 'La Ligue du Nord et l'invention du "Padan"' ['The Northern League and the invention of "Padan"'], *Critique internationale*, 1(10), 2001, pp. 129–42.

11 Maddanu, Simone, 'La deuxième génération de musulmans en Italie: Nouvelles pratiques quotidiennes chez les jeunes de l'association GMI' ['Second generation Muslims in Italy: new daily practices among the youth in the GMI Association'], Doctoral thesis under the direction of Nilüfer Göle, defended 5 March 2009 at EHESS, Paris.

12 Ibid.

4. MUTE MINARETS, TRANSPARENT MOSQUES

1 Lambert, Elie, 'Les origines de la mosquée et l'architecture religieuse des Omeiyades' ['The origins of the mosque and the religious architecture of the Ummayad'], *Studia Islamica*, 6, 1956, pp. 5–18.

2 Eisenstadt, Shmuel N., 'The public sphere in Muslim societies,' in Nilüfer Göle and Ludwig Ammann (eds), *Islam in Public: Turkey, Iran, and Europe.* Istanbul: Bilgi University, 2006. See also M. Hoexter, N. Levtzion and S. N. Eisenstadt (eds), *The Public Sphere in Muslim Societies.* Albany, NY: Suny Press, 2002.

3 Allievi, *Conflicts over Mosques in Europe.*

4 Mayer, Jean-François, 'Minarets: entre variété architecturale et symbole de l'islam – autour d'un débat en Suisse' ['Minarets: between architectural variety and symbol of Islam – a Swiss debate'], *Religioscope*, 27 September 2009. religion.info/french/articles/article_445.shtml#.UNGopqx5eOI.

5 Allievi, Stefano, 'Conflicts over Mosques in Europe: between symbolism and territory,' in Nilüfer Göle (ed.), *Islam and Public Controversy in Europe.* Surrey: Ashgate Global Connections Series, forthcoming.

6 Ibid.

7 BBC Online, 29 November 2008.

8 *Le Monde*, 6 January 2009.

9 *The Şakirin Mosque, within the Legacy of the Karacaahmet Cemetery*, Semiha Şakir Foundation, Istanbul, 2011.

10 See the documentary 'Itinerary of European research' by the Euro PublicIslam project.

11 There are exceptions; for example, the Fittja mosque in Sweden (2013) and the Hamburg mosque in Germany (2009) received authorization to use minarets for the Friday call to prayer.

12 Allievi, *Conflicts over Mosques in Europe*, pp. 39–45.

13 The DITIB (Diyanet işleri Türk İslam Birliği) is a union of Islamic associations under the Turkish Presidency of Religious Affairs. The DITIB was created in the 1980s by the Turkish state after immigrants in Europe realized that their religious needs were not being respected. It manages imams, organizes the annual pilgrimage to Mecca and guarantees the transfer of remains for burial. See Citak, Zana, 'D'acteur national à transnational: La Diyanet en Europe' ['From national to transnational actor: the Diyanet in Europe']. *Cahiers de l'Obtic*, 2, December 2012, pp. 9–14.

5. ART, SACREDNESS AND VIOLENCE

1 Mohammed Arkoun distinguishes between several modalities of the divine word because it refers to the Preserved Tablet (*Lawḥ maḥfūẓ*), Koranic discourse as oral transmission of this word to the Prophet Mohammed, and the written text as a complete corpus (*muṣḥaf*) that becomes an Official Closed Corpus. However, traditional Ash'ari and Hanabalite theology identify the *muṣḥaf* as 'the transcendent Word of God.'

2 Gril, Denis, 'Le Corps du Prophète' ['The Prophet's body'], *Revue des mondes musulmans et de la Méditerranée*, 113/114, November 2006, pp. 37–57.

3 Ramadan, Tariq, *Muhammad, Vie du Prophète* [*In the Footsteps of the Prophet*]. Paris: Archipoche, 2006.

4 Esposito, John L. (ed.), *The Oxford Dictionary of Islam*. New York: Oxford University Press, 2003, p. 305.

5 Naef, Silvia, *Y a-t-il une question de l'image en islam?* [*Is Imagery an Issue in Islam?*]. Paris: Téraèdre, 2004.

6 Poizat, Jean-Claude, 'Débat entre Abdennour Bidar et Catherine Kintzler sur la laïcité et la place de la religion dans l'espace public,'

Le Philosophoire, 29, 2007, p. 243; see also Abdennour Bidar, *Self Islam. Histoire d'un islam personnel*. Paris: Seuil, 2006.

7 Tolan, John, *Les Sarrasins, l'islam dans l'imagination européenne au Moyen Age* [*Saracens: Islam in the European Imagination in the Middle Ages*]. Paris: Aubier, 2003.

8 Ibid., p. 18.

9 Ibid., pp. 201–2.

10 For a detailed analysis of the controversy surrounding this fresco, see Leone, Massimo, 'The sacred, (in)visibility, and communication: an inter-religious dialogue between Goethe and Hafez,' *Christian–Muslim Relations*, 21(4), 2010, pp. 373–84.

11 Kalin, Ibrahim, 'Sources of tolerance and intolerance in Islam: the case of the people of the book,' *Religions*, 2009, pp. 36–67.

12 Flood, Finbarr Barry, 'Inciting modernity? Images, alterities and the contexts of the "Cartoon wars,"' in Spyer, Patricia and Mary Margaret Steedly, *Images that Move*, Santa Fe: SAR Press, 2013, pp. 41–72.

13 Göle, *Islam in Europe*.

14 For a detailed description of the event, see Jytte Klausen, *The Cartoons that Shook the World*. New Haven and London: Yale University Press, 2009.

15 There is no direct translation of blasphemy in Arabic. However, the Arab language has several interconnected terms to designate similar questions in Islamic theology. In Islam, the notion of *tawhid*, the absolute uniqueness of the Creator, the impossibility of representing him and the veracity of His word revealed in the Koran, are fundamental and immutable principles. The Arab term *shirk*, which signifies the act of associating or admitting other divinities alongside God – in other words, idolatry – is an essential motive for accusation of those who oppose the affirmation and the uniqueness of God. The notion *kufr* signifies hiding or denying divine revelation, miscreance, the refusal of belief, and also forgetting God. Those who renounce Islam or some of its rules can be accused of apostasy, *ridda*, and condemned to death. The terms *shirk*, *kufr*, *ridda* are interconnected and overlap with the notion of blasphemy. Despite the fact that Islam, like Judaism, is a God-centric religion, the targets of blasphemy have always concerned the representation of the Prophet and Koranic revelation.

16 IUMS – International Union of Muslim Scholars – Statement on Insulting Cartoons, 19 January 2006. www.central-mosque.com/figh/iumsttmnt.htm.

17 Interview with Sheikh Faiz Siddiqi, Hijaz College, Muslim Arbitration Tribunal, 29 May 2009.

18 Mahmood, Saba, 'Religious reason and secular affect: an incommensurable divide?,' in T. Asad, W. Brown, J. Butler and S. Mahmood (eds), *Is Critique Secular? Blasphemy, Injury, and Free Speech*. California: University of California Press, 2009, pp. 64–100; p. 78.

19 Asad, Talal, 'Free speech, blasphemy, and secular criticism,' in T. Asad, W. Brown, J. Butler and S. Mahmood (eds), *Is Critique Secular? Blasphemy, Injury, and Free Speech*. California: University of California Press, 2009, p–;pp. 33–4.

20 Klausen, *The Cartoons that Shook the World*, p. 18.

21 Ibid., p. 14.

22 Butler, Judith, *Gender Trouble: Feminism and the Subversion of Identity*. New York: Routledge, 1990.

23 The European Muslim Network (EMN) is a think tank that brings together European Muslim intellectuals and activists. Its aim is to promote expert communication, opinion and analysis on key themes related to the presence of Muslims in Europe. www.euro-muslims.eu/#/home.

24 Ruby, Christian, 'L'art public dans la ville' ['Public art in the city'], EspacesTemps.net, Actuel, 2002, p. 2.

25 Ibid., p. 4.

6. VEILING AND ACTIVE MINORITIES

1 Benkheira, Mohammed Hocine, 'Sexualité' ['Sexuality'], in Amir-Moezzi, Mohammad Ali (ed.), *Dictionnaire du Koran*. Paris: under the direction of Editions Robert Laffont, 2007, pp. 815–18.

2 Terray, Emmanuel, 'L'hystérie politique' ['Political hysteria'], in C. Nordmann et al. (eds), *Le Foulard Islamique en Questions* [*The Islamic Headscarf in Questions*], Paris: Amsterdam, 2004, pp. 103–17.

3 Marzouki, Nadia, *L'islam, une religion américaine?* [*Islam, an American Religion?*]. Paris: Seuil/La couleur des idées, 2013, pp. 365–6.

4 Elster, Jon, 'L'usage stratégique de l'argumentation' ['The strategic use of argumentation'], *Négociations*, 2(4), 2005, pp. 59–82.

5 Baubérot, Jean, *La laïcité en question?* [*Secularism in question?*], , Introduction by Christophe Bertossi, Policy Paper 12. Paris: French Institute of International Relations, December 2004.

6 Cf. Baubérot, Jean, *La laïcité falsifiée* [*Falsified Secularism*]. Paris: La Découverte, 2012; Baubérot, *Histoire de la laïcité en France*; Baubérot, *Laïcité 1905–2005, entre passion et raison*.

7 To read the secularism charter in its entirety, see www.education.gouv.fr/cid73666/charte-de-la-laicite-a-l-ecole.html.

8 Scott, Joan W., *The Politics of the Veil*. Princeton: Princeton University Press, 2007, p. 97.

9 Bowen, John R., *Why the French Do Not Like Headscarves: Islam, the state and public space*. Princeton: Princeton University Press, 2007.

10 Beck, Ulrich, 'La condition cosmopolite et le piège du nationalisme méthodologique' ['The cosmopolitan condition and the nationalism trap'], in M. Wieviorka (ed.), *Les Sciences sociales en mutation*. Paris: Editions Sciences Humaines, 2007, pp. 223–38.

11 The Deutsche Islamkonferenz was founded in 2006 by the then minister of the interior, M. Wolfgang Schäuble. On the history of the organization of the DIK, see www.deutsche-islam-konferenz.de.

12 Amir-Moazami, Schirin, 'Pitfalls of consensus oriented dialogue, the German Islam Conference (Deutsche Islam Konferenz),' *Approaching Religion*, 1, May 2011, pp. 2–15.

13 Ibid., p. 8.

14 Derrida, Jacques, *Limited, Inc.*, Introduction and trans. Elizabeth Weber. Paris: Galilée, 1990.

15 Turkish secularism has the particularities unique to an Islamic culture. The question of women was central from the outset in the secularization of Islam in Turkey. See Göle, Nilufer, *The Forbidden Modern: Civilization and Veiling*. Ann Arbor: University of Michigan Press, 1997.

16 Weil, Patrick, *Être français. Les quatre piliers de la nationalité* [*Being French: The Four Pillars of Nationality*]. Ville: Editions de l'Aube, 2011.

17 Barakat, Sidi Mohammed, 'La loi contre le droit' ['Law against rights'], in Nordmann et al., *Le Foulard Islamique en Questions*, pp. 28–35.

18 Ibid.

19 Oubrou, Tareq, 'Pour une visibilité musulmane discrète,' *Le Monde*, 3 October 2013. abonnes.lemonde.fr/idees/article/2013/10/03/pour-une-

visibilite-musulmane-discrete-par-l-imam-tareq-oubrou_3488919_3232.html.

20 Andreassen, Rikke, 'Political Muslim women in the news media,' in H. Akman (ed.), *Negotiating Identity in Scandinavia: Women, Migration and the Diaspora*, New York and Oxford: Berghahn, forthcoming.

21 Ibid.

22 Hivert, Anne Françoise, 'Asmaa Abdol Hamid: la politique du voile' [Asmaa Abdol Hamid: the politics of the veil'], *Libération*, 12 November 2007. www.liberation.fr/jour/2007/11/12/asmaa-abdol-hamid-la-politique-du-voile_106017.

23 Fassin, Éric, 'La démocratie sexuelle et le conflit des civilisations' ['Sexual democracy and the conflict of civilizations'], *Multitudes*, 26, Autumn 2006, pp. 123–31.

24 Ibid.

25 Ibid., p. 131

26 Foucault, Michel, *The History of Sexuality*, vol. 1: *The Will to Knowledge*. New York: Pantheon Books, 1978.

27 Moscovici, Serge, *Psychologie des minorités actives* [*Psychology of Active Minorities*]. Paris: PUF. 1991, p. 11.

28 Ali, Zahra, *Féminismes islamiques* [*Islamic feminisms*]. Paris: La Fabrique, 2012.

29 Ounissi, Saida, 'La France refuse les mutations du monde' ['France is denying the changes in the world'], *Le Monde*, 1 November 2013. www.lemonde.fr/idees/article/2013/11/01/la-france-refuse-les-mutations-du-monde_3506462_3232.html.

30 Scott, *The Politics of the Veil*, p. 105.

31 Andreassen, 'Political Muslim women in the news media.'

32 The exhibition took place in Copenhagen in April 2010, during our visit for our inquiry. An art book of the exhibit was published. *'Strude,'* Trine Søndergaard, *Statens Kunstfond*, 2010.

7. WHAT ABOUT SHARIA?

1 See Dupret, Badouin, *La Charia aujourd'hui. Usages de la référence au droit islamique* [*Sharia Today: Uses of the Reference to Islamic Law*]. Paris: La Découverte, 2012; and Dupret, Badouin, *La Charia. Des sources à la pratique, un concept pluriel* [*Sharia: From Sources to Practice, A Plural Concept*]. Paris: La Découverte, 2014.

2 Zubaida, Sami, *Law and Power in the Islamic World*, New York and London: I. B. Tauris, 2005.

3 Gaborieau, Marc and Malika Zeghal, 'Autorités religieuses en islam' ['Religious authorities in Islam'], *Archives de sciences sociales des religions*, 125, January–March 2004, pp. 5–21.

4 Zeghal, Malika, *Gardiens de l'islam: les oulémas d'Al-Azhar dans l'Egypte contemporaine* [*Guardians of Islam: the Ulemas of Al-Azhar in Contemporary Egypt*]. Paris: Presses de Sciences Po, 1996, p. 22.

5 Masud, Muhammad Khalid, 'Shari'a et *fatwa*: un regard musulman' ['Sharia and fatwa: a Muslim view'], *Religioscope*, url.ca/i8zdg, 13 April 2002.

6 Ibid.

7 Fregosi, Franck, 'Usages sociaux de la référence à la charia chez les musulmans d'Europe' ['Social uses of references to sharia by Muslims of Europe'], in Dupret, *La Charia aujourd'hui*, pp. 65–77.

8 Meddeb, Abdelwahab, *Contre-Prêches* [*Counter Preachings*]. Paris: Seuil, 2006 (cited by Fregosi, 'Usages sociaux,' p. 68).

9 Oubrou, Tareq, 'La *sharî'a* de minorité: réflexion sur une intégration légale de l'islam' ['Minority sharia: reflection on a legal integration of Islam'], in Fregosi, Franck (ed.), *Lectures contemporaines du droit islamique, Europe–monde arabe*. Strasbourg: PUS, 2004, p. 206.

10 Interview with Salima, Geneva, 12 December 2009.

11 Interview with David, Geneva, 11 November 2009.

12 Interview with Issam, Toulouse, 25 April 2009.

13 Ramadan, *Western Muslims and the Future of Islam*.

14 Ibid., p. 101.

15 Roussillon, *La pensée islamique contemporaine*.

16 Ramadan, *Radical Reform*, pp. 10–11.

17 Ramadan, Tariq, *L'autre en nous. Pour une philosophie du pluralisme* [*The Other in Us: For a Philosophy of Pluralism*], Paris: Presses du Châtelet, 2009, p. 31.

18 Ibid.

19 Ibid., p. 35.

20 Ibid., p. 32.

21 Ibid., p. 44.

22 Ibid., p. 45.

23 Ibid., p. 67.

24 Fregosi, 'Usages sociaux,' p. 70; Fregosi, Franck, 'Les contours discursifs d'une religiosité citoyenne laïcité et identité islamique chez Tariq Ramadan' ['Discursive contours of a secular citizen's religiousness and Islamic identity in Tariq Ramadan'], in Dassetto, Felice (ed.), *Paroles d'islam. Individus, sociétés et discours dans l'islam européen contemporain*. Paris: Maisonneuve et Larose, 2000, pp. 205–21.

25 Williams, Rowan, 'Civil and religious law in England: a religious perspective,' urr.ca/19hr9, 7 February 2008.

26 Williams, Rowan, *Faith in the Public Square*. London: Bloomsbury Continuum, 2012.

27 Rawls, John, *A Theory of Justice*. Cambridge, Mass: Belknap Press of Harvard University Press, 1971.

28 Bras, Jean-Philippe, 'The British debate over Sharia Councils: a French-style controversy?,' in Göle, *Islam and Public Controversy in Europe*, pp. 151–8.

29 Pearl, David and Menski, Werner, *Muslim Family Law*. London: Sweet and Maxwell, 1998.

30 Yilmaz, Ihsan, 'Muslim law in Britain: reflections in the socio-legal sphere and differential legal treatment,' *Journal of Muslim Minority Affairs*, 20, 2001, pp. 353–60.

31 Interview with Faiz Siddiqi, Hijaz College, Nuneaton, 28 May 2009.

32 Bowen, John R., 'How could English courts recognize Sharia?,' *University of St Thomas Law Journal*, 7(3), 2010, pp. 411–35.

33 Bras, Jean-Philippe, 'Conclusion: des métamorphoses de la charia' ['Conclusion: metamorphoses of sharia'], in Dupret, *La Charia aujord'hui*, p. 290.

34 Interview with Imam Raza, Muslim College, London, 29 May 2009.

35 Interview with Khurshid Drabu, Winchester, 11 May 2009.

36 Bras, 'Conclusion: des métamorphoses de la charia,' p. 289.

37 See Mernissi, Fatima, *Le Harem politique. Le Prophète et les femmes* [*The Political Harem: The Prophet and His Wives*]. Paris: Albin Michel, 1987; and Ahmed, Leila, *A Quiet Revolution: The Veil's Resurgence, from the Middle East to America*. New Haven and London: Yale University Press, 2011.

38 Billaud, Julie, 'Ethics and affects in British Sharia Councils: "a simple way of getting to paradise,"' in Göle, *Islam and Public Controversy in Europe*, pp. 159–73.

8. HALAL LIFESTYLES

1 Benkheira, Mohammed Hocine, *L'Amour de la loi. Essai sur la normativité en islam* [*Love of the Law: Essay on Normativity in Islam*]. Paris: PUF, 1997.
2 Ibid., p. 28.
3 Ibid., p. 201.
4 Al-Qaradawi, Yusuf, *Le Licite et l'illicite en islam* [*The Licit and the Illicit in Islam*]. Paris: Al-Qalam, 2005, p. 42.
5 Ibid., pp. 44–5.
6 Benkheira, Mohammed Hocine, *Islam et interdits alimentaires* [*Islam and Food Bans*]. Paris: PUF, 2000, pp. 174–5.
7 Ibid., p. 131.
8 Ibid., p. 178.
9 *L'Abattage rituel en islam* [*Ritual Slaughter in Islam*], a report published by the Islamic Educational, Scientific and Cultural Organization (ISESCO) and the World Health Organization, Regional Office for the Eastern Mediterranean, Cairo, 1999.
10 Hames, Constant, 'Le sacrifice animal au regard des textes islamiques canoniques' ['Animal sacrifice in canonical Islamic texts'], *Archives de sciences sociales des religions*, 43(101), January–March 1998, pp. 5–25; see also Bonte, Pierre, Annee-Marie Brisebarre and Altan Gokalp (eds), *Sacrifices en Islam. Espaces et temps d'un rituel* [*Sacrifices in Islam: Ritual Spaces and Times*]. Paris: CNRS Éditions, 2013 (first edn 1999).
11 Benkheira, *Islam et interdits alimentaires*, p. 202.
12 In the framework of the European Commission, the DIALREL project (www.dialrel.eu) discusses ritual slaughter in a dialogue between religions in order to facilitate the adoption of 'good practices.'
13 Delahaye, Léa, 'Le végétarisme est-il *halal*?' ['Is vegetarianism *halal*?'], *Le Monde des religions*, 21 August 2014.
14 Caeiro, Alexandre, 'The Making of the Fatwa,' *Archives de sciences sociales des religions*, 155, July–September 2011; see also Al-Qaradawi, Yusuf, *Fatwas contemporaines*. Paris: Maison d'Ennour, 2009.
15 Esposito, *The Oxford Dictionary of Islam*, p. 105.
16 Yassine, Rachide Id, 'Eclectic usage of *halal* and conflicts of authority,' in Göle, *Islam and Public Controversy in Europe*, pp. 173–86.

17 Saïd Nursi (1877–1960) was the founder of the Nourdjou movement in Turkey. His thinking renewed the Muslim religious tradition of science and his book *Risale-i Nur* (*The Epitomes of Light*) is a major reference for Muslims the world over; see Ulu Sametoglu, Sümeyye, 'Les *sohbet*: un espace alternatif de socialisation et formation du sujet pieux féminin en France et Allemagne' ['*Sohbet*: an alternative place for the socialization and education of the pious woman subject in France and Germany'], in Göle, *En quête de l'islam européen*.

18 Ibid.

19 Haenni, Patrick, 'L'économie politique de la consommation musulmane' ['The political economy of Muslim consumption'], *Religioscope*, 18, November 2008; see also Haenni, Patrick, *L'Islam de marché. L'autre révolution conservatrice* [*Market Islam: The Other Conservative Revolution*]. Paris: Seuil, 2005.

20 Yassine, Rachid Id, 'Eclectic usage of *Halal* and conflicts of authority,' p. 179.

21 Brooks, David, *Bobos in Paradise: The New Upper Class and How They Got There*. New York: Simon & Schuster, 2001. The expression 'bobo,' a contraction of the oxymoron 'bourgeois bohemian,' signals the hybridization of capitalist values with the hippie counterculture of the 1960s. These new bobo elites distinguish themselves primarily by their taste and their ethical principles on ecology, organics and the environment, which is evident in the way they live, eat and engage politically.

22 Hadjab, Warda, 'Le bien-être islamique en Europe' ['Islamic well-being in Europe'], presented at the graduate student conference 'Les normes publiques à l'épreuve de l'intime,' organized by Nilüfer Göle, Paris, 2 June 2014.

23 Ural, Yasemin, 'La place des défunts musulmans dans les cimetières français et allemand' ['The place of Muslim deceased in French and German cemeteries'] in Göle, *En quête de l'islam européen*.

24 Roberts, Isabelle and Raphaël Garrigos, 'M6 censure une enquête de "Zone interdite"' ['M6 censors "Zone interdite"'s enquiry'], *Libération*, 23 October 2009.

25 Kepel, Gilles, *Quatre-Vingt-Treize*. Paris: Gallimard, 2012, p. 66.

26 'Marine Le Pen s'attaque de nouveau au *halal*' ['Marine Le Pen attacks *halal* again'], *Le Nouvel Observateur*, 18 February 2012.

27 Papi, Stéphane, 'Islam, laïcité et commensalité dans les cantines scolaires publiques. Ou comment continuer à manger ensemble "à la table de la République?"' [Islam, secularism and solidarity in public school cafeterias: or how to eat "at the republican table" again'], *Hommes et migrations*, 1296, 2012; see also Brisebarre, Anne-Marie, 'Manger *halal* en France aujourd'hui: des nourritures domestiques à la restauration collective' ['Eating *halal* in France today: from domestic food to collective dining'], www.lemangeur-ocha.com, 4 October 2007.

28 Jean-Pierre Elkabbach's interview with François Fillon, Europe 1, 5 March 2012.

29 Birnbaum, Pierre, *La République du Cochon*. Paris: Seuil, 2013.

30 Ibid., p. 77.

31 Bergeaud-Blackler, Florence, 'Animal rights movements and ritual slaughtering: autopsy of a moribund campaign,' in Göle, *Islam and Public Controversy in Europe*, pp. 187–200.

32 Macé, Eric, *As Seen on TV. Les Imaginaires médiatiques.* Paris: Amsterdam, 2006.

33 See especially Porcher, Jocelyne, *Vivre avec les animaux. Une utopie pour le XXIe siècle* [*Living with Animals: A 21st Century Utopia*]. Paris: La Découverte, 2014.

34 Étudiants musulmans de France (EMF) is a student association created in 1989, and was initially called the Union Islamique des étudiants de France (Islamic Union of French Students). Associated with the Union des organizations islamiques de France (Union of Islamic Organizations of France) (UOIF), in 2009 this group was present on more than sixteen university campuses; it works in the social, cultural and syndical fields of student life.

35 Médecins du monde is a French association for international solidarity (NGO) dependent on the charity of health professionals to provide humanitarian aid to vulnerable populations across the world.

36 Riposte laïque is a website created in 2007 that brings together French people from the left and right who claim to fight the 'Islamicization' of France. The site's editorial line reveals an openly declared Islamophobia. Presenting itself as a secular and republican movement, Riposte laïque's activists participated in joint action with the Bloc identitaire and the far right.

37 Ni putes ni soumises (NPNS) is a French feminist movement founded in 2003 by Fadéla Amara following organized marches against local violence. The association quickly gained a significant audience in the media, and the founder became the city's Secretary of State from 2007 to 2010.

38 *Le Jambon* (*Ham*), a film made in Bordeaux with Frédéric Guerbert, Pédro and Abie, ur1.ca/ilqho, 2008. The name of the website is 'Besides that, it's all good. Muslim Humor and Islamic Comedy' (www.apartcatoutvabien.com/). Since then, the site, now called 'Besides that, it's all good. The projects make movies,' has been home to a number of short films in the same vein, as funny as they are instructive.

39 Roy, Olivier, *La Sainte ignorance. Le temps de la religion sans culture* [*Holy Ignorance: The Time of Religion without Culture*]. Paris: Seuil, 2008.

40 Haenni, 'L'économie politique de la consommation musulmane'.

41 See El Asri, Farid, 'Islam européenne en musique: les rythmes de l'identité religieux' ['European Islam in music: rhythms of religious identity'], *SociologieS*, 7 March 2014.

42 Ibid.

43 Al-Qaradawi, *Le Licite et l'illicite en islam*, pp. 299–303.

44 The notion of *awra* defines Koranic modesty prescribed for body parts – for women as well as for men – which must be hidden from others' view. According to different legal traditions, the feminine voice is or is not included in the feminine *awra* (see the definition given by Éric Chaumont in Amir-Moezzi, Mohamed Ali (ed.), *Le Dictionnaire du Coran*. Paris: Robert Laffont, 2007, pp. 925–6.

45 Bowen, Innes, *Medina in Birmingham, Najaf in Brent. Inside British Islam*. London: Hurst & Co., 2014. This book is based on interviews with leaders and members of Islamic groups such as the Deobandis, the Tablighi Jamaat and the Barelwis, who have headquarters or central branches in Birmingham.

46 This mosque was created by the HM2F Association (Muslim Homosexuals of France) in order to end policies of ostracism of Muslim dissidents: see Brault, Jean-François, 'Une visibilité islamique dissidente. De HM2F à MPF: l'"intrusion" d'une mosquée inclusive dans l'espace public français' ['Islamic dissident visibility from HM2F to MPF: the "intrusion" of an inclusive mosque in French public space'], *Tumultes*, 41, 2013, pp. 223–40.

47 Cunillera, Zehra, 'Des imams "importés" aux oulémas "natifs" d'Europe' ['From "imported" imams to "native" ulemas'], Doctoral thesis in sociology (in progress) under the direction of Nilüfer Göle, EHESS, Paris.

9. THE JEWISH CURSOR

1 Allievi, *Conflicts over Mosques in Europe*, pp. 40–41.
2 European Monitoring Center on Racism and Islamophobia, *Muslims in the EU: Racism and Islamophobia*, fra.europa.eu/sites/default/files/fra_uploads/156-Manifestations_EN.pdf, Vienna, 2006, p. 79.
3 Collectif contre l'Islamophobie en France, *L'Islamophobie en France*, www.islamophobie.net, 2009, p. 23.
4 Interview with Yassine, Bologna, 27 May 2009.
5 Birnbaum, *La République du Cochon*, p. 28.
6 Like Muslim sharia, the Halakhah defines practical law, codes of customary conduct and communitarian norms in Judaism. See Ackerman-Lieberman, Phillip, 'Halakha et charia, les chemins de la Loi' ['Halakha and sharia, the paths of Law'], in Abdelwahab Meddeb and Benjamin Stora (eds), *Histoire des relations entre juifs et musulmans des origines à nos jours*. Paris: Albin Michel, 2013, pp. 683–93.
7 Benbassa, Esther, *La République face à ses minorités. Les juifs hier, les musulmans aujourd'hui* [*The Republic and Its Minorities: Jews Yesterday, Muslims Today*]. Paris: Mille et une Nuits, 2004.
8 Cohen, Mark R., 'Modern myths of Muslim anti-Semitism,' in Moshe Maoz (ed.), *Muslim Attitudes to Jews and Israel*. Brighton: Sussex Academic Press, 2010, pp. 41–7. See also Cohen, Mark R., *Under Crescent and Cross. The Jews in the Middle Ages*. Princeton, NJ: Princeton University Press, 1994.
9 The word *dhimmi* means 'protected,' those who benefit from great legal autonomy and freedom of religion, a counterpart to the obligatory payment of specific capitation, *djizye*. Laurens, Henry, John Tolan and Gilles Veinstein, *L'Islam en Europe. Quinze siècles d'histoire* [*Islam in Europe: Fifteen Centuries of History*]. Paris: Odile Jacob, 2009.
10 In the Ottoman Empire, a *millet* was a separate legal court ruling on 'personal law' under which a confessional community (a group abiding by the laws of Muslim sharia, Christian canon law or Jewish Halakhah) was allowed to rule itself under its own system. Phillips Cohen, Julia,

Becoming Ottomans. Sephardi Jews and Imperial Citizenship in the Modern Era. New York: Oxford University Press, 2014.

11 Cohen, 'Modern myths of Muslim anti-Semitism.'

12 Lavi, Shai J., 'Unequal rites: Jews, Muslims and the history of ritual slaughter in Germany,' in Jose Brunner and Shai J. Lavi (eds), *Juden und Muslime in Deutschland. Recht, Religion, Identität.* Göttingen: Wallstein Verlag, 2009, pp. 164–84.

13 Lavi, Shai J., 'Enchanting a disenchanted law: on Jewish ritual and secular history in nineteenth-century Germany,' *UC Irvine Law Review*, 1.3, 2011, pp. 813–42.

14 Judd, Robin, *Contested Rituals. Circumcision, Kosher Butchering, and Jewish Political Life in Germany, 1843–1933.* Ithaca, NY/London: Cornell University Press, 2007, pp. 3–5.

15 'Un tribunal allemand condamne la circoncision d'un enfant pour des motifs religieux,' *Le Monde*, 26 June 2012.

16 Amir-Moezzi, *Le Dictionnaire du Coran*, p. 167.

17 A film by the French director Nurtih Aviv, featuring non-practicing men and women, nonetheless shows how circumcision is for them a source of questioning. Their interrogations begin with the mark on the body but also question the filiation, the cultural heritage and its transmission. For mixed couples, it can become a source of conflict. (Aviv, Nurithi, *Circoncision.* Arte, 2000).

18 Kiesow, Rainer Maria, 'Le jugement du tribunal de grande instance de Cologne de 2012,' *Grief*, 1, 2014, pp. 48–61.

19 Ibid., p. 60.

20 Matussek, Mathias, 'Tolerance and taboos: why circumcision is not a crime,' *Der Spiegel*, 22 July 2012. In his work, Navid Kermani reflects on the connection of Jewish and Islamic traditions with modernity (Kermani, Navid, *The Terror of God. Attar, Job and the Metaphysical Revolt.* Cambridge: Polity Press, 2011).

21 'Allemagne: le gouvernement réagit pour endiguer la polémique sur la circoncision' ['Germany: the government attempts to contain the polemic on circumcision'], *Le Nouvel Observateur*, 13 July 2012.

22 Schnapper, Dominique, 'La sensibilité démocratique et la circoncision,' *Grief*, 1, 2014, pp. 62–7.

23 Heimbach-Steins, Marianne, 'Religious freedom and the German circumcision debate,' European University Institute/Robert Schuman

Centre for Advanced Studies, RELIGIOWEST, EUI Working Paper RSCAS 2013/18.

24 Lavi, 'Enchanting a disenchanted law,' pp. 823–7.

25 Ibid., p. 840.

26 Asad, Talal, *Genealogies of Religion: Discipline and Reasons of Power in Christianity and Islam*. Baltimore, MD, and London: Johns Hopkins University Press, 1993, pp. 5–79.

27 Lavi, 'Enchanting a disenchanted law,' p. 826.

28 Batnitzky, Leora, *How Judaism Became a Religion: An Introduction to Modern Jewish Thought*. Princeton, NJ/Oxford: Princeton University Press, 2011.

29 Ibid., p. 834.

30 Ibid.

31 See Raz Krakotzkin, Amnon, *The Censor, the Editor and the Text*. University of Pennsylvanya Press, 2007.

32 Anidjar, Gil, *The Jew, the Arab: A History of the Enemy, Cultural Memory in the Present*. Palo Alto, CA: Stanford University Press, 2003.

33 Gouguenheim, Sylvain, *Aristote au Mont-Saint-Michel. Les racines grecques de l'Europe chrétienne*. Paris: Seuil, 2008.

34 Ibid., p. 123.

35 See the articles by Roger-Pol Droit in *Le Monde*, 2 April 2008, and by Stéphane Boiron in *Le Figaro*, 17 April 2008; several French intellectuals and researchers supported Sylvain Gouguenheim, if not his thesis itself (Jacques Le Goff, Paul-François Paoli, Jean Sévillia, Rémi Brague, Christian Jambet ...). See notably the opinion piece in response to a collective of fifty-six researchers criticizing the work, which 'is an outlet for cultural racism': 'Oui, l'Occident chrétien est redevable au monde islamique' ['Yes, the Christian West is indebted to the Islamic world'], *Libération*, 30 April 2008.

36 De Libera, Alain, *Penser au Moyen Âge*. Paris: Seuil, 1991.

37 Buttgen, Philippe, Alain de Libera, Marwan Rashed and Irène Rosier-Catach (eds), *Les Grecs, les Arabes et nous. Enquête sur l'islamophobie savante*. Paris: Fayard, 2009, pp. 7–17.

38 L'Yvonnet, François, 'L'hellénisation de l'Europe chrétienne: une controverse,' *Post-Laicity and Beyond*. Rio de Janeiro: Academy of Latinity, Candido Mendes University, 2009, pp. 41–54.

39 See Göle, *Islam in Europe*.

40 Dakhlia, Jocelyne and Bernard Vincent (eds), *Les Musulmans dans l'histoire de l'Europe*, vol. 1: *Une intégration invisible*. Paris: Albin Michel, 2011.
41 Bossuat, Gérard, 'Histoire d'une controverse: la référence aux héritages spirituels dans la constitution européenne,' *Matériaux pour l'histoire de notre temps*, 78, 2005, pp. 68–82.
42 Topolski, Anya, 'A genealogy of the "Judeo-Christian" signifier: a tale of Europe's identity crisis,' www.academia.edu.
43 Ibid.
44 Nusseibeh, Sari with Anthony David, *Once Upon a Country: A Palestinian Life*. New York: Farrar, Straus and Giroux, 2007.
45 Vergès, Françoise et al., *Ruptures postcoloniales*. Paris: La Découverte, 2010.
46 Rothberg, Michael and Yasemin Yildiz, 'Memory citizenship: migrant archives of Holocaust remembrance in contemporary Germany,' *Parallax*, 17(4), 2011, pp. 32–48; p. 34.
47 Rothberg, Michael, *Multidirectional Memory: Remembering the Holocaust in the Age of Decolonization*. Palo Alto, CA: Stanford University Press, 2009.
48 Adelson, Leslie A., *The Turkish Turn in Contemporary German Literature: Toward a New Critical Grammar of Migration*. New York: Palgrave Macmillan, 2005.
49 Senocak, Zafer, *Atlas of Tropical Germany: Essays on Politics and Culture, 1990–1998*. Lincoln and London: University of Nebraska Press, 2000, p. 6.
50 Anidjar, *The Jew, the Arab*, pp. 112–49. See also Agamben, Giorgio, *Remnants of Auschwitz: The Witness and the Archive*. New York: Zone Books, 1999, and Benslama, Fethi, 'La représentation et l'impossible,' *Le Genre humain*, December 2001, pp. 59–80.
51 Launched in 2009, the Aladdin project aims to create 'a bridge of understanding between Jews and Muslims' around recognition of the Shoah (www.projetaladin.org). Made up of politicians, academics and intellectuals, this delegation went to Auschwitz on 1 February 2011 at the invitation of the Aladdin project, UNESCO and the city of Paris with the support of the French government.
52 Kertész, Imre, *Fatelessness*. Vintage Books, 1975.

53 Aktar, Cengiz, *L'Appel au pardon. Des Turcs s'adressent aux Arméniens.* Paris: CNRS Éditions, 2009. Signed by 30,000 people, this text notably affirmed 'My conscience does not accept the insensitivity shown to and the denial of the Great Catastrophe that the Ottoman Armenians were subjected to in 1915, which is denied. I reject this injustice and, for my part, I empathize with the feelings and pain of my Armenian brothers and sisters. I apologize to them.'

54 Isin, Engin F., 'Claiming European citizenship,' in Isin, Engin F. and Michael Saward (eds), *Enacting European Citizenship.* New York: Cambridge University Press, 2003, pp. 19–46.

55 Pinto, Diana, 'The Third Pillar: toward a European Jewish identity,' in Kovács, András and Eszter Andor (eds), *Jewish Studies at the Central European University. Public Lectures 1996–1999.* Budapest, 2000, pp. 177–201.

56 Ibid.

CONCLUSION

1 Göle, Nilüfer, 'Islam resetting the European agenda,' *Public Culture*, 18(1), Winter 2005/06, pp. 11–14.

2 Depardon, Raymond, 'Berlin m'a toujours accompagné' ['Berlin has always been with me'], 'Le mur de Berlin: vingt ans après,' Special issue of *Télérama horizons*, 1, September 2009, pp. 8–19.

3 Pascal-Moussellard, Olivier, 'Sarajevo en mille morceaux' ['Sarajevo in a thousand pieces'], *Télérama horizons*, 1, Septermber 2009, pp. 66–73. For more on Haris Pasovic's role as a model of resistance during the siege of Sarajevo, see Wallon, Emmanuel, 'Portrait de l'artiste en témoin' ['Portrait of the artist as a witness'], in Lescot, David and Laurent Verjay (eds), *Les Mises en scène de la guerre au XX*[e] siècle, théâtre et cinéma. Paris: Nouveau Monde editions, 2011, pp. 381–417.

4 On 9 April 2004, the Appeals Court of the International Criminal Court for the former Yugoslavia confirmed that the massacre of 8,000 men and young boys in Srebrenica in 1995 by Serbian forces constituted genocide. On 11 June 2005, on the tenth anniversary of the event, it was commemorated as the worst massacre in Europe since the Second World War.

5 Hauland Groenneberg, Cyril, 'Rencontre avec Gilles Péqueux, ingénieur responsable de la reconstruction du pont Mostar' ['Meeting with Gilles Péqueux, the engineer responsible for the reconstruction of the Mostar Bridge'], *Le Courrier des Balkans*, uri.ca/jaorg, 21 April 2003.

6 Ricœur, Paul, *Memory, History, Forgetting*. Chicago, IL: University of Chicago Press, 2004, pp. 161–2.

7 Delanty, Gerard, 'The making of a post-Western Europe: a civilizational analysis,' *Thesis Eleven*, 72, February 2003, pp. 8–25. See by the same author *The Cosmopolitan Imagination: The Renewal of Critical Social Theory*. Cambridge: Cambridge University Press, 2009.

8 See Dakhlia and Vincent, *Les Musulmans dans l'histoire de l'Europe*, vol. 1, and Dakhlia, Jocelyne and Wolfgang Kaiser (eds), *Les Musulmans dans l'histoire de l'Europe*, vol. 2: *Passages et contacts en Méditerranée.* Paris: Albin Michel, 2013.

9 Hirschkind, Charles, 'The contemporary afterlife in Moorish Spain,' in Göle, *Islam and Public Controversy in Europe*, pp. 227–40.

10 Riera, Jean-Michel, *Mosquées de Paris*, Documentary produced by L5A3 PROD with the support of the City of Paris and the Institute of Cultures of Islam, France Ô, 2009, 60 mins.

11 Stierlien, Henri, *Cordoue, la grande mosquée*. Paris: Imprimerie nationale, 2012.

12 Mansur Abdussalam Escudero (1947–2010) was a respected figure in the Spanish Muslim community. In 1989, he created the Junta islámica de España, which he led until his death, promoting a 'universalist and humanist' Islam.

13 Donadio, Rachel, 'The Great Mosque of Córdoba: name debate echoes an old clash of faiths,' *New York Times*, 4 November 2010.

14 The term 'Moor' was a synonym for 'Muslim' in medieval Andalusia. The 'hunt for *moros*' signals the political expulsion of Spanish Muslims after the Reconquista in 1492.

15 Necipoglu, Gülru, 'The life of an imperial monument: *Hagia Sophia* after Byzantium,' in Mark, Robert and Ahmet Çakmak (eds), *Hagia Sophia from the Age of Justinian to the Present.* Cambridge: Cambridge University Press, 1992, pp. 195–225.

16 Ibid., pp. 198–9.

17 Habermas, Jürgen, *Europe, the Faltering Project*. Cambridge: Polity Press, 2009.

18 Lévi-Strauss, Claude, 'Le champ de l'anthropologie' ['The field of anthropology'], Inaugural lesson of the Chair of Social Anthropology at the Collège de France, 5 January 1960); Lévi-Strauss, Claude, *Structural Anthropology*, vol. II, trans. from the French by Monique Layton. University of Chicago Press, 1983 (1st edn 1976).

19 In March 2008, during a parliamentary debate on Islamic activism in the Netherlands, Geert Wilders called for a ban on the Koran.

20 Tolan, John, 'Miroir de nos phantasmes? L'islam dans l'imaginaire européen: perspectives historiques,' in Göle, *Islam and Public Controversy in Europe*, pp. 113–22.

21 Like Theo Van Gogh and Ayaan Hirsi Ali, a woman of Somali origin in the Netherlands, Thilo Sarazzin and Necla Kelek, of Turkish origin in Germany, and Oriana Fallaci and Magdi Allam, of Egyptian origin in Italy.

22 Goffman, Erving, *Frame Analysis: An essay on the organization of experience.* London: Harper and Row, 1974, p. 417.

23 Lefort, Claude, *Democracy and Political Theory*, trans. from the French by David Macey. MIT Press, 1989; *The Political Forms of Modern Society: Bureaucracy, Democracy, Totalitarianism*. MIT Press, 1986.

24 Remaud, Olivier, 'How do you become contemporary? On controversies and common sense,' in Göle, *Islam and Public Controversy in Europe*, pp. 21–36.

25 Scholz, Bernard F., 'Bakhtin's concept of chronotope: the Kantian connection,' in Shepherd, David (ed.), *The Contexts of Bakhtin. Philosophy, Authorship, Aesthetics.* London and New York: Routledge, 1998, pp. 146, 164.

26 Bakhtin, Mikhail, *Esthétique et théorie du roman*. Paris: Gallimard, 1987, p. 235.

27 For a rehabilitation of the phenomenality of politics in a reading of Arendt's works, see Tassin, Etienne, *Hannah Arendt, l'humaine condition politique*. Paris: L'Harmattan, 2003.

28 Quéré, Louis, 'L'espace public: de la théorie politique à la méthodologie sociologique,' *Quaderni*, 18, 1992, pp. 75–92.

29 Interview with Saida, Paris, 21 April 2009.

30 'Islam et Europe: pourquoi un concours du plus beau minaret?,' *CaféBabel*, url.ca/jaefw, 7 February 2011.

31 Guidi, Diletta, 'Les réactions artistiques aux controverses. L'espace artistique comme lieu de dédramatisation des grands débats de société liés à l'islam,' in Göle, *En quête de l'islam européen.*

32 Power, Carla, 'Updating the mosque for the 21st century,' *Time*, 2 April 2009.

33 In the video launching the campaign (url.ca/jaeqe), we see different Muslims, men and women (veiled and not), adolescents, from different ethnic backgrounds, standing facing the camera and calmly repeating the following message: 'ISIS do not represent Islam or any Muslim. Because it's totally un-Islamic, because they're killing innocent people, because you're unjust. We must all unite together and try and stop this group from damaging Islam and damaging Muslims. Not in my name. Because your leader is a liar, because your actions do not represent the actions of the rightly guided companions, because your caliphate doesn't represent Ummah, because what you're doing is inhumane, because you abuse hearts and minds, because you have no compassion, because my religion promotes tolerance for women and you have no respect for women. Not in my name!'

BIBLIOGRAPHY

Adelson, Leslie A. (2005) *The Turkish Turn in Contemporary German Literature: Toward a New Critical Grammar of Migration*, New York: Palgrave Macmillan.

Adler, Laure (2011) *Françoise*, Paris: Grasset.

Agamben, Giorgio (1999) *Remnants of Auschwitz: The Witness and the Archive*, New York: Zone Books.

Ahmed, Leila (2011) *A Quiet Revolution: The Veil's Resurgence, from the Middle East to America*, New Haven, CT, and London: Yale University Press.

Aktar, Cengiz (2009) *L'Appel au pardon. Des Turcs s'adressent aux Arméniens* [*Call to forgiveness: Turks speaking to Armenians*], Paris: CNRS Éditions.

Ali, Zahra (2012) *Féminismes islamiques* [*Islamic feminisms*], Paris: La Fabrique.

Allievi, Stefano (2009) *Conflicts over Mosques in Europe: Policy Issues and Trends*, London: NEF/Alliance Publishing Trust.

—— (forthcoming) 'Conflicts over mosques in Europe: between symbolism and territory,' in Nilüfer Göle (ed.), *Islam and Public Controversy in Europe*, Surrey: Ashgate Global Connections Series.

Al-Qaradawi, Yusuf (2005) *Le Licite et l'illicite en islam* [*The Licit and the Illicit in Islam*], Paris: Al-Qalam.

—— (2009) *Fatwas contemporaines* [*Contemporary Fatwas*], Paris: Maison d'Ennour.

Amir-Moezzi, Mohamed Ali (ed.) (2007) *Le Dictionnaire du Coran* [*Dictionary of the Koran*], Paris: Robert Laffont.

Andreassen, Rikke (forthcoming) 'Political Muslim women in the news media,' in H. Akman (ed.), *Negotiating Identity in Scandinavia: Women, Migration and the Diaspora*, New York and Oxford: Berghahn.

Anidjar, Gil (2003) *The Jew, the Arab: A History of the Enemy, Cultural Memory in the Present*, Palo Alto, CA: Stanford University Press.

Arendt, Hannah (1971) *The Life of the Mind*, New York: Harcourt Brace Jovanovich.

Asad, Talal (1993) *Genealogies of Religion: Discipline and Reasons of Power in Christianity and Islam*, Baltimore, MD, and London: Johns Hopkins University Press.

——— (2009) 'Free speech, blasphemy, and secular criticism,' in T. Asad, W. Brown, J. Butler and S. Mahmood (eds), *Is Critique Secular? Blasphemy, Injury, and Free Speech*, California: University of California Press, pp. 20–63.

Aviv, Nurithi (2000) *Circoncision* [*Circumcision*], Arte.

Aykac, Cagla (2010) 'Personnage publics de l'islam en Europe: scandales, controverses, et performances' ['The public personas of Islam in Europe: scandals, controversies and performances'], Unpublished doctoral thesis, dir. Nilüfer Göle, École des Hautes Études en Sciences Sociales, Paris, 2 March 2010.

Bakhtin, Mikhail (1987) *Esthétique et théorie du roman* [*Aesthetics and Theory of the Novel*], Paris: Gallimard.

Batnitzky, Leora (2011) *How Judaism Became a Religion: An Introduction to Modern Jewish Thought*, Princeton, NJ, and Oxford: Princeton University Press.

Baubérot, Jean (2004) 'La laïcité en question?' ['Secularism in question?'], Introduction by Christophe Bertossi, Policy Paper 12, Paris: French Institute of International Relations, December.

——— (2004) *Laïcité 1905–2005: entre passion et raison* [*Secularism 1905–2005, between passion and reason*], Paris: Seuil.

——— (2005) *Histoire de la laïcité en France* [*History of Secularism in France*], Paris: PUF.

——— (2012) *La laïcité falsifiée* [*Falsified Secularism*], Paris: La Découverte.

Beck, Ulrich (2007) 'La condition cosmopolite et le piège du nationalisme méthodologique' ['The cosmopolitan condition and the nationalism trap'], in M. Wieviorka (ed.), *Les Sciences sociales en mutation* [*The Transformation of Social Sciences*], Paris: Editions Sciences Humaines.

Benbassa, Esther (2004) *La République face à ses minorités. Les juifs hier, les musulmans aujourd'hui* [*The Republic and Its Minorities: Jews Yesterday, Muslims Today*], Paris: Mille et une Nuits.

Benkheira, Mohammed Hocine (1997) *L'Amour de la loi. Essai sur la normativité en islam* [*Love of the Law: Essay on Normativity in Islam*], Paris: PUF.

—— (2000) *Islam et interdits alimentaires* [*Islam and Food Bans*], Paris: PUF.

—— (2007) 'Sexualité' ['Sexuality'], in Mohammad Ali Amir-Moezzi (ed.), *Dictionnaire du Coran* [*Dictionary of the Koran*], Paris: under the direction of Editions Robert Laffont.

Bidar, Abdennour (2006) *Self Islam. Histoire d'un islam personnel*, Paris: Seuil.

Birnbaum, Pierre (2013) *La République du Cochon* [*The Republic of the Pig*], Paris: Seuil.

Boal, Augusto (2000) *Theater of the Oppressed*, trans. Emily Fryer, London: Pluto Press.

Boltanski, Luc (2012) Énigmes et complots. Une enquête à propos d'enquêtes [*Puzzles and Plots. A Survey about Surveys*], Paris: Gallimard.

Bonte, Pierre, Annee-Marie Brisebarre and Altan Gokalp (eds), *Sacrifices en Islam. Espaces et temps d'un rituel* [*Sacrifices in Islam: Ritual Spaces and Times*], Paris: CNRS Éditions (1st edn 1999).

Bosetti, Giancarlo (2008) 'Madame et son ennemi' ['Madame and her enemy'], *Reset DOC*, 5 February.

Bowen, Innes (2014) *Medina in Birmingham, Najaf in Brent. Inside British Islam*, London: Hurst & Co.

Bowen, John R. (2007) *Why the French Do Not Like Headscarves: Islam, the state and public space*, Princeton, NJ: Princeton University Press.

Brooks, David (2001) *Bobos in Paradise: The New Upper Class and How They Got There*, New York: Simon & Schuster.

Bruckner, P. (2010) 'L'invention de l'"islamophobie"' [The invention of Islamophobia], *Libération*, 23 November.

Brunner, Jose and Shai J. Lavi (eds) (2009) *Juden und Muslime in Deutschland. Recht, Religion, Identität* [*Jews and Muslims in Germany. Law, Religion, Identity*], Göttingen: Wallstein Verlag.

Butler, Judith (1990) *Gender Trouble: Feminism and the Subversion of Identity*, New York: Routledge.

Buttgen, Philippe, Alain de Libera, Marwan Rashed and Irène Rosier-Catach (eds) (2009) *Les Grecs, les Arabes et nous. Enquête sur l'islamophobie savante* [*Greeks, Arabs and Us. Survey on Scholarly Islamophobia*], Paris: Fayard.

Canto-Sperber, Monique (2005) *Le Bien, La Guerre et la Terreur* [*Good, War and Terror*], Paris: Plon.

Cohen, Mark R. (1994) *Under Crescent and Cross. The Jews in the Middle Ages*, Princeton, NJ: Princeton University Press.

Collectif contre l'Islamophobie en France (2009) *L'Islamophobie en France* [*Islamophobia in France*], www.islamophobie.net.

Cousin, Bruno (2005) 'Quand le racisme se fait best-seller. Pourquoi les Italiens lisent-ils Oriana Fallaci?' ['When racism becomes a bestseller: why do Italians read Oriana Fallaci?'], *La vie des idées*, 3: 71–7.

Cousin, Bruno and Tommaso Vitale, 'Italian intellectuals and the promotion of Islamophobia after 9/11,' in George Morgan and Scott Poynting (eds), *Global Islamophobia. Muslims and Moral Panic in the West*, Farnham: Ashgate, pp. 47–65.

Dakhlia, Jocelyne and Bernard Vincent (eds) (2011) *Les Musulmans dans l'histoire de l'Europe*, vol. 1: *Une intégration invisible* [*Muslims in the History of Europe*, vol. 1: *An Invisible Integration*], Paris: Albin Michel.

Dakhlia, Jocelyne and Wolfgang Kaiser (eds) (2013) *Les Musulmans dans l'histoire de l'Europe*, vol. 2: *Passages et contacts en Méditerranée* [*Muslims in the History of Europe*, vol. 2: *Crossings and Contacts in the Mediterranean*], Paris: Albin Michel.

De Libera, Alain (1991) *Penser au Moyen Âge* [*Thinking of the Middle Ages*], Paris: Seuil.

Delanty, Gerard (2009) *The Cosmopolitan Imagination: The Renewal of Critical Social Theory*, Cambridge: Cambridge University Press.

Derrida, Jacques (1990) *Limited, Inc.*, Introduction and trans. Elizabeth Weber, Paris: Galilée.

Dupret, Badouin (2012) *La Charia aujourd'hui. Usages de la référence au droit islamique* [*Sharia Today: Uses of the Reference to Islamic Law*], Paris: La Découverte.

—— (2014) *La Charia. Des sources à la pratique, un concept pluriel* [*Sharia: From Sources to Practice, a Plural Concept*], Paris: La Découverte.

Eisenstadt, Shmuel N. (2006) 'The public sphere in Muslim societies,' in Nilüfer Göle and Ludwig Ammann (eds), *Islam in Public: Turkey, Iran, and Europe*, Istanbul: Bilgi University.

Esposito, John L. (ed.) (2003) *The Oxford Dictionary of Islam*, New York: Oxford University Press.

European Monitoring Center on Racism and Islamophobia (2006) *Muslims in the EU: Racism and Islamophobia*, fra.europa.eu/sites/default/files/fra_uploads/156-Manifestations_EN.pdf, Vienna.

Fallaci, Oriana (1990) *Inshallah*, Milan: Rizzoli.

——— (2002) *The Rage and the Pride*, New York: Rizzoli.

Fassin, Éric (2006) 'La démocratie sexuelle et le conflit des civilisations' ['Sexual democracy and the conflict of civilizations'], *Multitudes*, 26, Autumn, pp. 123–31.

Flood, Finbarr Barry (2013) 'Inciting modernity? Images, alterities and the contexts of the "Cartoon wars,"' in Patricia Spyer and Mary Margaret Steedly, *Images that Move*, Santa Fe: SAR Press, pp. 41–72.

Foucault, Michel (1978) *The History of Sexuality*, vol. 1: *The Will to Knowledge*, New York: Pantheon Books.

Fourest, Caroline (2004) *Frère Tariq. Discours, stratégie et méthode de Tariq Ramadan* [*Brother Tariq: Tariq Ramadan's discourse, strategy and method*], Paris: Grasset & Fasquelle.

Fourest, Caroline and Fiammetta Venner (2003) 'Islamophobie?' ['Islamophobia?'], *ProChoix*, 26/27.

Fregosi, Franck (2000) 'Les contours discursifs d'une religiosité citoyenne laïcité et identité islamique chez Tariq Ramadan' ['Discursive contours of a secular citizen's religiousness and Islamic identity in Tariq Ramadan'], in Felice Dassetto (ed.), *Paroles d'islam. Individus, sociétés et discours dans l'islam européen contemporain* [*Words of Islam. Individuals, Societies and Speeches in Contemporary European Islam*], Paris: Maisonneuve et Larose.

——— (ed.) (2004) *Lectures contemporaines du droit islamique, Europe–monde arabe* [*Contemporary Readings of Islamic Law, Europe–Arab World*], Strasbourg: PUS.

——— (2014) 'Usages sociaux de la référence à la charia chez les musulmans d'Europe' ['Social uses of references to sharia by Muslims of Europe'], in Badouin Dupret, *La Charia. Des sources à la pratique, un concept pluriel* [*Sharia: From Sources to Practice, A Plural Concept*], Paris: La Découverte.

Frontisi-Ducroux, Françoise (2009) *Ouvrages de dames. Ariane, Héléne, Pénélope …* [*Women's Handiwork. Ariane, Helena, Penelope …*], Paris: Seuil.

Gauchet, Marcel (1998) *La religion dans la démocratie: Parcours de la laïcité* [*Religion in Democracies: The Path of Secularism*], Paris: Gallimard.

Geisser, Vincent (2003) *La nouvelle islamophobie* [*The New Islamophobia*], Paris: La Découverte.

Goffman, Erving (1959) *The Presentation of Self in Everyday Life*, New York: Doubleday/Anchor Press.

—— (1974) *Frame Analysis: An essay on the organization of experience*, London: Harper and Row.

Göle, Nilüfer (1993) *Musulmanes et Modernes. Voile et civilisation en Turquie*, Paris: La Découverte; trans. as *The Forbidden Modern: Civilization and Veiling*.

—— (1997) *The Forbidden Modern: Civilization and Veiling*, Ann Arbor: University of Michigan Press.

—— (2010) *Islam in Europe: The Lure of Fundamentalism and the Allure of Cosmopolitanism*, trans. from the French by Steven Rendall, Princeton, NJ: Markus Wiener.

—— (ed.) (2014) *Islam and Public Controversy in Europe*, London: Ashgate.

—— (ed.) (2015) *En quête de l'islam européen* [*In Search of European Islam*], Perpignan: Halfa.

Gouguenheim, Sylvain (2008) *Aristote au Mont-Saint-Michel. Les racines grecques de l'Europe chrétienne* [*Aristotle at Mont-Saint-Michel. The Greek Roots of Christian Europe*], Paris: Seuil.

Gresh, Alain (2004) 'A propos de l'islamophobie: Plaidoyer en faveur d'un concept controversé' ['On Islamophobia: A plea in favor of a controversial concept'], Les mots sont important Net, 4 March, lmsi.net/A-propos-de-l-islamophobie.

Haag, Pascale and Cyril Lemieux (eds) (2012) *Faire des sciences sociales: critiquer*, vol. 1 [*Practicing Social Sciences: Critics*, vol. 1], Paris: Editions de l'EHESS.

Habermas, Jürgen (2009) *Europe, the Faltering Project*, Cambridge: Polity Press.

—— (2011) 'L'Europe malade de la xénophobie' ['Europe is sick with xenophobia'], *Le Monde*, 4 January.

Haenni, Patrick (2005) *L'Islam de marché. L'autre révolution conservatrice* [*Market Islam: The Other Conservative Revolution*], Paris: Seuil.

Hirsi Ali, Ayaan (2007) *Infidel*, New York: Free Press.

Hoexter, M., N. Levtzion and S. N. Eisenstadt (eds) (2002) *The Public Sphere in Muslim Societies*, Albany, NY: Suny Press.

Houellebecq, Michel (2002) *Platform*, trans. Frank Wynne, London: Random House.

Isin, Engin F. and Michael Saward (eds) (2003) *Enacting European Citizenship*, New York: Cambridge University Press.

Judd, Robin (2007) *Contested Rituals. Circumcision, Kosher Butchering, and Jewish Political Life in Germany, 1843–1933*. Ithaca, NY, and London: Cornell University Press.

Kepel, Gilles (2012) *Quatre-Vingt-Treize* [*Ninety-three*], Paris: Gallimard.

Kermani, Navid (2011) *The Terror of God. Attar, Job and the Metaphysical Revolt*, Cambridge: Polity Press.

Klausen, Jytte (2009) *The Cartoons that Shook the World*, New Haven, CT, and London: Yale University Press.

Laurens, Henry, John Tolan and Gilles Veinstein (2009) *L'Islam en Europe. Quinze siècles d'histoire* [*Islam in Europe: Fifteen Centuries of History*], Paris: Odile Jacob.

Lefort, Claude (1986) *The Political Forms of Modern Society: Bureaucracy, Democracy, Totalitarianism*, MIT Press.

—— (1989) *Democracy and Political Theory*, trans. from the French by David Macey, MIT Press.

Lévi-Strauss, Claude (1983) *Structural Anthropology*, vol. II, trans. from the French by Monique Layton, University of Chicago Press (1st edn 1976).

Macé, Eric (2006) *As Seen on TV. Les Imaginaires médiatiques* [*As Seen on TV. Mediatic Imaginaries*], Paris: Amsterdam.

Mahmood, Saba (2005) *Politics of Piety: The Islamic Revival and the Feminist Subject*, Princeton, NJ: Princeton University Press.

—— (2009) 'Religious reason and secular affect: an incommensurable divide?,' in T. Asad, W. Brown, J. Butler and S. Mahmood (eds), *Is Critique Secular? Blasphemy, Injury, and Free Speech*, California: University of California Press, pp. 64–100.

Maoz, Moshe (ed.) (2010) *Muslim Attitudes to Jews and Israel*, Brighton: Sussex Academic Press.

Mark, Robert and Ahmet Çakmak (eds) (1992) *Hagia Sophia from the Age of Justinian to the Present*, Cambridge: Cambridge University Press.

Marzouki, Nadia (2013) *L'islam, une religion américaine?* [*Islam, an American Religion?*], Paris: Seuil/La couleur des idées.

Meddeb, Abdelwahab and Benjamin Stora (eds) (2013) *Histoire des relations entre juifs et musulmans des origines à nos jours* [*History of Relations between Jews and Muslims. From Their Origins to Today*], Paris: Albin Michel.

Meizoz, Jérôme (2004) L'œil sociologue et la littérature [*The Sociological Eye and Literature*], Geneva: Slaktine Érudition.

Mernissi, Fatima (1987) *Le Harem politique. Le Prophète et les femmes* [*The Political Harem: The Prophet and His Wives*], Paris: Albin Michel.

Modood, Tariq (2007) *Multiculturalism: A Civic Idea*. Cambridge: Polity Press.

Moscovici, Serge (1991) *Psychologie des minorités actives* [*Psychology of Active Minorities*], Paris: PUF.

Naef, Silvia (2004) *Y a-t-il une question de l'image en islam?* [*Is Imagery an Issue in Islam?*], Paris: Téraèdre.

Noiriel, Gérard (2007) À quoi sert l'identité 'nationale'? [*What is 'National' Identity For?*], Marseille: Agone.

Nordmann, C. et al. (eds) (2004) *Le Foulard Islamique en Questions* [*The Islamic Headscarf in Questions*], Paris: Amsterdam.

Nusseibeh, Sari with Anthony David (2007) *Once Upon a Country: A Palestinian Life*, New York: Farrar, Straus and Giroux.

Ockrent, Christine (2003) *Françoise Giroud, une ambition française* [*Françoise Giroud: A French Ambition*], Paris: Fayard.

Pamuk, Orhan (2008) *Other Colors. Essays and a Story*, New York: Vintage International.

Pearl, David and Werner Menski (1998) *Muslim Family Law*, London: Sweet and Maxwell.

Phillips Cohen, Julia (2014) *Becoming Ottomans. Sephardi Jews and Imperial Citizenship in the Modern Era*, New York: Oxford University Press.

Pinto, Diana (2000) 'The Third Pillar: toward a European Jewish identity,' in András Kovács and Eszter Andor (eds), *Jewish Studies at the Central European University. Public Lectures 1996–1999*, Budapest.

Porcher, Jocelyne (2014) *Vivre avec les animaux. Une utopie pour le XXIe siècle* [*Living with Animals: A 21st Century Utopia*], Paris: La Découverte.

Ramadan, Tariq (2004) *Western Muslims and the Future of Islam*, New York: Oxford University Press.

—— (2006) *Muhammad, Vie du Prophète* [*In the Footsteps of the Prophet*], Paris: Archipoche.

—— (2009) *Radical Reform: Islamic Ethics and Liberation*, New York: Oxford University Press.

—— (2009) *L'autre en nous. Pour une philosophie du pluralisme* [*The Other in Us: For a Philosophy of Pluralism*], Presses du Châtelet.

—— (2012) *The Quest for Meaning: Developing a Philosophy of Pluralism*, London: Penguin.

Rancière, Jacques (2010) 'Racisme, une passion d'en haut' ['Racism, a passion from above'], *Médiapart*, 11 September, www.mediapart.fr/node/92825.

Rawls, John (1971) *A Theory of Justice*, Cambridge, MA: Belknap Press of Harvard University Press.

Raz Krakotzkin, Amnon (2007) *The Censor, the Editor and the Text*, University of Pennsylvanya Press.

Ricœur, Paul (2004) *Memory, History, Forgetting*, Chicago, IL: University of Chicago Press.

Riegl, Alois (2002) *Questions du style. Fondements d'une histoire de l'ornementation* [*Questions of Style. Foundations of a History of Ornamentation*], Paris: Hazan.

Rosanvallon, Pierre (1998) *Le Peuple introuvable: Histoire de la représentation démocratique en France* [*The Lost People: History of Democratic Representation in France*], Paris: Gallimard.

Rothberg, Michael (2009) *Multidirectional Memory: Remembering the Holocaust in the Age of Decolonization*, Palo Alto, CA: Stanford University Press.

Roussillon, Alain (2005) *La pensée islamique contemporaine: acteurs et enjeux* [*Contemporary Islamic Thought: Actors and Stakes*], Paris: Téraèdre.

Roy, Olivier (2008) *La Sainte ignorance. Le temps de la religion sans culture* [*Holy Ignorance: The Time of Religion without Culture*], Paris: Seuil.

Sarrazin, Thilo (2010) *Deutschland schafft sich ab. Wie wir unser Land aufs Spiel setzen* [*Germany Does Away with Itself: How We Are Gambling Away Our Country*], Muncih: Deutsche Verlag-Anstalt.

Scheffer, Paul (2000) 'The multicultural drama,' *NRC Handelsblad*, 29 January.

Scott, Joan W. (2007) *The Politics of the Veil*, Princeton, NJ: Princeton University Press.

Sennett, Richard (2008) *The Craftsman*, New Haven, CT: Yale University Press.

Senocak, Zafer (2000) *Atlas of Tropical Germany: Essays on Politics and Culture, 1990–1998*, Lincoln and London: University of Nebraska Press.

Shepherd, David (ed.) (1998) *The Contexts of Bakhtin. Philosophy, Authorship, Aesthetics*, London and New York: Routledge.

Stierlien, Henri (2012) *Cordoue, la grande mosquée* [*Cordoba, the Great Mosque*], Paris: Imprimerie nationale.

Tassin, Etienne (2003) *Hannah Arendt, l'humaine condition politique*, Paris: L'Harmattan.

—— (2013) 'Les gloires ordinaires, actualité du concept arendtien d'espace public' ['Common glories, Arendt's public space concept'], *Sens public*, 15/16, July, pp. 23–38.

Taylor, Charles (2007) *A Secular Age*, Cambridge, MA: Harvard University Press.

Terray, Emmanuel (2004) 'L'hystérie politique' ['Political hysteria'], in C. Nordmann et al. (eds), *Le Foulard Islamique en Questions* [*The Islamic Headscarf in Questions*], Editions Amsterdam.

Tolan, John (2003) *Les Sarrasins, l'islam dans l'imagination européenne au Moyen Age* [*Saracens: Islam in the European Imagination in the Middle Ages*], Paris: Aubier.

Vergès, Françoise et al. (2010) *Ruptures postcoloniales* [*Postcolonial Ruptures*], Paris: La Découverte.

Weil, Patrick (2011) *Être français. Les quatre piliers de la nationalité* [*Being French: The Four Pillars of Nationality*], Ville: Editions de l'Aube.

Williams, Rowan (2012) *Faith in the Public Square*, London: Bloomsbury Continuum.

Zeghal, Malika (1996) *Gardiens de l'islam: les oulémas d'Al-Azhar dans l'Egypte contemporaine* [*Guardians of Islam: the Ulemas of Al-Azhar in Contemporary Egypt*], Paris: Presses de Sciences Po.

Zubaida, Sami (2005) *Law and Power in the Islamic World*, New York and London: I. B. Tauris.

INDEX